Accelerate Deep Learning Workloads with Amazon SageMaker

Train, deploy, and scale deep learning models effectively using Amazon SageMaker

Vadim Dabravolski

BIRMINGHAM—MUMBAI

Accelerate Deep Learning Workloads with Amazon SageMaker

Publishing Product Manager: Gebin George
Content Development Editor: Priyanka Soam
Technical Editor: Sweety Pagaria
Copy Editor: Safis Editing
Project Coordinator: Farheen Fathima
Proofreader: Safis Editing
Indexer: Rekha Nair
Production Designer: Aparna Bhagat
Marketing Coordinators: Shifa Ansari, Abeer Riyaz Dawe

First published: October 2022

Production reference: 1191022

Published by Packt Publishing Ltd.
Livery Place
35 Livery Street
Birmingham
B3 2PB, UK.

ISBN 978-1-80181-644-1

www.packt.com

Contributors

About the Author

Vadim Dabravolski is a Solutions Architect and Machine Learning Engineer. He has had a career in software engineering for over 15 years, with a focus on data engineering and machine learning. During his tenure in AWS, Vadim helped many organizations to migrate their existing ML workloads or engineer new workloads for the Amazon SageMaker platform. Vadim was involved in the development of Amazon SageMaker capabilities and the adoption of them in practical scenarios.

Currently, Vadim works as an ML engineer, focusing on training and deploying large NLP models. His areas of interest include engineering distributed model training and evaluation, complex model deployment use cases, and optimizing inference characteristics of DL models.

About the reviewer

Brent Rabowsky is a manager and principal data science consultant at AWS, with over 10 years of experience in the field of ML. At AWS, he manages a team of data scientists and leverages his expertise to help AWS customers with their ML projects. Prior to AWS, Brent was on an ML and algorithms team at Amazon.com, and worked on conversational AI agents for a government contractor and a research institute. He also served as a technical reviewer of *Data Science on AWS* published by O'Reilly, and the following from Packt: *Learn Amazon SageMaker*, *SageMaker Best Practices*, and *Getting Started with Amazon SageMaker Studio*.

Table of Contents

Part 2: Building and Training Deep Learning Models

5

6

7

Part 3: Serving Deep Learning Models

8

Considering Hardware for Inference 173

9

Implementing Model Servers 193

10

Operationalizing Inference Workloads 217

Preface

Deep Learning (DL) is a relatively new type of machine learning which demonstrates incredible results in tasks such as natural language understanding and computer vision. At times, DL can be more accurate than humans.

Thanks to the proliferation of open source frameworks, publicly available model architectures and pertained models, many people and organizations can successfully apply cutting-edge DL models to their practical use cases. However, developing, training, and deploying DL models also requires highly specialized and costly types of hardware, software stacks, expertise, and management capabilities which may considerably slow down the adoption.

This book focuses on how to engineer and manage Deep Learning workloads on Amazon SageMaker, which allows you to overcome the aforementioned barriers. SageMaker is a sprawling AWS cloud Machine Learning platform with a variety of capabilities. This book does not intend to cover all available SageMaker capabilities in detail, but rather dive deep into the features relevant to DL workloads. We prioritized depth over breadth when writing this book. The goal of this book is to provide you with practical guidelines on how to efficiently implement real-time use cases involving Deep Learning models on Amazon SageMaker.

Since cloud adoption and machine learning adoption are both accelerating, this book may be of interest to a wide audience, from beginners to experienced ML practitioners. Specifically, this book is for ML engineers who work on DL model development and training, and Solutions Architects who are in charge of designing and optimizing DL workloads.

It is assumed that you are familiar with the Python ecosystem, and the principles of Machine Learning and Deep Learning. Familiarity with AWS and practical experience working with it are also helpful.

The complexity of the chapters increases as we move from introductory and overview topics to advanced implementation and optimization techniques. You may skip certain chapters, or select specific topics which are relevant to your specific task at hand.

Most chapters of this book have corresponding code examples so you can develop practical experience working with Amazon SageMaker. It's recommended that you try to run the code samples yourself, however, you may also review them. We also provide commentary for code samples as part of each chapter.

Please note that running code examples will results in AWS charges. Make sure to check the Amazon SageMaker pricing page for details.

We welcome your feedback and suggestions on this book, and hope that you enjoy your learning journey.

Who this book is for

This book is written for DL and AI engineers who have a working knowledge of the DL domain and who want to learn and gain practical experience in training and hosting DL models in the AWS cloud using the Amazon SageMaker service capabilities.

What this book covers

Chapter 1, Introducing Deep Learning with Amazon SageMaker, will introduce Amazon SageMaker: how it simplifies infrastructure and workload management, and what the key principles of this AWS service and its main capabilities are. We will then focus on the managed training, hosting infrastructure, and integration with the rest of the AWS services it provides.

Chapter 2, Deep Learning Frameworks and Containers on SageMaker, will review in detail how SageMaker extensively utilizes Docker containers. We will start by diving into pre-built containers for popular DL frameworks (Tensorflow, PyTorch, and MXNet). Then, we will consider how to extend pre-build SageMaker containers and BYO containers. For the latter case, we will review the technical requirements for training and serving containers in SageMaker.

Chapter 3, Managing SageMaker Development Environment, will discuss how to manage SageMaker resources programmatically using a CLI, SDKs, and CloudFormation. We will discuss how to organize an efficient development process using SageMaker Studio and Notebooks as well as how to integrate with your favorite IDE. We will also review troubleshooting your DL code using SageMaker Local Mode. We will review various SageMaker capabilities that allow us to organize and manage datasets and discuss various storage options on AWS and their application use cases.

Chapter 4, Managing Deep Learning Datasets, will provide practical guidance on setting up the first DL project on SageMaker and then building, training, and using a simple DL model. We will provide a follow-along implementation of this project so that readers can learn and experiment with the core SageMaker capabilities themselves.

Chapter 5, Considering Hardware for Deep Learning Training, will consider the price performance characteristics of the most suitable instances for DL models and cover in which scenarios to use one instance type or another for optimal performance.

Chapter 6, Engineering Distributed Training, will focus on understanding the common approaches to distributing your training processes and why you may need to do so for DL models. Then, we will provide an overview of both open source training distribution frameworks as well as innate SageMaker libraries for distributed training.

Chapter 7, Operationalizing Deep Learning Training, will discuss how to monitor and debug your DL training job using SageMaker Debugger and its Profiler as well as how to optimize for cost using Managed Spot Training, early stopping, and other strategies.

Chapter 8, Considering Hardware for Inference, will provide practical guidance on building NLP state-of-the-art models using the PyTorch and Hugging Face frameworks. Readers will follow along with the code to learn how to prepare a training script for distributed training on Amazon SageMaker and then monitor and further optimize the training job. We will use the SageMaker Data Parallel library for distributing training computations.

Chapter 9, Implementing Model Servers, will start by reviewing key components of SageMaker Managed Hosting, such as real-time endpoints and batch inference jobs, model registry, and serving containers. Readers will learn how to configure their endpoint deployment and batch inference jobs using a Python SDK.

Chapter 10, Operationalizing Inference Workloads, will focus on the software stack of DL servers, specifically, on model servers. We will review the model servers provided by the popular TensorFlow and PyTorch solutions as well as framework-agnostic model servers such as SageMaker Multi Model Server. We will discuss when to choose one option over another.

To get the most out of this book

Software/hardware covered in the book	Operating system requirements
local SageMaker-compatible environment established	Windows, macOS, or Linux

If you are using the digital version of this book, we advise you to type the code yourself or access the code from the book's GitHub repository (a link is available in the next section). Doing so will help you avoid any potential errors related to the copying and pasting of code.

Download the example code files

You can download the example code files for this book from GitHub at `https://github.com/PacktPublishing/Accelerate-Deep-Learning-Workloads-with-Amazon-SageMaker`. If there's an update to the code, it will be updated in the GitHub repository.

We also have other code bundles from our rich catalog of books and videos available at `https://github.com/PacktPublishing/`. Check them out!

Download the color images

We also provide a PDF file that has color images of the screenshots/diagrams used in this book. You can download it here: `https://packt.link/FXLPc`.

Conventions used

There are a number of text conventions used throughout this book.

`Code in text`: Indicates code words in text, database table names, folder names, filenames, file extensions, pathnames, dummy URLs, user input, and Twitter handles. Here is an example: "In the following code block, we use the `'_build_tf_config()'` method to set up this variable."

A block of code is set as follows:

```
estimator.fit({
"train":"s3://unique/path/train_files/",
"test":"s3://unique/path/test_files"}
)
```

Any command-line input or output is written as follows:

```
conda create -n sagemaker python=3.9
```

When we wish to draw your attention to a particular part of a code block, the relevant lines or items are set in bold:

```
tensorboard --logdir ${tb_debug_path}
```

Bold: Indicates a new term, an important word, or words that you see onscreen. For instance, words in menus or dialog boxes appear in **bold**. Here is an example: "In the **Create the default IAM role** popup window, select **Any S3 bucket**."

> **Tips or Important Notes**
> Appear like this.

Get in touch

Feedback from our readers is always welcome.

General feedback: If you have questions about any aspect of this book, mention the book title in the subject of your message and email us at customercare@packtpub.com.

Errata: Although we have taken every care to ensure the accuracy of our content, mistakes do happen. If you have found a mistake in this book, we would be grateful if you would report this to us. Please visit www.packtpub.com/support/errata, selecting your book, clicking on the Errata Submission Form link, and entering the details.

Piracy: If you come across any illegal copies of our works in any form on the Internet, we would be grateful if you would provide us with the location address or website name. Please contact us at copyright@packt.com with a link to the material.

If you are interested in becoming an author: If there is a topic that you have expertise in and you are interested in either writing or contributing to a book, please visit authors.packtpub.com.

Share Your Thoughts

Once you've read *Accelerate Deep Learning Workloads with Amazon SageMaker*, we'd love to hear your thoughts! Scan the QR code below to go straight to the Amazon review page for this book and share your feedback.

https://packt.link/r/1-801-81644-1

Your review is important to us and the tech community and will help us make sure we're delivering excellent quality content.

Download a free PDF copy of this book

Thanks for purchasing this book!

Do you like to read on the go but are unable to carry your print books everywhere? Is your eBook purchase not compatible with the device of your choice?

Don't worry, now with every Packt book you get a DRM-free PDF version of that book at no cost.

Read anywhere, any place, on any device. Search, copy, and paste code from your favorite technical books directly into your application.

The perks don't stop there, you can get exclusive access to discounts, newsletters, and great free content in your inbox daily

Follow these simple steps to get the benefits:

1. Scan the QR code or visit the link below

https://packt.link/free-ebook/9781801816441

2. Submit your proof of purchase
3. That's it! We'll send your free PDF and other benefits to your email directly

Part 1:
Introduction to Deep Learning on Amazon SageMaker

In the first part, we will start with a brief introduction to deep learning and Amazon SageMaker and then focus on the key SageMaker capabilities that will be used throughout the book.

This section comprises the following chapters:

- *Chapter 1, Introducing Deep Learning with Amazon SageMaker*
- *Chapter 2, Deep Learning Frameworks and Containers on SageMaker*
- *Chapter 3, Managing SageMaker Development Environment*
- *Chapter 4, Managing Deep Learning Datasets*

1
Introducing Deep Learning with Amazon SageMaker

Deep learning (**DL**) is a fairly new but actively developing area of **machine learning** (**ML**). Over the past 15 years, DL has moved from research labs to our homes (such as smart homes and smart speakers) and cars (that is, self-driving capabilities), phones (for example, photo enhancement software), and applications you use every day (such as recommendation systems in your favorite video platform).

DL models are achieving and, at times, exceeding human accuracy on tasks such as computer vision (object detection and segmentation, image classification tasks, and image generation) and language tasks (translation, entity extraction, and text sentiment analysis). Beyond these areas, DL is also actively applied to complex domains such as healthcare, information security, robotics, and automation.

We should expect that DL applications in these domains will only grow over time. With current results and future promises also come challenges when implementing DL models. But before talking about the challenges, let's quickly refresh ourselves on what DL is.

In this chapter, we will do the following:

- We'll get a quick refresher on DL and its challenges
- We'll provide an overview of Amazon SageMaker and its value proposition for DL projects
- We'll provide an overview of the foundational SageMaker components – that is, managed training and hosting stacks
- We'll provide an overview of other key AWS services

These will be covered in the following topics:

- Exploring DL with Amazon SageMaker
- Choosing Amazon SageMaker for DL workloads
- Exploring SageMaker's managed training stack

- Using SageMaker's managed hosting stack
- Integration with AWS services

Technical requirements

There are several hands-on code samples in this chapter. To follow along with them, you will need the following:

- An AWS account and IAM user with permission to manage Amazon SageMaker resources.
- A computer or cloud host with Python3 and SageMaker SDK installed (`https://pypi.org/project/sagemaker/`).
- Have the AWS CLI installed (see `https://docs.aws.amazon.com/cli/latest/userguide/install-cliv2.html`) and configured to use IAM user (see the instructions at `https://docs.aws.amazon.com/cli/latest/userguide/cli-configure-quickstart.html`).
- To use certain SageMaker instance types for training purposes, you will likely need to request a service limit increase in your AWS account. For more information, go to `https://docs.aws.amazon.com/general/latest/gr/aws_service_limits.html`.

All of the code in this chapter can be downloaded from `https://github.com/PacktPublishing/Accelerate-Deep-Learning-Workloads-with-Amazon-SageMaker`.

Exploring DL with Amazon SageMaker

DL is a subset of the ML field, which uses a specific type of architecture: layers of learnable parameters connected to each other. In this architecture, each layer is "learning" a representation from a training dataset. Each new training data sample slightly tweaks the learnable parameters across all the layers of the model to minimize the loss function. The number of stacked layers constitutes the "depth" of the model. At inference time (that is, when we use our model to infer output from the input signal), each layer receives input from the previous layer's output, calculates its representation based on the input, and sends it to the next layer.

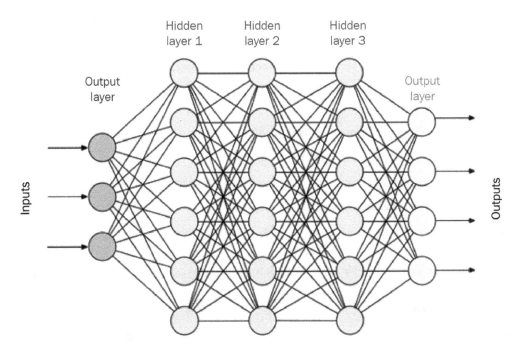

Figure 1.1 – Fully connected DL network

Simple DL models can consist of just a few fully connected layers, while **state-of-the-art (SOTA)** models have hundreds of layers with millions and billions of learnable parameters. And the model size continues to grow. For example, let's take a look at the evolution of the GPT family of models for various NLP tasks. The GPT-1 model was released in 2018 and had 110 million parameters; the GPT-2 model released in 2019 had 1,500 million parameters; the latest version, GPT-3, was released in 2020 and has 175 billion parameters!

As the number of parameters grows, DL practitioners deal with several engineering problems:

- How do we fit models into instance memory at training time? If it's not possible, then how do we split the model between the memory of multiple GPU devices and/or compute nodes?

- How can we organize communication between multiple nodes at training time so that the overall model can aggregate learnings from individual nodes?

Layer internals are also becoming more complex and require more computing power. DL models also typically require vast amounts of data in specific formats.

So, to be able to successfully train and use SOTA DL models, ML engineers need to solve the following tasks (beyond implementing the SOTA model, of course):

- Gain access to a large number of specialized compute resources during training and inference
- Set up and maintain a software stack (for example, GPU libraries, DL frameworks, and acceleration libraries)
- Implement, manage, and optimize distributed training jobs
- Implement, deploy, and monitor inference pipelines
- Organize time- and cost-efficient experiments when tuning model performance
- Pre-process, label, and access large datasets (GBs and TBs of data)

As you can see, these tasks are not necessarily related to solving any specific business problem. However, you need to get all these components right to ensure that a particular business case can be solved using DL models with the highest possible accuracy in time and within expected budgets.

Using SageMaker

Amazon SageMaker is an AWS service that promises to simplify the lives of ML practitioners by removing "undifferentiated heavy lifting" (such as the tasks mentioned previously) and lets you focus on actually solving business problems instead. It integrates various functional capabilities to build, train, and deploy ML models. SageMaker was first introduced in late 2017 and has since expanded greatly, adding more than 200 features in 2020 alone according to AWS's *Re:invent 2020* keynotes.

Amazon SageMaker caters to a broad audience and set of use cases, including the following (this is a non-exclusive list):

- Developers without much ML background
- Enterprise data science teams
- Leading research organizations who are looking to run cutting-edge research

SageMaker is a managed service as it abstracts the management of underlying compute resources and software components via APIs. AWS customers use these APIs to create training jobs, manage model artifacts, and deploy models for inference on Amazon SageMaker. AWS is responsible for the high availability of SageMaker resources and provides respective **Service-Level Agreements (SLAs)**. Amazon SageMaker has a "pay as you go" model, with customers paying only for the resources they consume.

In this book, we will explore SageMaker capabilities that are relevant for DL models and workloads, and we will build end-to-end solutions for popular DL use cases, such as **Natural Language Processing (NLP)** and **Computer Vision (CV)**.

We will focus on the following Amazon SageMaker capabilities:

- Model development phase:

  - Data preparation using SageMaker GroundTruth

  - Data pre- and post-processing using SageMaker Processing

  - Integration with data storage solutions – Amazon S3, Amazon EFS, and Amazon FSx for Lustre

  - Developing models using SageMaker Studio IDE and Notebooks

- Training phase:

  - Managed training instances and software stack

  - DL containers for TensorFlow and Pytorch frameworks

  - Implementing distributed training using SageMaker's DataParallel and ModelParallel libraries

  - Monitoring and debugging training with SageMaker Debugger

- Inference:

  - Managed hosting platform for batch and real-time inference

  - Model monitoring at inference time

  - Compute instances for DL serving

As we progress through the book, we will also learn how to use the SageMaker API and SDKs to programmatically manage our resources. Additionally, we will discuss optimization strategies and SageMaker capabilities to reduce cost and time-to-market.

This book focuses on DL capabilities, so we will set several SageMaker features and capabilities aside. You can explore Amazon SageMaker further by reading the SageMaker documentation (`https://docs.aws.amazon.com/sagemaker/latest/dg/whatis.html`) and practical blog posts (`https://aws.amazon.com/blogs/machine-learning/category/artificial-intelligence/sagemaker/`).

In the next section, we'll find out exactly how SageMaker can help us with DL workloads.

Choosing Amazon SageMaker for DL workloads

As discussed earlier, DL workloads present several engineering challenges due to their need to access high quantities of specialized resources (primarily GPU devices and high-throughput storage solutions). However, managing a software stack can also present a challenge as new versions of ML and DL frameworks are released frequently. Due to high associated costs, it's also imperative to organize your training and inference efficiently to avoid waste.

Let's review how SageMaker can address these challenges.

Managed compute and storage infrastructure

SageMaker provides a fully managed compute infrastructure for your training and inference workloads. SageMaker Training and Inference clusters can scale to tens and up to hundreds of individual instances within minutes. This can be particularly useful in scenarios where you need to access a large compute cluster with short notice and for a limited period (for example, you need to train a complex DL model on a large dataset once every couple of months). As with other AWS services, SageMaker resources provide advanced auto-scaling features for inference endpoints so that customers can match demand without resource overprovisioning.

You can also choose from a growing number of available compute instances based on the requirements of specific DL models and types of workload. For instance, in many scenarios, you would need to use a GPU-based instance to train your DL model, while it may be possible to use cheaper CPU instances at inference time without this having an impact on end user performance. SageMaker gives you the flexibility to choose the most optimal instances for particular DL models and tasks.

In case of failure, AWS will automatically replace faulty instances without any customer intervention.

These SageMaker features greatly benefit customers as SageMaker simplifies capacity planning and operational management of your ML infrastructure.

Managed DL software stacks

To build, train, and deploy DL models, you need to use various frameworks and software components to perform specialized computations and communication between devices and nodes in distributed clusters. Creating and maintaining software stacks across various development environments can be labor-intensive.

To address these needs, as part of the SageMaker ecosystem, AWS provides multiple pre-built open source Docker containers for popular DL frameworks such as PyTorch, TensorFlow, MXNet, and others. These containers are built and tested by AWS and optimized for specific tasks (for instance, different containers for training and inference) and compute platforms (CPU or GPU-based containers, different versions of CUDA toolkits, and others).

Since Docker containers provide interoperability and encapsulation, developers can utilize pre-built SageMaker containers to build and debug their workloads locally before deploying them to a cloud cluster to shorten the development cycle. You also have the flexibility to extend or modify SageMaker containers based on specific requirements.

Advanced operational capabilities

While Amazon SageMaker utilizes several popular open source solutions for DL, it also provides several unique capabilities to address certain challenges when operationalizing your ML workloads, such as the following:

- SageMaker Debugger
- SageMaker Model Monitor
- SageMaker's DataParallel/ModelParallel distributed training libraries

Let's move on next to look at integration with other AWS services.

Integration with other AWS services

Amazon SageMaker is well integrated with other AWS services so that developers can build scalable, performant, and secure workloads.

In the next section, we'll see how Amazon SageMaker's managed training stack can be leveraged to run DL models.

Exploring SageMaker's managed training stack

Amazon SageMaker provides a set of capabilities and integration points with other AWS services to configure, run, and monitor ML training jobs. With SageMaker managed training, developers can do the following:

- Choose from a variety of built-in algorithms and containers, as well as BYO models
- Choose from a wide range of compute instances, depending on the model requirements
- Debug and profile their training process in near-real-time using SageMaker Debugger
- Run bias detection and model explainability jobs
- Run incremental training jobs, resume from checkpoints, and use spot instances

> **Spot instances**
>
> Amazon EC2 Spot Instances provides customers with access to unused compute capacity at a lower price point (up to 90%). Spot instances will be released when someone else claims them, which results in workload interruption.

- Run model tuning jobs to search for optimal combinations of model hyperparameters
- Organize training jobs in a searchable catalog of experiments

Amazon SageMaker provides the following capabilities out of the box:

- Provisioning, bootstrapping, and tearing down training nodes
- Capturing training job logs and metrics

In this section, we will go over all the stages of a SageMaker training job and the components involved. Please refer to the following diagram for a visual narrative that provides a step-by-step guide on creating, managing, and monitoring your first SageMaker training job. We will address the advanced features of SageMaker's managed training stack in *Part 2* of this book:

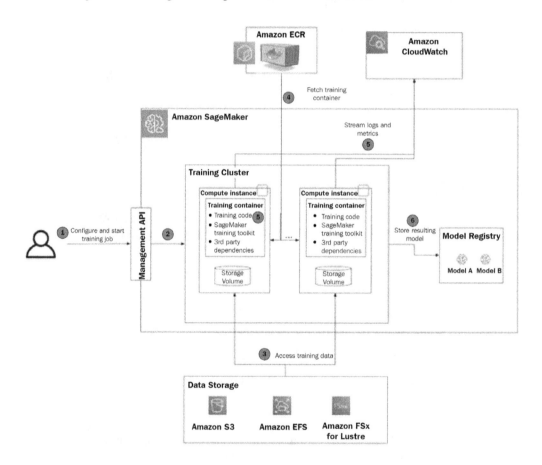

Figure 1.2 – Amazon SageMaker training stack

Let's walk through each step in turn.

We will also provide code snippets to illustrate how to perform a SageMaker training job configuration using the SageMaker Python SDK (https://sagemaker.readthedocs.io/en/stable/).

Step 1 – configuring and creating a training job

You can instantiate a SageMaker training job via an API call.

SageMaker defines several mandatory configuration parameters that need to be supplied by you. They are listed as follows.

Choosing an algorithm to train

Amazon SageMaker supports several types of ML algorithms:

- **Built-in algorithms** are available out of the box for all SageMaker users. At the time of writing, 18 built-in algorithms cover a variety of use cases, including DL algorithms for computer vision and NLP tasks. The user is only responsible for providing algorithm hyperparameters.

- **Custom algorithms** are developed by the user. AWS is not responsible for training logic in this case. The training script will be executed inside a Docker container. Developers can choose to use AWS-authored Docker images with pre-installed software dependencies or can use BYO Docker images.

- **Marketplace algorithms** are developed by third-party vendors and available via the AWS Marketplace. Similar to built-in algorithms, they typically offer a fully managed experience where the user is responsible for providing algorithm hyperparameters. Unlike built-in algorithms, which are free to use, the user usually pays a fee for using marketplace algorithms.

Defining an IAM role

Amazon SageMaker relies on the Amazon IAM service and, specifically, IAM roles to define which AWS resources and services can be accessed from the training job. That's why, whenever scheduling a SageMaker training job, you need to provide an IAM role, which will be then assigned to training nodes.

Defining a training cluster

Another set of required parameters defines the hardware configuration of the training cluster, which includes several compute instances, types of instances, and instance storage.

It's recommended that you carefully choose your instance type based on specific requirements. At a minimum, ML engineers need to understand which compute device is used at training time. For example, in most cases for DL models, you will likely need to use a GPU-based instance, while many classical ML algorithms (such as linear regression or Random Forest) are CPU-bound.

ML engineers also need to consider how many instances to provision. When provisioning multiple nodes, you need to make sure that your algorithm and training script support distributed training.

Built-in algorithms usually provide recommended instance types and counts in their public documentation. They also define whether distributed training is supported or not. In the latter case, you should configure a single-node training cluster.

Defining training data

Amazon SageMaker supports several storage solutions for training data:

- **Amazon S3**: This is a low-cost, highly durable, and highly available object storage. This is considered a default choice for storing training datasets. Amazon S3 supports two types of input mode (also defined in training job configuration) for training datasets:

  - **File**: Amazon SageMaker copies the training dataset from the S3 location to a local directory

  - **Pipe**: Amazon SageMaker streams data directly from S3 to the container via a Unix-named pipe

  - **FastFile**: A new file streaming capability provided by Amazon SageMaker.

- **Amazon EFS**: This is an elastic filesystem service. If it's used to persist training data, Amazon SageMaker will automatically mount the training instance to a shared filesystem.

- **Amazon FSx for Luster**: This is a high-performant shared filesystem optimized for the lowest latency and highest throughput.

Before training can begin, you need to make sure that data is persisted in one of these solutions, and then provide the location of the datasets.

Please note that you can provide the locations of several datasets (for example, training, test, and evaluation sets) in your training job.

Picking your algorithm hyperparameters

While it's not strictly mandatory, in most cases, you will need to define certain hyperparameters of the algorithm. Examples of such hyperparameters include the batch size, number of training epochs, and learning rate.

At training time, these hyperparameters will be passed to the training script as command-line arguments. In the case of custom algorithms, developers are responsible for parsing and setting hyperparameters in the training script.

Defining the training metrics

Metrics are another optional but important parameter. SageMaker provides out-of-the-box integration with Amazon CloudWatch to stream training logs and metrics. In the case of logs, SageMaker will automatically stream `stdout` and `stderr` from the training container to CloudWatch.

---

stdout and stderr

`stdout` and `stderr` are standard data streams in Linux and Unix-like OSs. Every time you run a Linux command, these data streams are established automatically. Normal command output is sent to `stdout`; any error messages are sent to `stderr`.

In the case of metrics, the user needs to define the regex pattern for each metric first. At training time, the SageMaker utility running on the training instance will monitor `stdout` and `stderr` for the regex pattern match, then extract the value of the metric and submit the metric name and value to CloudWatch. As a result, developers can monitor training processes in CloudWatch in near-real time.

Some common examples of training metrics include loss value and accuracy measures.

Configuring a SageMaker training job for image classification

In the following Python code sample, we will demonstrate how to configure a simple training job for a built-in **image classification** algorithm (https://docs.aws.amazon.com/sagemaker/latest/dg/image-classification.html):

1. Begin with your initial imports:

    ```
    import sagemaker
    from sagemaker import get_execution_role
    ```

2. The `get_execution_role()` method allows you to get the current IAM role. This role will be used to call the SageMaker APIs, whereas `sagemaker.Session()` stores the context of the interaction with SageMaker and other AWS services such as S3:

    ```
    role = get_execution_role()
    sess = sagemaker.Session()
    ```

3. The `.image_uris.retrieve()` method allows you to identify the correct container with the built-in image classification algorithm. Note that if you choose to use custom containers, you will need to specify a URI for your specific training container:

    ```
    training_image = sagemaker.image_uris.retrieve('image-
    classification', sess.boto_region_name)
    ```

4. Define the number of instances in the training cluster. Since image classification supports distributed training, we can allocate more than one instance to the training cluster to speed up training:

    ```
    num_instances = 2
    ```

5. The image classification algorithm requires GPU-based instances, so we will choose to use a SageMaker P2 instance type:

    ```
    instance_type = "ml.p2.xlarge"
    ```

6. Next, we must define the location of training and validation datasets. Note that the image classification algorithm supports several data formats. In this case, we choose to use the JPG file format, which also requires .1st files to list all the available images:

```
data_channels = {
    'train': f"s3://{sess.default_bucket()}/data/train",
    'validation': f"s3://{sess.default_bucket()}/data/
validation",
    'train_lst': f"s3://{sess.default_bucket()}/data/
train.lst",
    'vadidation_lst': f"s3://{sess.default_bucket()}/
data/validation.lst",
}
```

7. Configure the training hyperparameters:

```
hyperparameters=dict(
    use_pretrained_model=1,
    image_shape='3,224,224',
    num_classes=10,
    num_training_samples=40000, # TODO: update it
    learning_rate=0.001,
    mini_batch_size= 8
)
```

8. Configure the Estimator object, which encapsulates training job configuration:

```
image_classifier = sagemaker.estimator.Estimator(
    training_image,
    role,
    train_instance_count= num_instances,
    train_instance_type= instance_type,
    sagemaker_session=sess,
    hyperparameters=hyperparameters,
)
```

9. The `fit()` method submits the training job to the SageMaker API. If there are no issues, you should observe a new training job instance in your AWS Console. You can do so by going to **Amazon SageMaker | Training | Training Jobs**:

    ```
    image_classifier.fit(inputs=data_channels, job_
    name="sample-train")
    ```

Next, we'll provision the training cluster.

Step 2 – provisioning the SageMaker training cluster

Once you submit a request for the training job, SageMaker automatically does the following:

- Allocates the requested number of training nodes
- Allocates the Amazon EBS volumes and mounts them on the training nodes
- Assigns an IAM role to each node
- Bootstraps various utilities (such as Docker, SageMaker toolkit libraries, and so on)
- Defines the training configuration (hyperparameters, input data configuration, and so on) as an environment variable

Next up is the training data.

Step 3 – SageMaker accesses the training data

When your training cluster is ready, SageMaker establishes access to training data for compute instances. The exact mechanism to access training data depends on your storage solution:

- If data is stored in S3 and the input mode is **File**, then data will be downloaded to instance EBS volumes. Note that depending on the dataset's size, it may take minutes to download the data.
- If the data is stored in S3 and the input mode is **Pipe**, then the data will be streamed from S3 at training time as needed.
- If the data is stored in S3 and the input mode is **FastFile**, then the training program will access the files as if they are stored on training nodes. However, under the hood, the files will be streamed from S3.
- If the data is stored in EFS or FSx for Luster, then the training nodes will be mounted on the filesystem.

The training continues with deploying the container.

Step 4 – SageMaker deploys the training container

SageMaker automatically pulls the training images from the ECR repository. Note that built-in algorithms abstract the underlying training images so that users don't have to define the container image, just the algorithm to be used.

Step 5 – SageMaker starts and monitors the training job

To start the training job, SageMaker issues the following command on all training nodes:

```
docker run [TrainingImage] train
```

If the training cluster has instances with GPU devices, then `nvidia-docker` will be used.

Once the training script has started, SageMaker does the following:

- Captures `stdout/stderr` and sends it to CloudWatch logs.
- Runs a regex pattern match for metrics and sends the metric values to CloudWatch.
- Monitors for a `SIGTERM` signal from the SageMaker API (for example, if the user decides to stop the training job earlier).
- Monitors if an early stopping condition occurs and issues `SIGTERM` when this happens.
- Monitors for the exit code of the training script. In the case of a non-zero exit code, SageMaker will mark the training job as "failed."

Step 6 – SageMaker persists the training artifacts

Regardless of whether the training job fails or succeeds, SageMaker stores artifacts in the following locations:

- The `/opt/ml/output` directory, which can be used to persist any training artifacts after the job is completed.
- The `/opt/ml/model` directory, the content of which will be compressed into `.tar` format and stored in the SageMaker model registry.

Once you have your first model trained to solve a particular business problem, the next step is to use your model (in ML parlance, **perform inference**). In the next few sections, we will learn what capabilities SageMaker provides to run ML inference workloads for various use cases.

Using SageMaker's managed hosting stack

Amazon SageMaker supports several types of managed hosting infrastructure:

- A persistent synchronous HTTPS endpoint for real-time inference
- An asynchronous endpoint for near-real-time inference
- A transient Batch Transform job that performs inference across the entire dataset

In the next section, we will discuss use cases regarding when to use what type of hosting infrastructure, and we'll review real-time inference endpoints in detail.

Real-time inference endpoints

Real-time endpoints are built for use cases where you need to get inference results as soon as possible. SageMaker's real-time endpoint is an HTTPS endpoint: model inputs are provided by the client via a POST request payload, and inference results are returned in the response body. The communication is synchronous.

There are many scenarios when real-time endpoints are applicable, such as the following:

- To provide movie recommendations when the user opens a streaming application, based on the user's watch history, individual ratings, and what's trending now
- To detect objects in a real-time video stream
- To generate a suggested next word as the user inputs text

SageMaker real-time endpoints provide customers with a range of capabilities to design and manage their inference workloads:

- Create a fully managed compute infrastructure with horizontal scaling (meaning that a single endpoint can use multiple compute instances to serve high traffic load without performance degradation)
- There is a wide spectrum of EC2 compute instance types to choose from based on model requirements including AWS' custom chip Inferentia and SageMaker Elastic Inference
- Pre-built inference containers for popular DL frameworks
- Multi-model and multi-container endpoints
- Model production variants for A/B testing
- Multi-model inference pipelines
- Model monitoring for performance, accuracy, and bias
- SageMaker Neo and SageMaker Edge Manager to optimize and manage inference at edge devices

Since this is a managed capability, Amazon SageMaker is responsible for the following aspects of managing users' real-time endpoints:

- Provisioning and scaling the underlying compute infrastructure based on customer-defined scaling policies

- Traffic shaping between model versions and containers in cases where multiple models are deployed on a single SageMaker endpoint.

- Streaming logs and metrics at the level of the compute instance and model.

Creating and using your SageMaker endpoint

Let's walk through the process of configuring, provisioning, and using your first SageMaker real-time endpoint. This will help to build your understanding of its internal workings and the available configuration options. The following diagram provides a visual guide:

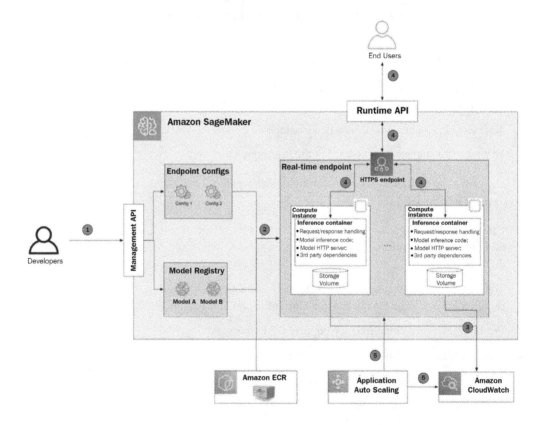

Figure 1.3 – SageMaker inference endpoint deployment and usage

Step 1 – initiating endpoint creation

There are several ways to initiate SageMaker endpoint creation: the SageMaker Python SDK, the boto3 SDK, the AWS CLI, or via a CloudFormation template. As part of the request, there are several parameters that you need to provide, as follows:

- **Model definition** in SageMaker Model Registry, which will be used at inference time. The model definition includes references to serialized model artifacts in S3 and a reference to the inference container (or several containers in the case of a multi-container endpoint) in Amazon ECR.

- **Endpoint configuration**, which defines the number and type of compute instances, and (optional) a combination of several models (in the case of a multi-model endpoint) or several model production variants (in the case of A/B testing).

Step 2 – configuring the SageMaker endpoint for image classification

The following Python code sample shows how to create and deploy an endpoint using the previously trained image classification model:

1. Begin with your initial imports, IAM role, and SageMaker session instantiation:

```
import sagemaker
from sagemaker import get_execution_role
role = get_execution_role()
sess = sagemaker.Session()
```

2. Retrieve the inference container URI for the image classification algorithm:

```
image_uri = sagemaker.image_uris.retrieve('image-
classification', sess.boto_region_name)
```

3. Define where the model artifacts (such as trained weights) are stored in S3:

```
model_data = f"s3://{sess.default_bucket}/model_location"
```

4. Create a SageMaker Model object that encapsulates the model configuration:

```
model = Model(
image_uri=image_uri,
model_data=model_data,
name="image-classification-endpoint",
sagemaker_session=sess,
role=role
)
```

5.   Define the endpoint configuration parameters:

```
endpoint_name = "image-classification-endpoint"
instance_type = "ml.g4dn.xlarge"
instance_count = 1
```

6.   The `.predict()` method submits a request to SageMaker to create an endpoint with a specific model deployed:

```
predictor = model.deploy(
instance_type=instance_type,
initial_instance_count=instance_count,
endpoint_name=endpoint_name,
)
```

With that done, SageMaker gets to work.

Step 3 – SageMaker provisions the endpoint

Once your provision request is submitted, SageMaker performs the following actions:

- It will allocate several instances according to the endpoint configuration
- It will deploy an inference container
- It will download the model artifacts

It takes several minutes to complete endpoint provisioning from start to finish. The provisioning time depends on the number of parameters, such as instance type, size of the inference container, and the size of the model artifacts that need to be uploaded to the inference instance(s).

Please note that SageMaker doesn't expose inference instances directly. Instead, it uses a fronting load balancer, which then distributes the traffic between provisioned instances. As SageMaker is a managed service, you will never interact with inference instances directly, only via the SageMaker API.

Step 4 – SageMaker starts the model server

Once the endpoint has been fully provisioned, SageMaker starts the inference container by running the following command, which executes the ENTRYPOINT command in the container:

```
docker run image serve
```

This script does the following:

- Starts the model server, which exposes the HTTP endpoint
- Makes the model server load the model artifacts in memory
- At inference time, it makes the model server execute the inference script, which defines how to preprocess data

In the case of SageMaker-managed Docker images, the model server and startup logic are already implemented by AWS. If you choose to BYO serving container, then this needs to be implemented separately.

SageMaker captures the `stdout/stderr` streams and automatically streams them to CloudWatch logs. It also streams instances metrics such as the number of invocations total and per instance, invocation errors, and latency measures.

Step 5 – the SageMaker endpoint serves traffic

Once the model server is up and running, end users can send a `POST` request to the SageMaker endpoint. The endpoint authorizes the request based on the authorization headers (these headers are automatically generated when using the SageMaker Python SDK or the AWS CLI based on the IAM profile). If authorization is successful, then the payload is sent to the inference instance.

The running model server handles the request by executing the inference script and returns the response payload, which is then delivered to the end user.

Step 6 – SageMaker scales the inference endpoint in or out

You may choose to define an auto-scaling policy to scale endpoint instances in and out. In this case, SageMaker will add or remove compute nodes behind the endpoint to match demand more efficiently. Please note that SageMaker only supports horizontal scaling, such as adding or removing compute nodes, and not changing instance type.

SageMaker supports several types of scaling events:

- Manual, where the user updates the endpoint configuration via an API call
- A target tracking policy, where SageMaker scales in or out based on the value of the user-defined metric (for example, the number of invocations or resource utilization)
- A step scaling policy, which provides the user with more granular control over how to adjust the number of instances based on how much threshold is breached
- A scheduled scaling policy, which allows you to scale the SageMaker endpoint based on a particular schedule (for example, scale in during the weekend, where there's low traffic, and scale out during the weekday, where there's peak traffic)

Advanced model deployment patterns

We just reviewed the anatomy of a simple, single-model real-time endpoint. However, in many real-life scenarios where there are tens or hundreds of models that need to be available at any given point in time, this approach will lead to large numbers of underutilized or unevenly utilized inference nodes.

This is a generally undesirable situation as it will lead to high compute costs without any end user value. To address this problem, Amazon SageMaker provides a few advanced deployment options that allow you to combine several models within the same real-time endpoint and, hence, utilize resources more efficiently.

Multi-container endpoint

When deploying a multi-container endpoint, you may specify up to 15 different containers within the same endpoint. Each inference container has model artifacts and its own runtime environment. This allows you to deploy models built in various frameworks and runtime environments within a single SageMaker endpoint.

At creation time, you define a unique container hostname. Each container can then be invoked independently. During endpoint invocation, you are required to provide this container hostname as one of the request headers. SageMaker will automatically route the inference request to a correct container based on this header.

This feature comes in handy when there are several models with relatively low traffic and different runtime environments (for example, Pytorch and TensorFlow).

Inference pipeline

Like a multi-container endpoint, the inference pipeline allows you to combine different models and container runtimes within a single SageMaker endpoint. However, the containers are called sequentially. This feature is geared toward scenarios where an inference request requires pre and/or post-processing with different runtime requirements; for example:

- The pre-processing phase is done using the scikit-learn library
- Inference is done using a DL framework
- Post-processing is done using a custom runtime environment, such as Java or C++

By encapsulating different phases of the inference pipeline in separate containers, changes in one container won't impact adversely other containers, such as updating the dependency version. Since containers within inference pipelines are located on the same compute node, this guarantees low latency during request handoff between containers.

Multi-model endpoint

Multi-model endpoints allow you to deploy hundreds of models within a single endpoint. Unlike multi-container endpoints and inference pipelines, a multi-model endpoint has a single runtime environment. SageMaker automatically loads model artifacts into memory and handles inference requests. When a model is no longer needed, SageMaker unloads it from memory to free up resources. This leads to some additional latency when invoking the model for the first time after a while. Model artifacts are stored on Amazon S3 and loaded by SageMaker automatically.

At the core of the multi-model endpoint is the AWS-developed open source Multi-Model Server, which provides model management capabilities (loading, unloading, and resource allocation) and an HTTP frontend to receive inference requests, execute inference code for a given model, and return the resulting payload.

Multi-model endpoints are optimal when there's a large number of homogeneous models and end users can tolerate warmup latency.

SageMaker asynchronous endpoints

So far, we have discussed SageMaker real-time endpoints, which work synchronously: users invoke the endpoint by sending a POST request, wait for the endpoint to run inference code, and then return the inference results in the response payload. The inference code is expected to complete within 60 seconds; otherwise, the SageMaker endpoint will return a timeout response.

In certain scenarios, however, this synchronous communication pattern can be problematic:

- Large models can take a considerable time to perform inference
- Large payload sizes (for instance, high-resolution imagery)

For such scenarios, SageMaker provides Asynchronous Endpoints, which allow you to queue inference requests and process them asynchronously, avoiding potential timeouts. Asynchronous endpoints also allow for a considerably larger payload size of up to 1 GB, whereas SageMaker real-time endpoints have a limit of 5 MB. Asynchronous endpoints can be scaled to 0 instances when the inference queue is empty to provide additional cost savings. This is specifically useful for scenarios with sporadic inference traffic patterns.

The main tradeoff of asynchronous endpoints is that the inference results are delivered in *near* real-time and may not be suited for scenarios where consistent latency is expected:

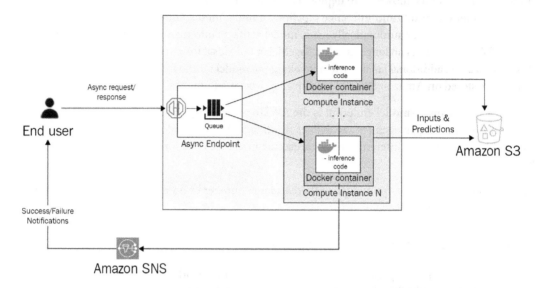

Figure 1.4 – SageMaker asynchronous endpoint

SageMaker Batch Transform

SageMaker Batch Transform allows you to get predictions for a batch of inference inputs. This can be useful for scenarios where there is a recurrent business process and there are no strict latency requirements. An example is a nightly job that calculates risks for load applications.

SageMaker Batch Transform is beneficial for the following use cases:

- Customers only pay for resources that are consumed during job execution
- Batch Transform jobs can scale to GBs and tens of compute nodes

When scheduling a Batch Transform job, you define the cluster configuration (type and number of compute nodes), model artifacts, inference container, the input S3 location for the inference dataset, and the output S3 location for the generated predictions. Please note that customers can use the same container for SageMaker real-time endpoints and the Batch Transform job. This allows developers to use the same models/containers for online predictions (as real-time endpoints) and offline (as Batch Transform jobs):

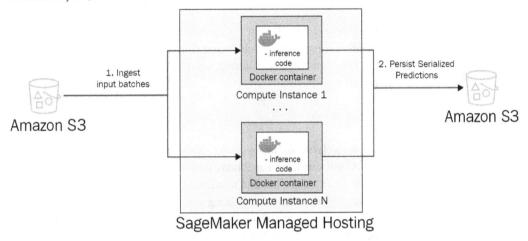

Figure 1.5 – SageMaker Batch Transform job

With that, you understand how to train a simple DL model using a SageMaker training job and then create a real-time endpoint to perform inference. Before we proceed further, we need to learn about several foundational AWS services that are used by Amazon SageMaker that you will see throughout this book.

Integration with AWS services

Amazon SageMaker relies on several AWS services, such as storage and key management. In this section, we will review some key integrations with other AWS services and use cases when they can be useful.

Data storage services

Data storage services are key to building any ML workload. AWS provides several storage solutions to address a wide range of real-life use cases.

Amazon S3 is a form of serverless object storage and one of AWS's foundational services. SageMaker utilizes S3 for a wide range of use cases, such as the following:

- To store training datasets
- To store model artifacts and training output
- To store inference inputs and outputs for Asynchronous Endpoints and Batch Transform jobs

Amazon S3 is a highly durable, scalable, and cost-efficient storage solution. When accessing data stored on S3, developers may choose to either download the full dataset from the S3 location to SageMaker compute nodes or stream the data. Downloading a large dataset from S3 to SageMaker compute nodes to add to the training job's startup time.

Amazon EFS

Amazon Elastic File System (**EFS**) is an elastic filesystem service. Amazon SageMaker supports storing training datasets in EFS locations. At training time, SageMaker nodes mount to the EFS location and directly access the training datasets. In this case, no data movement is required for nodes to access data, which typically results in reduced startup times for training jobs. EFS also allows multiple nodes to persist and seamlessly share data (since this is a shared system). This can be beneficial when the cache or system state needs to be shared across training nodes.

Amazon FSx for Lustre

Amazon FSx for Lustre is a shared filesystem service designed specifically for low-latency, high-performance scenarios. Amazon FSx automatically copies data from the S3 source and makes it available for SageMaker compute nodes. Amazon FSx has similar benefits to EFS – that is, a reduced startup time for training jobs and a shared filesystem.

Orchestration services

Orchestration services allow you to integrate SageMaker-based workloads with the rest of the IT ecosystem.

AWS Step Functions

AWS Step Functions is a serverless workflow service that allows you to orchestrate business processes and interactions with other AWS services. With Step Functions, it's easy to combine individual steps into reusable and deployable workflows. It supports visual design and branching and conditional logic.

Step Functions provides native integration with SageMaker resources. Step Functions can be useful in scenarios where you need to orchestrate complex ML pipelines using multiple services in addition to SageMaker. AWS provides developers with the AWS Step Functions Data Science Python SDK to develop, test, and execute such pipelines.

Amazon API Gateway

Amazon API Gateway is a fully managed API management service that's used to develop, monitor, and manage APIs. API Gateway supports several features that can be helpful when developing highly-scalable and secure ML inference APIs:

- Authentication and authorization mechanisms

- Request caching, rate limiting, and throttling

- Firewall features

- Request headers and payload transformation

API Gateway allows you to insulate SageMaker real-time endpoints from external traffic and provide an additional layer of security. It also allows you to provide end users with a unified API without exposing the specifics of the SageMaker runtime API.

Security services

Robust security controls are a must-have for any ML workload, especially when dealing with private and sensitive data. While this book does not focus on security, it's important to understand the basic aspects of permissions and data encryption on AWS.

AWS IAM

AWS Identity and Access Management (**IAM**) allows customers to manage access to AWS services and resources. In the case of SageMaker, IAM has a twofold function:

- IAM roles and policies define which AWS resources SageMaker jobs can access and manage – for example, whether the training job with the assumed IAM role can access the given dataset on S3 or not.

- IAM roles and policies define which principal (user or service) can access and manage SageMaker resources. For instance, it defines whether the given user can schedule a SageMaker training job with a specific cluster configuration.

Reviewing IAM is outside the scope of this book, but you need to be aware of it. Setting up IAM permissions and roles are prerequisites when working with SageMaker.

Amazon VPC

Amazon Virtual Private Cloud (**VPC**) is a service that allows you to run your cloud workloads in logically isolated private networks. This network-level isolation provides an additional level of security and control over who can access your workload. SageMaker allows you to run training and inference workloads inside a dedicated VPC so that you can control egress and ingress traffic to and from your SageMaker resources.

AWS KMS

AWS Key Management Service (KMS) is used to encrypt underlying data. It also manages access to cryptographic keys when encrypting and decrypting data. In the context of SageMaker, KMS is primarily used to encrypt training data, model artifacts, and underlying disks in SageMaker clusters. KMS is integrated with all available storage solutions, such as S3, EFS, and EBS (underlying disk volumes).

Monitoring services

AWS has dedicated services to monitor the management, auditing, and execution of other AWS resources.

Amazon CloudWatch

CloudWatch provides monitoring and observability capabilities. In the context of SageMaker, it's used primarily for two purposes:

- To store and manage logs coming from SageMaker resources such as endpoints or training jobs. By default, SageMaker ships `stdout/stderr` logs to CloudWatch.

- To store time series metrics. SageMaker provides several metrics out of the box (for example, for real-time endpoints, it streams latency and invocation metrics). However, developers can implement custom metrics.

Amazon CloudTrail

CloudTrail captures all activities (such as API calls) related to managing any AWS resources, including SageMaker resources. Typically, CloudTrail is used for governance and auditing purposes, but it can be used to build event-driven workflows. For instance, developers can use it to monitor resource creation or update requests and programmatically react to specific events.

Summary

We started this chapter by providing a general overview of the DL domain and its challenges, as well as the Amazon SageMaker service and its value proposition for DL workloads. Then, we reviewed the core SageMaker capabilities: managed training and managed hosting. We examined the life cycle of a SageMaker training job and real-time inference endpoint. Code snippets demonstrated how to configure and provision SageMaker resources programmatically using its Python SDK. We also looked at other relevant AWS services as we will be using them a lot in the rest of this book. This will help us as we now have a good grounding in their uses and capabilities.

In the next chapter, we will dive deeper into the foundational building blocks of any SageMaker workload: runtime environments (specifically, supported DL frameworks) and containers. SageMaker provides several popular pre-configured runtime environments and containers, but it also allows you to fully customize them via its "BYO container" feature. We will learn when to choose one of these options and how to use them.

2
Deep Learning Frameworks and Containers on SageMaker

Amazon SageMaker supports many popular ML and DL frameworks. Framework support in SageMaker is achieved using prebuilt Docker containers for inference and training tasks. Prebuilt SageMaker containers provide a great deal of functionality, and they allow you to implement a wide range of use cases with minimal coding. There are also real-life scenarios where you need to have a custom, runtime environment for training and/or inference tasks. To address these cases, SageMaker provides a flexible **Bring-Your-Own (BYO)** container feature.

In this chapter, we will review key supported DL frameworks and corresponding container images. Then, we will focus our attention on the two most popular DL frameworks, TensorFlow and PyTorch, and learn how to use them in Amazon SageMaker. Additionally, we will review a higher-level, state-of-the-art framework, Hugging Face, for NLP tasks, and its implementation for Amazon SageMaker.

Then, we will understand how to use and extend prebuilt SageMaker containers based on your use case requirements, as well as learning about the SageMaker SDK and toolkits, which simplify writing training and inference scripts that are compatible with Amazon SageMaker.

In later sections, we will dive deeper into how to decide whether to use prebuilt SageMaker containers or BYO containers. Then, we will develop a SageMaker-compatible BYO container.

These topics will be covered in the following sections:

- Exploring DL frameworks on SageMaker
- Using SageMaker DL containers
- Developing BYO containers

By the end of this chapter, you will be able to decide which container strategy to choose based on your specific problem requirements and chosen DL framework. Additionally, you will understand the key aspects of training and inference script development, which are compatible with Amazon SageMaker.

Technical requirements

In the *Using SageMaker DL containers* and *Developing BYO containers* sections, we will provide walk-through code samples, so you can develop practical skills. Full code examples are available at `https://github.com/PacktPublishing/Accelerate-Deep-Learning-Workloads-with-Amazon-SageMaker/blob/main/chapter2/`.

To follow along with this code, you will need the following:

- An AWS account and IAM user with the permissions to manage Amazon SageMaker resources.
- Python 3 and the SageMaker SDK (`https://pypi.org/project/sagemaker/`) installed on your development machine.
- Docker installed on your development machine.
- To use SageMaker P2 instances for training purposes, you will likely need to request a service limit increase on your AWS account. For more details, please view `https://docs.aws.amazon.com/general/latest/gr/aws_service_limits.html`.

Exploring DL frameworks on SageMaker

At the time of writing this book, Amazon SageMaker supports the following frameworks, where DL frameworks are marked with an asterisk:

- scikit-learn
- SparkML Serving
- Chainer*
- Apache MXNet*
- Hugging Face*
- PyTorch*
- TensorFlow*
- Reinforcement learning containers – including TensorFlow- and PyTorch-enabled containers
- XGBoost

The preceding list of supported frameworks could change in the future. Be sure to check the official SageMaker documentation at `https://docs.aws.amazon.com/sagemaker/latest/dg/frameworks.html`.

In this book, we will primarily focus on the two most popular choices: **TensorFlow** and **PyTorch**. Both are open source frameworks with a large and vibrant communities. Depending on the specific use case or model architecture, one or the other framework might have a slight advantage. However, it's safe to assume that both frameworks are comparable in terms of features and performance. In many practical scenarios, the choice between TensorFlow or PyTorch is made based on historical precedents or individual preferences.

Another framework that we will discuss in this book is **Hugging Face**. This is a high-level framework that provides access to SOTA models, training, and inference facilities for NLP tasks (such as text classification, translation, and more). Hugging Face is a set of several libraries (transformers, datasets, tokenizers, and accelerate) designed to simplify building SOTA NLP models. Under the hood, Hugging Face libraries use TensorFlow and PyTorch primitives (collectively known as "backends") to perform computations. Users can choose which backend to use based on specific runtime requirements. Given its popularity, Amazon SageMaker has recently added support for the Hugging Face libraries in separate prebuilt containers for training and inference tasks.

Container sources

Sources of SageMaker DL containers are available on the public GitHub repository at `https://github.com/aws/deep-learning-containers`. In certain cases, it can be helpful to review relevant Dockerfiles to understand the runtime configuration of prebuilt containers. Container images are available in AWS public registries at `https://github.com/aws/deep-learning-containers/blob/master/available_images.md`.

For each of the supported frameworks, SageMaker provides separate training and inference containers. We have separate containers for these two tasks because of the following considerations:

- Training and inference tasks might have different runtime requirements. For example, you might choose to run your training and inference tasks on different compute platforms. This will result in different sets of accelerators and performance optimization tweaks in your container, depending on your specific task.

- Training and inference tasks require different sets of auxiliary scripts; for instance, standing up a model server in the case of inference tasks. Not separating training and inference containers could result in bloated container sizes and intricate APIs.

For this reason, we will always explicitly identify the container we are using depending on the specific task.

Specific to DL containers, AWS also defines separate GPU-based and CPU-based containers. GPU-based containers require the installation of additional accelerators to be able to run computations on GPU devices (such as the CUDA toolkit).

Model requirements

When choosing a SageMaker DL container, always consider the model requirements for compute resources. For the majority of SOTA models, it's recommended that you use GPU-based compute instances to achieve acceptable performance. Choose your DL container accordingly.

TensorFlow containers

A TensorFlow container has two major versions: 1.x (maintenance mode) and 2.x (the latest version). Amazon SageMaker supports both versions and provides inference and training containers. In this book, all of the code examples and general commentary are done assuming TensorFlow v2.x.

AWS updates with frequently supported minor TensorFlow versions. The latest supported major version is 2.10.0.

PyTorch containers

Amazon SageMaker provides inference and training containers for PyTorch. The latest version is 1.12.1.

Hugging Face containers

AWS provides Hugging Face containers in two flavors: PyTorch and TensorFlow backends. Each backend has separate training and inference containers.

Using SageMaker Python SDK

AWS provides a convenient Python SDK that simplifies interactions with supported DL frameworks via the Estimator, Model, and Predictor classes. Each supported framework has a separate module with the implementation of respective classes. For example, here is how you import Predict, Estimator, and Model classes for the PyTorch framework:

```
from sagemaker.pytorch.estimator import PyTorch
from sagemaker.pytorch.model import PyTorchModel,
PyTorchPredictor
```

The following diagram shows the SageMaker Python SDK workflow:

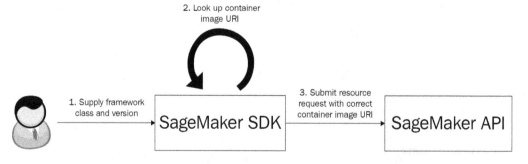

Figure 2.1 – How SageMaker Python SDK works with image URIs

To build a better intuition, let's do a quick example of how to run a training job using a PyTorch container with a specific version using SageMaker Python SDK. For a visual overview, please refer to *Figure 2.1*:

1. First, we decide which framework to use and import the respective `Pytorch estimator` class:

    ```
    from sagemaker.pytorch.estimator import PyTorch
    ```

    When instantiating the PyTorch `estimator` object, we need to provide several more parameters including the framework version and the Python version:

    ```
    estimator = PyTorch(
        entry_point="training_script.py",
        framework_version="1.8",
        py_version="py3",
        role=role,
        instance_count=1,
        instance_type="ml.p2.xlarge"
    )
    ```

2. When executing this code, SageMaker Python SDK automatically validates user input, including the framework version and the Python version. If the requested container exists, then SageMaker Python SDK retrieves the appropriate container image URI. If there is no container with the requested parameters, SageMaker Python SDK will throw an exception.

3. During the `fit()` call, a correct container image URI will be provided to the SageMaker API, so the training job will be running inside the SageMaker container with PyTorch v1.8 and Python v3.7 installed. Since we are requesting a GPU-based instance, a training container with the CUDA toolkit installed will be used:

    ```
    estimator.fit()
    ```

> **Using custom images**
>
> Please note that if, for some reason, you would prefer to provide a direct URI to your container image, you can do it using the `image_uri` parameter that is supported by the `model` and `estimator` classes.

Now, let's take a deep dive into SageMaker DL containers, starting with the available prebuilt containers for the TensorFlow, PyTorch, and Hugging Face frameworks.

Using SageMaker DL containers

Amazon SageMaker supports several container usage patterns. Also, it provides you with Training and Inference Toolkits that simplify using prebuilt containers and developing BYO containers.

In this section, we will learn how to choose the most efficient container usage pattern for your use case and how to use the available SageMaker toolkits to implement it.

Container usage patterns

Amazon SageMaker provides you with the flexibility to choose whether to use prebuilt containers "as is" (known as **Script Mode**), **BYO containers**, or modify prebuilt containers.

Typically, the choice of approach is driven by specific model runtime requirements, available resources, and engineering expertise. In the next few subsections, we will discuss when to choose one approach over another.

Script Mode

In script mode, you define which prebuilt container you'd like to use and then provide one or more scripts with the implementation of your training or inference logic. Additionally, you can provide any other dependencies (proprietary or public) that will be exported to the containers.

Both training and inference containers in script mode come with preinstalled toolkits that provide common functionality such as downloading data to containers and model artifacts, starting jobs, and others. We will look at further details of the SageMaker **Inference Toolkit** and **Training Toolkit** later in this chapter.

Script Mode is suitable for the following scenarios:

- Prebuilt containers satisfy your runtime requirements, or you can install any dependencies without needing to rebuild the container
- You want to minimize the time spent on developing and testing your containers or you don't have the required expertise to do so

In the following sections, we will review how to prepare your first training and inference scripts and run them on SageMaker in script mode.

Modifying prebuilt containers

Another way to use SageMaker's prebuilt containers is to modify them. In this case, you will use one of the prebuilt containers as a base image for your custom container.

Modifying prebuilt containers can be beneficial in the following scenarios:

- You need to add additional dependencies (for instance, ones that need to be compiled from sources) or reconfigure the runtime environment
- You want to minimize the development and testing efforts of your container and rely for the most part on the functionality of the base container tested by AWS

Please note that when you extend a prebuilt container, you will be responsible for the following aspects:

- Creating the Dockerfile with the implementation of your runtime environment
- Building and storing your container in a Container registry such as **Amazon Elastic Container Registry (ECR)** or private Docker registries

Later in this chapter, we see an example of how to extend a prebuilt PyTorch container for a training task.

BYO containers

There are many scenarios in which you might need to create a custom container, such as the following:

- You have unique runtime requirements that cannot be addressed by extending the prebuilt container
- You want to compile frameworks and libraries from sources for specific hardware platforms
- You are using DL frameworks that are not supported natively by SageMaker (for instance, JAX)

Building a custom container compatible with SageMaker inference and training resources requires development efforts, an understanding of Docker containers, and specific SageMaker requirements. Therefore, it's usually recommended that you consider script mode or extending a prebuilt container first and choose to use a BYO container only if the first options do not work for your particular use case.

SageMaker toolkits

To simplify the development of custom scripts and containers that are compatible with Amazon SageMaker, AWS created Python toolkits for training and inference tasks.

Toolkits provide the following benefits:

- Establish consistent runtime environments and locations for storing code assets
- `ENTRYPOINT` scripts to run tasks when the container is started

Understanding these toolkits helps to simplify and speed up the development of SageMaker-compatible containers, so let's review them in detail.

The Training Toolkit

The SageMaker Training Toolkit has several key functions:

- It establishes a consistent runtime environment, setting environment variables and a directory structure to store the input and output artifacts of model training:

```
/opt/ml
├── input
│    ├── config
│    │    ├── hyperparameters.json
│    │    └── resourceConfig.json
│    └── data
│         └── <channel_name>
│              └── <input data>
├── model
│
├── code
│
├── output
│
└── failure
```

Figure 2.2 – The directory structure in SageMaker-compatible containers

The Training Toolkit sets up the following directories in the training container:

- The /opt/ml/input/config directory with the model hyperparameters and the network layout used for distributed training as JSON files.
- The /opt/ml/input/data directory with input data when S3 is used as data storage.
- The /opt/ml/code/ directory, containing code assets to run training job.
- The /opt/ml/model/ directory, containing the resulting model; SageMaker automatically copies it to Amazon S3 after training completion.

- It executes the entrypoint script and handles success and failure statuses. In the case of a training job failure, the output will be stored in /opt/ml/output/failure. For successful executions, the toolkit will write output to the /opt/ml/success directory.

By default, all prebuilt training containers already have a training toolkit installed. If you wish to use it, you will need to install it on your container by running the following:

```
RUN pip install sagemaker-training
```

Also, you will need to copy all of the code dependencies into your container and define a special environmental variable in your main training script, as follows:

```
COPY train_scipt.py /opt/ml/code/train_script.py
ENV SAGEMAKER_PROGRAM train_scipt.py
```

The training toolkit package is available in the PyPI (`pypi.org`) package and the SageMaker GitHub repository (`https://github.com/aws/sagemaker-training-toolkit`).

Inference Toolkit

The **Inference Toolkit** implements a model serving stack that is compatible with SageMaker inference services. It comes together with an open source **Multi-Model Server** (**MMS**) to serve models. It has the following key functions:

- To establish runtime environments, such as directories to store input and output artifacts of inference and environmental variables. The directory structure follows the layout of the training container.

- To implement a handler service that is called from the model server to load the model into memory, and handle model inputs and outputs.

- To implement default serializers and deserializers to handle inference requests.

The Inference Toolkit package is available in the PyPi (`pypi.org`) package and the GitHub repository (`https://github.com/aws/sagemaker-inference-toolkit`).

Developing for script mode

Now that we have an understanding of SageMaker's container ecosystem, let's implement several learning projects to build practical skills. In this first example, we will use SageMaker script mode to train our custom NLP model and deploy it for inference.

Problem overview

In this example, we will learn how to develop training and inference scripts using the Hugging Face framework. We will leverage prebuilt SageMaker containers for Hugging Face (with the PyTorch backend).

We chose to solve a typical NLP task: text classification. We will use the 20 Newsgroups dataset, which assembles ~20,000 newsgroup documents across 20 different newsgroups (categories). There are a number of model architectures that can address this task. Usually, current SOTA models are based on Transformer architecture. Autoregressive models such as **BERT** and its various derivatives are suitable for this task. We will use a concept known as **transfer learning**, where a model that is pretrained for one task is used for a new task with minimal modifications.

As a baseline model, we will use model architecture known as **DistilBERT**, which provides high accuracy on a wide variety of tasks and is considerably smaller than other models (for instance, the original BERT model). To adapt the model for a classification task, we would need to add a classification layer, which will be trained during our training to recognize articles:

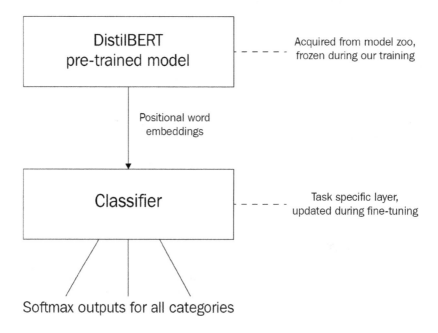

Figure 2.3 – The model architecture for the text classification task

The Hugging Face Transformers library simplifies model selection and modification for fine-tuning in the following ways:

- It provides a rich model zoo with a number of pretrained models and tokenizers
- It has a simple model API to modify the baseline model for fine-tuning a specific task
- It implements inference pipelines, combining data preprocessing and actual inference together

The full source code of this learning project is available at `https://github.com/` `PacktPublishing/Accelerate-Deep-Learning-Workloads-with-Amazon-` `SageMaker/blob/main/chapter2/1_Using_SageMaker_Script_Mode.ipynb`.

Developing a training script

When running SageMaker training jobs, we need to provide a training script. Additionally, we might provide any other dependencies. We can also install or modify Python packages that are installed on prebuilt containers via the `requirements.txt` file.

In this example, we will use a new feature of the Hugging Face framework to fine-tune a multicategory classifier using the Hugging Face Trainer API. Let's make sure that the training container has the newer Hugging Face Transformer library installed. For this, we create the `requirements.txt` file and specify a minimal compatible version. Later, we will provide this file to our SageMaker training job:

```
transformers >= 4.10
```

Next, we need to develop the training script. Let's review some key components of it.

At training time, SageMaker starts training by calling `user_training_script --arg1 value1` `--arg2 value2 ....` Here, `arg1..N` are training hyperparameters and other miscellaneous parameters provided by users as part of training job configuration. To correctly kick off the training process in our script, we need to include `main guard` within our script:

1. To correctly capture the parameters, the training script needs to be able to parse command-line arguments. We use the Python `argparse` library to do this:

    ```python
    if __name__ == "__main__":
        parser = argparse.ArgumentParser()
        parser.add_argument("--epochs", type=int, default=1)
        parser.add_argument("--per-device-train-batch-size",
    type=int, default=16)
        parser.add_argument("--per-device-eval-batch-size",
    type=int, default=64)
        parser.add_argument("--warmup-steps", type=int,
    default=100)
        parser.add_argument("--logging-steps", type=float,
    default=100)
        parser.add_argument("--weight-decay", type=float,
    default=0.01)
        args, _ = parser.parse_known_args()
        train(args)
    ```

2. The `train()` method is responsible for running end-to-end training jobs. It includes the following components:

    -   Calling `_get_tokenized_dataset` to load and tokenize datasets using a pretrained DistilBERT tokenizer from the Hugging Face library.

    -   Loading and configuring the DistilBERT model from the Hugging Face model zoo. Please note that we update the default configuration for classification tasks to adjust for our chosen number of categories.

    -   Configuring Hugging Face Trainer and starting the training process.

    -   Once the training is done, we save the trained model:

```
def train(args):
    train_enc_dataset, test_enc_dataset = _get_tokenized_
data()
    training_args = TrainingArguments(
        output_dir=os.getenv(
            "SM_OUTPUT_DIR", "./"
        ),  # output directory, if runtime is not
        num_train_epochs=args.epochs,
        per_device_train_batch_size=args.per_device_
train_batch_size,
        per_device_eval_batch_size=args.per_device_eval_
batch_size,
        warmup_steps=args.warmup_steps,
        weight_decay=args.weight_decay,
        logging_steps=args.logging_steps,
    )
    config = DistilBertConfig()
    config.num_labels = NUM_LABELS
    model = DistilBertForSequenceClassification.from_
pretrained(
        MODEL_NAME, config=config
    )
    trainer = Trainer(
        model=model,  # model to be trained
        args=training_args,  # training arguments,
defined above
        train_dataset=train_enc_dataset,  # training
```

```
dataset
        eval_dataset=test_enc_dataset,   # evaluation
dataset
    )
    trainer.train()
    model.save_pretrained(os.environ["SM_MODEL_DIR"])
```

So far in our script, we have covered key aspects: handling configuration settings and model hyperparameters, loading pretrained models, and starting training using the Hugging Face Trainer API.

Starting the training job

Once we have our training script and dependencies ready, we can proceed with the training and schedule a training job via SageMaker Python SDK. We start with the import of the Hugging Face Estimator object and get the IAM execution role for our training job:

```
from sagemaker.huggingface.estimator import HuggingFace
from sagemaker import get_execution_role
role=get_execution_role()
```

Next, we need to define the hyperparameters of our model and training processes. These variables will be passed to our script at training time:

```
hyperparameters = {
    "epochs":1,
    "per-device-train-batch-size":16,
    "per-device-eval-batch-size":64,
    "warmup-steps":100,
    "logging-steps":100,
    "weight-decay":0.01
}
estimator = HuggingFace(
    py_version="py36",
    entry_point="train.py",
    source_dir="1_sources",
    pytorch_version="1.7.1",
    transformers_version="4.6.1",
    hyperparameters=hyperparameters,
    instance_type="ml.p2.xlarge",
    instance_count=1,
```

```
    role=role
)
estimator.fit({
    "train":train_dataset_uri,
    "test":test_dataset_uri
})
```

After that, the training job will be scheduled and executed. It will take 10–15 minutes for it to complete, then the trained model and other output artifacts will be added to Amazon S3.

Developing an inference script for script mode

Now that we have a trained model, let's deploy it as a SageMaker real-time endpoint. We will use the prebuilt SageMaker Hugging Face container and will only provide our inference script. The inference requests will be handled by the **AWS MMS**, which exposes the HTTP endpoint.

When using prebuilt inference containers, SageMaker automatically recognizes our inference script. According to SageMaker convention, the inference script has to contain the following methods:

- `model_fn(model_dir)` is executed at the container start time to load the model into memory. This method takes the model directory as an input argument. You can use `model_fn()` to initialize other components of your inference pipeline, such as the tokenizer in our case. Note, Hugging Face Transformers have a convenient Pipeline API that allows us to combine data preprocessing (in our case, text tokenization) and actual inference in a single object. Hence, instead of a loaded model, we return an inference pipeline:

```
MODEL_NAME = "distilbert-base-uncased"
NUM_LABELS = 6 # number of categories
MAX_LENGTH = 512 # max number of tokens model can handle
def model_fn(model_dir):
    device_id = 0 if torch.cuda.is_available() else -1
    tokenizer = DistilBertTokenizerFast.from_
pretrained(MODEL_NAME)
    config = DistilBertConfig()
    config.num_labels = NUM_LABELS
    model = DistilBertForSequenceClassification.from_
pretrained(
        model_dir, config=config
    )
```

```
            inference_pipeline = pipeline(
                model=model,
                task="text-classification",
                tokenizer=tokenizer,
                framework="pt",
                device=device_id,
                max_length=MAX_LENGTH,
                truncation=True
            )
            return inference_pipeline
```

- `transform_fn(inference_pipeline, data, content_type, accept_type)` is responsible for running the actual inference. Since we are communicating with an end client via HTTP, we also need to do payload deserialization and response serialization. In our sample example, we expect a JSON payload and return a JSON payload; however, this can be extended to any other formats based on the requirements (for example, CSV and Protobuf):

```
    def transform_fn(inference_pipeline, data, content_type,
    accept_type):
        # Deserialize payload
        if "json" in content_type:
            deser_data = json.loads(data)
        else:
            raise NotImplemented("Only 'application/json'
    content type is implemented.")

        # Run inference
        predictions = inference_pipeline(deser_data)

        # Serialize response
        if "json" in accept_type:
            return json.dumps(predictions)
        else:
            raise NotImplemented("Only 'application/json'
    accept type is implemented.")
```

Sometimes, combining deserialization, inference, and serialization in a single method can be inconvenient. Alternatively, SageMaker supports a more granular API:

- `input_fn(request_body, request_content_type)` runs deserialization
- `predict_fn(deser_input, model)` performs predictions
- `output_fn(prediction, response_content_type)` runs the serialization of predictions

Note that the `transform_fn()` method is mutually exclusive with the `input_fn()`, `predict_fn()`, and `output_fn()` methods.

Deploying a Text Classification endpoint

Now we are ready to deploy and test our Newsgroup Classification endpoint. We can use the `estimator.create_model()` method to configure our model deployment parameters, specifically the following:

1. Define the inference script and other dependencies that will be uploaded by SageMaker to an endpoint.

2. Identify the inference container. If you provide the `transformers_version`, `pytorch_version`, and `py_version` parameters, SageMaker will automatically find an appropriate prebuilt inference container (if it exists). Alternatively, you can provide `image_uri` to directly specify the container image you wish to use:

```
from sagemaker.huggingface.estimator import
HuggingFaceModel
model = estimator.create_model(role=role,
                               entry_point="inference.
py",
                               source_dir="1_sources",
                               py_version="py36",
                               transformers_
version="4.6.1",
                               pytorch_version="1.7.1"
                               )
```

3. Next, we define the parameters of our endpoint such as the number and type of instances behind it. The `model.deploy()` method starts the inference deployment (which, usually, takes several minutes) and returns a `Predictor` object to run inference requests:

```
predictor = model.deploy(
    initial_instance_count=1,
    instance_type="ml.m5.xlarge"
)
```

Next, let's explore how to extend pre-built DL containers.

Extending the prebuilt containers

We will reuse code assets from the script mode example. However, unlike the previous container, we will modify our runtime environment and install the latest stable Hugging Face Transformer from the GitHub master branch. This modification will be implemented in our custom container image.

First off, we need to identify which base image we will use. AWS has published all of the available DL containers at `https://github.com/aws/deep-learning-containers/blob/master/available_images.md`.

Since we plan to use reinstall from scratch HugggingFace Transformer library anyway, we might choose the PyTorch base image. At the time of writing, the latest PyTorch SageMaker container was `763104351884.dkr.ecr.us-east-1.amazonaws.com/pytorch-training:1.9.0-gpu-py38-cu111-ubuntu20.04`. Note that this container URI is for the AWS East-1 region and will be different for other AWS regions. Please consult the preceding referenced AWS article on the correct URI for your region.

To build a new container, we will need to perform the following steps:

*   Create a Dockerfile with runtime instructions.

*   Build the container image locally.

*   Push the new container image to the **container registry**. In this example, we will use ECR as a container registry: a managed service from AWS, which is well integrated into the SageMaker ecosystem.

First, let's create a Dockerfile for our extended container.

Developing a Dockerfile for our extended container

To extend the prebuilt SageMaker container, we need to have at least the following components:

- A SageMaker PyTorch image to use as a base.

- The required dependencies installed, such as the latest PyTorch and Hugging Face Transformers from the latest Git master branch.

- Copy our training script from the previous example into the container.

- Define the SAGEMAKER_SUBMIT_DIRECTORY and SAGEMAKER_PROGRAM environmental variables, so SageMaker knows which training script to execute when the container starts:

```
FROM 763104351884.dkr.ecr.us-east-1.amazonaws.com/
pytorch-training:1.9.0-gpu-py38-cu111-ubuntu20.04
RUN pip3 install git+https://github.com/huggingface/
transformers
ENV SAGEMAKER_SUBMIT_DIRECTORY /opt/ml/code
ENV SAGEMAKER_PROGRAM train.py
COPY 1_sources/train.py $SAGEMAKER_SUBMIT_
DIRECTORY/$SAGEMAKER_PROGRAM
```

Now we are ready to build and push this container image to ECR. You can find the bash script to do this in the chapter repository.

Scheduling a training job

Once we have our extended PyTorch container in ECR, we are ready to execute a SageMaker training job. The training job configuration will be similar to the script mode example with one notable difference: instead of the HuggingFaceEstimator object, we will use a generic SageMaker Estimator object that allows us to work with custom images. Note that you need to update the image_uri parameter with reference to the image URI in your ECR instance. You can find it by navigating to the ECR service on your AWS Console and finding the extended container there:

```
from sagemaker.estimator import Estimator
estimator = Estimator(
    image_uri="<UPDATE WITH YOUR IMAGE URI FROM ECR>",
    hyperparameters=hyperparameters,
    instance_type="ml.p2.xlarge",
    instance_count=1,
    role=role
)
estimator.fit({
```

```
        "train":train_dataset_uri,
        "test":test_dataset_uri
})
```

After completing the training job, we should expect similar training outcomes as those shown in the script mode example.

Developing a BYO container for inference

In this section, we will learn how to build a SageMaker-compatible inference container using an official TensorFlow image, prepare an inference script and model server, and deploy it for inference on SageMaker Hosting.

Problem overview

We will develop a SageMaker-compatible container for inference. We will use the latest official TensorFlow container as a base image and use AWS MMS as a model server. Please note that MMS is one of many ML model serving options that can be used. SageMaker doesn't have any restrictions on a model server other than that it should serve models on port 8080.

Developing the serving container

When deploying a serving container to the endpoint, SageMaker runs the following command:

```
docker run <YOUR BYO IMAGE> serve
```

To comply with this requirement, it's recommended that you use the exec format of the ENTRYPOINT instruction in your Dockerfile.

Let's review our BYO Dockerfile:

- We use the latest TensorFlow container as a base
- We install general and SageMaker-specific dependencies
- We copy our model serving scripts to the container
- We specify ENTRYPOINT and the CMD instructions to comply with the SageMaker requirements

Now, let's put it into action:

1. Use the latest official TensorFlow container:

    ```
    FROM tensorflow/tensorflow:latest
    ```

2. Install Java, as required by MMS and any other common dependencies.

3. Copy the entrypoint script to the image:

    ```
    COPY 3_sources/src/dockerd_entrypoint.py /usr/local/bin/
    dockerd-entrypoint.py
    RUN chmod +x /usr/local/bin/dockerd-entrypoint.py
    ```

4. Copy the default custom service file to handle incoming data and inference requests:

    ```
    COPY 3_sources/src/model_handler.py /opt/ml/model/model_
    handler.py
    COPY 3_sources/src/keras_model_loader.py /opt/ml/model/
    keras_model_loader.py
    ```

5. Define an entrypoint script and its default parameters:

    ```
    ENTRYPOINT ["python3", "/usr/local/bin/dockerd-
    entrypoint.py"]
    CMD ["serve"]
    ```

In this example, we don't intend to cover MMS and the development of inference scripts in detail. However, it's worth highlighting some key script aspects:

- `dockerd_entrypoint.py` is an executable that starts the MMS server when the `serve` argument is passed to it.

- `model_handler.py` implements model-loading and model-serving logics. Note that the `handle()` method checks whether the model is already loaded into memory. If it's not, it will load a model into memory once and then proceed to the handling serving request, which includes the following:

  - Deserializing the request payload

  - Running predictions

  - Serializing predictions

Deploying the SageMaker endpoint

To schedule the deployment of the inference endpoint, we use the generic Model class from SageMaker Python SDK. Note that since we downloaded the model from a public model zoo, we don't need to provide a model_data parameter (hence, its value is None):

```
from sagemaker import Model
mms_model = Model(
    image_uri=image_uri,
    model_data=None,
    role=role,
    name=model_name,
    sagemaker_session=session
)
mms_model.deploy(
    initial_instance_count=1,
    instance_type="ml.m5.xlarge",
    endpoint_name=endpoint_name
)
```

It might take several minutes to fully deploy the endpoint and start the model server. Once it's ready, we can call the endpoint using the boto3.sagemaker-runtime client, which allows you to construct the HTTP request and send the inference payload (or image, in our case) to a specific SageMaker endpoint:

```
import boto3
client = boto3.client('sagemaker-runtime')
accept_type = "application/json"
content_type = 'image/jpeg'
headers = {'content-type': content_type}
payload = open(test_image, 'rb')
response = client.invoke_endpoint(
    EndpointName=endpoint_name,
    Body=payload,
    ContentType=content_type,
    Accept = accept_type
)
most_likely_label = response['Body'].read()
print(most_likely_label)
```

This code will, most likely, return an object in the image based on model predictions.

Summary

In this chapter, we reviewed how SageMaker provides support for the ML and DL frameworks using Docker containers. After reading this chapter, you should now know how to select the most appropriate DL container usage pattern according to your specific use case requirements. We learned about SageMaker toolkits, which simplifies developing SageMaker-compatible containers. In later sections, you gained practical knowledge of how to develop custom containers and scripts for training and inference tasks on Amazon SageMaker.

In the next chapter, we will learn about the SageMaker development environment and how to efficiently develop and troubleshoot your DL code. Additionally, we will learn about DL-specific tools and interfaces that the SageMaker development environment provides to simplify the building, deploying, and monitoring of your DL models.

3

Managing SageMaker Development Environment

In previous chapters, we learned about the fundamental components and capabilities of Amazon SageMaker. By now, you know how to build and deploy your first simple models on SageMaker. In many more complex cases, however, you will need to write, profile, and test your DL code before deploying it to SageMaker-managed training or hosting clusters. Being able to perform this action locally while mocking SageMaker runtime will shorten development cycles and will avoid any unnecessary costs associated with provisioning SageMaker resources for development.

In this chapter, we will explore how to organize your development environment to effectively develop and test your DL models for SageMaker. This chapter includes considerations for choosing your IDE software for development and testing, as well as simulated SageMaker runtimes on your local machine. We will also provide an overview of available SDKs and APIs to manage your SageMaker resources.

These topics will be covered in the following sections:

- Selecting a development environment for SageMaker
- Debugging SageMaker code locally

After reading this chapter, you will be able to set up an efficient development environment compatible with SageMaker, based on your specific use case requirements.

Technical requirements

In this chapter, you can use code walk-through samples, so you can develop practical skills. Full code examples are available here: `https://github.com/PacktPublishing/Accelerate-Deep-Learning-Workloads-with-Amazon-SageMaker/blob/main/chapter3/`. To follow along with this code, you will need to have the following:

- An AWS account and be an IAM user with permission to manage Amazon SageMaker resources.
- Have Docker and Docker Compose installed on your local machine. If your development environment has a GPU device, you will need to install `nvidia-docker` (`https://github.com/NVIDIA/nvidia-docker`).
- Have Conda installed (`https://docs.conda.io/en/latest/`).

Selecting a development environment for SageMaker

The choice of development environment and IDE is typically driven by personal preferences or corporate policies. SageMaker being a cloud platform doesn't restrict you from using an IDE of your choice. You can run an IDE on your local machine or cloud machine (such as Amazon EC2). SageMaker also provides a set of SDKs and packages to simulate SageMaker runtime environments, so you can first test your code using local mocks before deploying anything to the cloud.

With advances in data science, and machine learning specifically, a new type of development runtime environment has evolved – **interactive notebooks**, namely **Jupyter Notebooks** and **JupyterLab** (the next generation of Jupyter Notebooks with additional development capabilities such as code debugging). While not fully replacing a classical IDE, notebooks have become popular because they allow you to explore and visualize data, and develop and share your code with others.

SageMaker provides several managed notebook environments:

- The **SageMaker Studio** service – a proprietary serverless notebook IDE for ML development
- **SageMaker notebook instances** – a managed Jupyter Notebook/JupyterLab environment

All three options – a classical IDE, SageMaker notebook instances, and SageMaker Studio – have certain benefits and may be optimal for a specific set of scenarios. In the following sections, we will review IDE options in detail with their pros and cons as they relate to DL development.

Setting up a local environment for SageMaker

There are a number of benefits of doing your initial development locally, specifically the following:

- You don't incur any running costs for doing your development locally
- You can choose your preferred IDE, which results in more efficient development cycles

However, local development runtime also has certain limitations. For instance, you cannot test and profile your code on different hardware devices. Getting the latest GPU devices designed for DL workloads can be impractical and not cost-efficient. That's why, in many cases, you will do initial development and testing of your DL code using a CPU device to troubleshoot initial issues, and then do the final code profiling and tweaking on cloud instances with access to target GPU devices.

SageMaker provides a number of SDKs to allow integration between the local environment and the AWS cloud. Let's do a practical example of how to configure your local environment to work with remote SageMaker resources.

Configuring a Python environment

We start our configuration by setting up and configuring a Python environment with AWS integration. It's recommended to use Conda environment management software to isolate your SageMaker local environment:

1. You can start by installing Conda on your local machine using the appropriate installation method (it depends on your local OS). Once Conda is installed, you can create a new Python environment by running the following command in your terminal window:

   ```
   conda create -n sagemaker python=3.9
   ```

   Note that we are explicitly specifying which version of Python interpreter to use in this environment.

2. Next, we switch to create an environment and install the AWS and SageMaker SDKs:

   ```
   conda activate sagemaker
   pip install boto3 awscli sagemaker
   ```

   Let's review the SDKs we just installed:

   - `awscli` is an AWS CLI toolkit that allows you to programmatically work with any AWS service. It also provides a mechanism to store and use AWS credentials locally.

   - `boto3` is a Python SDK to manage your AWS resources. It uses credentials established by the AWS CLI toolkit to cryptographically sign any management requests and, thus, authenticate in AWS.

   - `sagemaker` – This Python SDK should be already familiar to you at this point of book, as we used it in previous chapters to interact with SageMaker resources such as training jobs or inference endpoints. Unlike `boto3`, the SageMaker SDK abstracts many aspects of the management of underlying resources and is generally recommended whenever you need to programmatically manage your SageMaker workloads.

3. Before we proceed, we first need to configure AWS credentials. To do so, you will need to run the following command in your terminal and provide your AWS access and secret keys:

```
aws configure
```

You can read the details of how to set up AWS credentials here: https://docs.aws.amazon.com/cli/latest/userguide/cli-configure-quickstart.html.

Configuring a Jupyter environment

Once we have the basic Python environments configured and our AWS credentials established, we are ready to start the Jupyter server. In this example, we will use the JupyterLab environment. However, you are free to configure your own IDE for this purpose, as many IDEs, such as PyCharm and Visual Studio Code, support Jupyter notebooks via plugins or natively. The additional benefit of such an approach is that you can easily switch between your notebooks and training and inference scripts within the same IDE:

1. To install JupyterLab and create a kernel, run the following commands in your terminal:

```
conda install -c conda-forge jupyterlabpython -m
ipykernel install --user --name sagemaker
```

2. Next, we start the JupyterLab server on our machine:

```
jupyter lab
```

Your JupyterLab server should be now available on http://localhost:8888.

Running model training on SageMaker

In the JupyterLab instance, let's run some tests to make sure that we can connect and manage SageMaker resources from our local machine:

1. The full notebook code and training script are in the chapter3 directory of this book's GitHub repository:

```
import sagemaker, boto3
from sagemaker import get_execution_role
session = sagemaker.Session()
account = boto3.client('sts').get_caller_identity().
get('Account')
role = f"arn:aws:iam::{account}:role/service-role/
AmazonSageMaker-ExecutionRole-<YOUR_ROLE_ID>"
```

> **SageMaker execution role**
>
> Please note that you will need to manually define your execution role. For SageMaker managed environments, such as SageMaker Studio or SageMaker notebook instances, you can use the `get_execution_role()` method to retrieve the execution role.

2. Now, we can configure and kick off our SageMaker training the same way as before:

```
from sagemaker.pytorch import PyTorch
import os
pytorch_estimator = PyTorch(
                    session=session,
                    entry_point=f'{os.getcwd()}/
sources/cifar10.py',
                    role=role,
                    instance_type="ml.m4.xlarge",
                    instance_count=1,
                    job_name="test",
                    framework_version="1.9.0",
                    py_version="py38",
                    hyperparameters={
                        "epochs": 1,
                        "batch-size": 16
                    }
                )
pytorch_estimator.fit()
```

3. Once the training job is done, you can explore locally training results and where output artifacts have been stored:

```
pytorch_estimator.latest_training_job.describe()
```

As you can see, having a local development environment provides you with the flexibility to choose your preferred IDE and avoid paying for SageMaker-managed development environments. At the same time, it requires you to carefully manage your development environment, which requires specific expertise and dedicated efforts. Another potential challenge is the synchronization of the development environment between team members.

Using SageMaker Notebook instances

SageMaker notebook instances are managed by an AWS Jupyter environment running on top of EC2 instances. You can choose an instance type from a list of CPU and GPU-based instances. SageMaker provides a number of preconfigured Jupyter kernels with Python runtimes. It includes preconfigured runtimes with versions of PyTorch, TensorFlow, MXNet, and other popular DL and ML frameworks. You can also customize existing kernels (for instance, install new packages) or create fully custom kernels using Conda environment management.

Since a Jupyter environment runs directly on top of an EC2 instance, you can directly observe resource consumption during local training or inference (for example, by monitoring the `nvidia-smi` utility output). You can also run Docker operations such as building custom containers and testing them using SageMaker local mode, which we will discuss in detail in the *Debugging SageMaker code locally* section of this chapter.

There are scenarios when using notebook instances can be beneficial, such as the following:

- You need to have access to a specific type of hardware to test and debug your model (for example, finding max training throughput without running into OOM issues)

- You want to baseline your model performance locally for a specific combination of hyperparameters and hardware before deploying to a remote environment

One downside of notebook instances is the lack of flexibility. You cannot change your instance type quickly if your hardware requirements have changed. That may lead to unnecessary costs when you have a combination of tasks with different resource requirements.

Let's consider a scenario where you want to locally preprocess training data and then debug your training script on this data. Typically, data processing is a CPU-bound process and doesn't require any GPU devices. However, training DL morning will require a GPU device. So, you will have to provision an instance that satisfies the highest hardware requirements among your tasks. Alternatively, you will have to store your work between tasks and reprovision your notebook instance altogether.

SageMaker addressed this lack of elasticity in a newer product called SageMaker Studio notebooks. Let's review it in detail.

Using SageMaker Studio

SageMaker Studio is a web-based interface that allows you to interact with various SageMaker capabilities, from visual data exploration, to Model Zoo and model training, to code development and endpoint monitoring. SageMaker Studio is intended to simplify and optimize all steps of ML development by providing a single environment to work and collaborate.

There are multiple capabilities within SageMaker Studio. Let's review two specific capabilities relevant for DL development:

- **Studio notebooks** allow fast access to different compute instances and runtimes without the need to leave your JupyterLab application

- **SageMaker JumpStart** is a collection of prebuilt solutions and Model Zoo that allows you to deploy your DL solutions in a couple of clicks

Next, let's discuss these capabilities and use cases.

Studio notebooks

Studio notebooks provide a fully managed JupyterLab environment with the ability to quickly switch between different kernels and compute instances. During the switch, your work is persisted in a shared filesystem automatically. A shared filesystem is highly available and scales seamlessly as needed. Studio notebooks come with a set of prebuilt kernels similar to notebook instances, which can be further customized. You can also create a fully custom kernel image for Studio notebooks.

You can choose a compute instance from a wide spectrum of EC2 instances, the latest CPU instances, and specialized GPU instances for training and inference tasks. Studio notebooks have access to two types of EC2 instances:

- **Fast instances**, which allows switching within 2 minutes.

- **Regular instances**, for which you need to allow around 5 minutes to start. Note that this is approximate timing that may be impacted by resource availability in a given AWS region.

Collaborative Capabilities

Studio notebooks support a sharing capability that allows you to share your code, kernel, and instance configuration with teammates in just a few clicks.

SageMaker notebook kernels run within Docker images. As a result, there are several limitations:

- You cannot build or run containers in your Studio notebooks

- Studio notebooks don't support local mode to debug containers before deployment on SageMaker

- AWS provides an **Image Build CLI** to circumvent this limitation and allow users to build custom containers while working in Studio notebooks

For most scenarios, Studio notebooks will be a convenient and cost-efficient alternative to running your own JupyterLab on an EC2 instance or using SageMaker notebook instances. However, you should be mindful of the constraints of Studio notebooks mentioned previously, and assess whether these are a dealbreaker for your particular use case or usage pattern. Additionally, Studio notebooks come as part of the SageMaker Studio platform, which provides additional benefits such as visual data exploration and processing, visual model monitoring, prebuilt solutions, UI conveniences for managing your feature stores, model building pipelines, endpoints, experiments, and more.

SageMaker JumpStart

SageMaker JumpStart is a library of prebuilt end-to-end ML and DL solutions, sample notebooks, and models that can be deployed on SageMaker in one click. JumpStart's library of solutions and models is large and continuously growing.

JumpStart solutions are designed for specific industry use cases, such as transaction fraud detection, document understanding, and predictive maintenance. Each solution includes multiple integrated components and once deployed can be immediately used by end users. Note that you will need to provide your own dataset to train JumpStart models.

JumpStart models provide access to the SOTA model zoo. Depending on your model architecture, you may choose to immediately deploy this model to inference, fine-tune, train from scratch, or resume incremental training on your own dataset. JumpStart allows users to fully customize user actions, such as defining a size and instance type of training cluster, a hyperparameter of a training job, and the location of data.

Model Zoo includes models for CV and NLP tasks from TensorFlow Hub, PyTorch Hub, and Hugging Face models.

SageMaker JumpStart can come in handy in scenarios when your business problem can be addressed using generic solutions with your proprietary data. JumpStart can also be a friendly introduction to DL on SageMaker or for non-technical users who are looking to experiment with DL on their own.

In this section, we reviewed available development environment options for SageMaker. All three options come with their pros and cons, and a specific choice is largely driven by personal preferences and use case requirements. It's generally a good idea to have both a local environment and SageMaker Studio notebooks or notebook instances available. This setup allows you to develop, test, and do initial debugging locally without paying for any cloud resources. Once your code is working locally, you can then easily run the same code on cloud hardware. Studio notebooks can be especially useful, as they allow you to easily switch between different CPU and GPU runtimes without leaving your Jupyter notebook, so you can experiment with your training config (for instance, tweak the batch size or gradient accumulation).

In the next section, we will focus on how to efficiently debug your SageMaker code locally before moving your workload to SageMaker cloud resources.

Debugging SageMaker code locally

To simplify code development and testing locally, SageMaker supports **local mode**. This mode allows you to run your training, inference, or data processing locally in SageMaker containers. This is particularly helpful when you want to troubleshoot your scripts before provisioning any SageMaker resources.

Local mode is supported for all SageMaker images as well as custom SageMaker-compatible images. It is implemented as part of the `sagemaker` Python SDK. When running your jobs in local mode, the SageMaker SDK under the hood creates a Docker Compose YAML file with your job parameters and starts a relevant container locally. The complexities of configuring a Docker runtime environment are abstracted from the user.

Local mode is supported for both CPU and GPU devices. You can run the following types of SageMaker jobs in local mode:

- Training job
- Real-time endpoint
- Processing job
- Batch transform job

Limitations of local mode

There are several limitations when running your SageMaker jobs locally:

- Only one local endpoint is supported.
- Distributed local training for a GPU is not supported. However, you can run distributed jobs on a CPU.
- EFS and FSx for Lustre are not supported as data sources.
- `Gzip` compression, Pipe mode, or manifest files for input are not supported.

Running training and inference in local mode

Let's train a simple model in local mode and then deploy an inference endpoint locally. The full notebook code and training script are in the `chapter3` directory of the book repository:

1. We start by installing all required dependencies for local mode:

   ```
   pip install 'sagemaker[local]' –upgrade
   ```

2. We then configure the SageMaker local runtime. Note that we are using the `LocalSession` class to let the SageMaker SDK know that we want to provision resources locally:

```
import boto3
from sagemaker.local import LocalSession
sagemaker_local_session = LocalSession()
sagemaker_local_session.config = {'local': {'local_code':
True}}
account = boto3.client('sts').get_caller_identity().
get('Account')
role = f"arn:aws:iam::{account}:role/service-role/
AmazonSageMaker-ExecutionRole-<YOUR_ROLE_ID>"
```

3. In this notebook, we intend to use a public PyTorch image from the SageMaker ECR repository. For this, we need to store credentials so that the Docker daemon can pull the images. Run the following command in your notebook (you can also run it in your terminal window; just remove !):

```
! aws ecr get-login-password --region us-east-1 | docker
login --username AWS --password-stdin 763104351884.dkr.
ecr.us-east-1.amazonaws.com
```

4. Now, we need to decide whether we will use a GPU (if available) or CPU device (the default choice). The following code snippet determines whether a CUDA-compatible device is available (the `"local_gpu"` value) and, if not, defaults to a CPU device (the `"local"` value):

```
import subprocess
instance_type = "local"
try:
    if subprocess.call("nvidia-smi") == 0:
        instance_type = "local_gpu"
except:
    print("GPU device with CUDA is not available")
print("Instance type = " + instance_type)
```

5. Once we define which local device to use, we configure and run a SageMaker training job:

```
from sagemaker.pytorch import PyTorch
import os
# Configure an MXNet Estimator (no training happens yet)
pytorch_estimator = PyTorch(
```

```
                                    session=sagemaker_local_session,
                                    entry_point=f'{os.getcwd()}/
        sources/cifar10.py',
                                    role=role,
                                    instance_type=instance_type,
                                    instance_count=1,
                                    job_name="test",
                                    framework_version="1.9.0",
                                    py_version="py38",
                                    hyperparameters={
                                        "epochs": 1,
                                        "batch-size": 16
                                        }
                                    )
        pytorch_estimator.fit()
```

6. The SageMaker Python SDK performs the following operations automatically:

    - Pulls the appropriate PyTorch image from a public ECR repository
    - Generates a `docker-compose.yml` file with appropriate volume mount points to access code and training data
    - Starts a Docker container with the `train` command

    SageMaker will output the Docker Compose command and the STDOUT/STDERR of the training container to a Jupyter cell.

> **Debugging code inside a container**
>
> Many modern IDEs support debugging an application running inside a container. For instance, you can set a breakpoint in your training code. The code execution inside the container will stop so that you can inspect whether it's executing correctly. Consult your IDE documentation on how to set it up.

After the training job has finished, let's see how we can deploy a trained model to a local real-time endpoint. Note that, by default, we are training only for a single epoch, so don't expect great results!

1. You can deploy an inference container locally just by running the `deploy()` method on your estimator:

    ```
    pytorch_estimator.deploy(initial_instance_count=1,
    instance_type=instance_type)
    ```

2. Once the endpoint is deployed, the SageMaker SDK will start sending the output of the model server to a Jupyter cell. You can also observe container logs in the Docker client UI or via the `docker logs CONTAINER_ID` terminal command.

3. We can now send a test image and observe how our inference scripts handle an inference request in the Docker logs:

```
import requests
import json
payload = trainset[0][0].numpy().tobytes()
url = 'http://127.0.0.1:8080/invocations'
content_type = 'application/x-npy'
accept_type = "application/json"
headers = {'content-type': content_type, 'accept':
accept_type}
response = requests.post(url, data=payload,
headers=headers)
print(json.loads(response.content)[0])
```

In the preceding code block, we did the following:

- Formed an inference payload and serialized it to `bytes` objects

- Formed `content-type` and `accept-type` HTTP headers to indicate to the inference server what type of content the client is sending and what it expects

- Sent a request to the local SageMaker endpoint

- Read the response output

If there are any issues, you can log in to a running inference container to examine the runtime environment or set up a debugging session using your IDE capabilities.

Summary

In this chapter, we reviewed some available solutions and best practices on how to organize the development of DL code for Amazon SageMaker. Depending on your use case requirements and personal preferences, you can choose a DIY environment locally or use one of SageMaker's notebook environments – notebook instances and Studio notebooks. You also learned how to test SageMaker DL containers locally to speed up your development efforts and avoid any additional testing costs.

In the next chapter, we will focus on data management and data processing for SageMaker. As many training datasets for DL problems are large and require pre- or post-processing, it's crucial to understand an optimal storage solution. We also discuss aspects of data labeling and data processing using SageMaker capabilities, as well as the best practices for accessing your training data.

4

Managing Deep Learning Datasets

Deep learning models usually require a considerable amount of training data to learn useful patterns. In many real-life applications, new data is continuously collected, processed, and added to the training dataset, so your models can be periodically retrained so that they can adjust to changing real-world conditions. In this chapter, we will look into SageMaker capabilities and other AWS services to help you manage your training data.

SageMaker provides a wide integration capability where you can use AWS general-purpose data storage services such as Amazon S3, Amazon EFS, and Amazon FSx for Lustre. Additionally, SageMaker has purpose-built storage for **machine learning** (**ML**) called SageMaker Feature Store. We will discuss when to choose one or another storage solution, depending on the type of data, consumption, and ingestion patterns.

In many cases, before you can use training data, you need to pre-process it. For instance, data needs to be converted into a specific format or datasets need to be augmented with modified versions of samples. In this chapter, we will review SageMaker Processing and how it can be used to process large-scale ML datasets.

We will close this chapter by looking at advanced techniques on how to optimize the data retrieval process for TensorFlow and PyTorch models using AWS data streaming utilities.

In this chapter, we will cover the following topics:

- Selecting storage solutions for ML datasets
- Processing data at scale
- Optimizing data storage and retrieval

After reading this chapter, you will know how to organize your DL dataset's life cycle for training and inference on SageMaker. We will also run through some hands-on examples for data processing and data retrieval to help you gain practical skills in those areas.

Technical requirements

In this chapter, we will provide code samples so that you can develop your practical skills. The full code examples are available at `https://github.com/PacktPublishing/Accelerate-Deep-Learning-Workloads-with-Amazon-SageMaker/blob/main/chapter4/`.

To follow this code, you will need the following:

- An AWS account and IAM user with permission to manage Amazon SageMaker resources
- A SageMaker Notebook, SageMaker Studio Notebook, or local SageMaker-compatible environment established

Selecting storage solutions for ML datasets

AWS Cloud provides a wide range of storage solutions that can be used to store inference and training data. When choosing an optimal storage solution, you may consider the following factors:

- Data volume and velocity
- Data types and associated metadata
- Consumption patterns
- Backup and retention requirements
- Security and audit requirements
- Integration capabilities
- Price to store, write, and read data

Carefully analyzing your specific requirements may suggest the right solution for your use case. It's also typical to combine several storage solutions for different stages of your data life cycle. For instance, you could store data used for inference consumption with lower latency requirements in faster but more expensive storage; then, you could move the data to cheaper and slower storage solutions for training purposes and long-term retention.

There are several types of common storage types with different characteristics: filesystems, object storage and block storage solutions. Amazon provides managed services for each type of storage. We will review their characteristics and how to use them in your SageMaker workloads in the following subsections. Then, we will focus on Amazon SageMaker Feature Store as it provides several unique features specific to ML workloads and datasets.

Amazon EBS – high-performance block storage

Block storage solutions are designed for quick data retrieval and manipulation. The data is broken into blocks on the physical device for efficient utilization. Block storage allows you to abstract and decouple data from the runtime environment. At data retrieval time, blocks are reassembled by the storage solution and returned to users.

Amazon EBS is a fully managed block storage solution that supports a wide range of use cases for different read-write patterns, throughput, and latency requirements. A primary use case of Amazon EBS is to serve as data volumes attached to Amazon EC2 compute nodes.

Amazon SageMaker provides seamless integration with EBS. In the following example, we are provisioning a training job with four nodes; each node will have an EBS volume with 100 GB attached to it. The training data will be downloaded and stored on EBS volumes by SageMaker:

```
from sagemaker.pytorch import PyTorch
pytorch_estimator = PyTorch(
                        session=session,
                        entry_point=f'path/to/train.py',
                        role=role,
                        instance_type="ml.m4.xlarge",
   volume_size=100,

                        instance_count=4,
                        framework_version="1.9.0",
                        )
```

Note that you cannot customize the type of EBS volume that's used. Only **general-purpose** SSD volumes are supported. Once the training job is completed, all instances and attached EBS volumes will be purged.

Amazon S3 – industry-standard object storage

Object storage implements a flat structure, where each file object has a unique identifier (expressed as a path) and associated data object. A flat structure allows you to scale object storage solutions linearly and sustain high-throughput data reads and writes while keeping costs low.

Object storage can handle objects of different types and sizes. Object storage also allows you to store metadata associated with each object. Data reads and writes are typically done via HTTP APIs, which allows for ease of integration. However, note that object storage solutions are generally slower than filesystems or block storage solutions.

Amazon S3 was the first petabyte-scale cloud object storage service. It offers durability, availability, performance, security, and virtually unlimited scalability at very low costs. Many object storage solutions follow the Amazon S3 API. Amazon S3 is used to store customer data, but it's also used for many internal AWS features and services where data needs to be persisted.

SageMaker provides seamless integration with Amazon S3 for storing input and output objects, such as datasets, log streams, job outputs, and model artifacts. Let's look at an example of a training job and how to define where we will store our inputs and outputs:

- The `model_uri` parameter specifies an S3 location of model artifacts, such as pre-trained weights, tokenizers, and others. SageMaker automatically downloads these artifacts to each training node.

- `checkpoint_s3_uri` defines the S3 location where training checkpoints will be uploaded during training. Note that it is the developer's responsibility to implement checkpointing functionality in the training script.

- `output_path` specifies the S3 destination of all output artifacts that SageMaker will upload from training nodes after training job completion.

- `tensorboard_output_config` defines where to store TensorBoard logs on S3. Note that SageMaker continuously uploads these logs during training job execution, so you can monitor your training progress in near real time in TensorBoard:

```
from sagemaker.huggingface.estimator import HuggingFace
from sagemaker.debugger import TensorBoardOutputConfig
from sagemaker import get_execution_role
role=get_execution_role()
estimator = HuggingFace(
    py_version="py36",
    entry_point="train.py",
    pytorch_version="1.7.1",
    transformers_version="4.6.1",
    instance_type="ml.p2.xlarge",
    instance_count=2,
    role=role,
    model_uri="s3://unique/path/models/pretrained-bert/",
    checkpoint_s3_uri="s3://unique/path/training/
checkpoints",
    output_path="s3://unique/path/training/output",
    tensorboard_output_config = TensorBoardOutputConfig(
        s3_output_path='s3://unique/path/tensorboard/ ',
```

```
        container_local_output_path='/local/path/'
    ),
)
```

We also use S3 to store our training dataset. Take a look at the following `estimator.fit()` method, which defines the location of our training data:

```
estimator.fit({
    "train":"s3://unique/path/train_files/",
    "test":"s3://unique/path/test_files"}
    )
```

Here, the `"train"` and `"test"` parameters are called **data channels** in SageMaker terminology. Data channel parameters are a way to tell SageMaker to automatically download any required data, such as training and validation datasets, embeddings, lookup tables, and more. SageMaker allows you to use arbitrary names for your data channels. Before you start the training job, the SageMaker training toolkit will download model artifacts to a specific location under the `/opm/ml/input/data/{channel_name}` directory. Additionally, the training toolkit will create `SM_CHANNEL_{channel_name}` environment variables, which you can use in your training script to access model artifacts locally.

As shown in the preceding code block, Amazon S3 can be used to store the input and output artifacts of SageMaker training jobs.

File, FastFile, and Pipe modes

S3 storage is a common place to store your training datasets. By default, when working with data stored on S3, all objects matching the path will be downloaded to each compute node and stored on its EBS volumes. This is known as **File** mode.

However, in many scenarios, training datasets can be hundreds of gigabytes or larger. Downloading such large files will take a considerable amount of time, even before your training begins. To reduce the time needed to start a training job, SageMaker supports **Pipe** mode, which allows you to stream data from the S3 location without fully downloading it. This allows you to start training jobs immediately and fetch data batches as needed during the training cycle.

One of the drawbacks of Pipe mode is that it requires using framework-specific implementations of data utilities to stream data. The recently introduced **FastFile** mode addresses this challenge. FastFile mode allows you to stream data directly from S3 without the need to implement any specific data loaders. In your training or processing scripts, you can treat **FastFiles** as if they are regular files stored on disk; Amazon SageMaker will take care of the read and write operations for you.

We will develop practical skills on how to organize training code for S3 streaming using **FastFile** and **Pipe** modes in the *Optimizing data storage and retrieval* section.

FullyReplicated and ShardedByKey

In many training and data processing tasks, we want to parallelize our job across multiple compute nodes. In scenarios where we have many data objects, we can split our tasks by splitting our full set of objects into unique subsets.

To implement such a scenario, SageMaker supports **ShardedByKey** mode, which attempts to evenly split all matching objects and deliver a unique subset of objects to each node. For instance, if you have n objects in your dataset and k compute nodes in your job, then each compute node will get a unique set of n/k objects.

Unless otherwise specified, the default mode, **FullyReplicated**, is used when SageMaker downloads all matching objects to all nodes.

We will acquire practical skills on how to distribute data processing tasks in the *Distributed data processing* section.

Amazon EFS – general-purpose shared filesystem

Amazon EFS is a managed file storage service that is easy to set up and automatically scales up to petabytes. It provides a filesystem interface and file semantics such as file locking and strong consistency. Unlike Amazon EBS, which allows you to attach storage to a single compute node, EFS can be simultaneously used by hundreds or thousands of compute nodes. This allows you to organize efficient data sharing between nodes without the need to duplicate and distribute data.

Amazon SageMaker allows you to use EFS to store training datasets. The following code shows an example of how to use Amazon EFS in the training job configuration using the `FileSystemInput` class. Note that in this case, we have configured read-only access to the data (the `ro` flag of the `file_system_access_mode` parameter), which is typically the case for the training job. However, you can also specify read-write permissions by setting `file_system_access_mode` to `rw`:

```
from sagemaker.tensorflow.estimator import TensorFlow
from sagemaker.inputs import FileSystemInput
from sagemaker import get_execution_role
role=get_execution_role()
estimator = TensorFlow(entry_point='train.py',
                       role=role,
                       image_uri="image/uri",
                       instance_count=4,
                       instance_type='ml.c4.xlarge')
file_system_input = FileSystemInput(file_system_id='fs-1',
                                    file_system_type='EFS',
                                    directory_path='/
tensorflow',
```

```
                                            file_system_access_
mode='ro')
estimator.fit(file_system_input)
```

Here, you can control other EFS resources. Depending on the latency requirements for data reads and writes, you can choose from several modes that define the latency and concurrency characteristics of your filesystem. At the time of writing this book, EFS can sustain 10+ GB per second throughput and scale up to thousands of connected compute nodes.

Amazon FSx for Lustre – high-performance filesystem

Amazon FSx for Lustre is a file storage service optimized for ML and **high-performance computing (HPC)** workloads. It is designed for sub-millisecond latency for read and write operations and can provide hundreds of GB/s throughput. You can also choose to store data in S3 and synchronize it with the Amazon FSx for Lustre filesystem. In this case, an FSx system presents S3 objects as files and allows you to update data back to the S3 origin.

Amazon SageMaker supports storing training data in the FSx for Lustre filesystem. Training job configuration is similar to using the EFS filesystem; the only difference is that the `file_system_type` parameter is set to `FSxLustre`. The following code shows a sample training job:

```
from sagemaker.inputs import FileSystemInput
from sagemaker import get_execution_role
role=get_execution_role()
estimator = TensorFlow(entry_point='train.py',
                        role=role,
                        image_uri="image/uri",
                        instance_count=4,
                        instance_type='ml.c4.xlarge')

file_system_input = FileSystemInput(
                        file_system_id='fs-XYZ',
                        file_system_type='FSxLustre',
                        directory_path='/tensorflow',
                        file_system_access_mode='ro')

estimator.fit(file_system_input)
```

Note that when provisioning your Lustre filesystem, you may choose either SSD or HDD storage. You should choose SSD for latency-sensitive workloads; HDD is a better fit for workloads with high-throughput requirements.

SageMaker Feature Store – purpose-built ML storage

So far, we've discussed general-purpose file and object storage services that can be used to store data in your SageMaker workloads. However, real-life ML workflows may present certain challenges when it comes to feature engineering and data management, such as the following:

- Managing the data ingestion pipeline to keep data up to date
- Organizing data usage between different teams in your organization and eliminating duplicative efforts
- Sharing data between inference and training workloads when needed
- Managing dataset consistency, its metadata and versioning
- Ad hoc analysis of data

To address these challenges, SageMaker provides an ML-specific data storage solution called **Feature Store**. It allows you to accelerate data processing and curation by reducing repetitive steps and providing a set of APIs to ingest, transform, and consume data for inference and model training.

Its central concept is a **feature** – a single attribute of a data record. Each data record consists of one or many features. Additionally, data records contain metadata such as record update time, unique record ID, and status (deleted or not). The feature can be of the string, integer, or fractional type. Data records and their associated features can be organized into logical units called **feature groups**.

Now, let's review the key features of SageMaker Feature Store.

Online and offline storage

Feature Store supports several storage options for different use cases:

- **Offline storage** is designed to store your data in scenarios where data retrieval latency is not critical, such as storing data for training or batch inference. Your dataset resides in S3 storage and can be queried using the Amazon Athena SQL engine.
- **Online storage** allows you to retrieve a single or batch of records with millisecond latency for real-time inference use cases.
- **Offline and online storage** allows you to store the same data in both forms of storage and use it in both inference and training scenarios.

Ingestion Interfaces

There are several ways to get your data in Feature Store. One way is using Feature Store's `PutRecord` API, which allows you to write either a single or a batch of records. This will write the records in both offline and online storage.

Another option is to use a Spark connector. This is a convenient way to ingest data if you already have your Spark-based data processing pipeline.

Analytical queries

When data is stored in offline storage, you can use Athena SQL to query the dataset using SQL syntax. This is helpful when you have a diverse team that has different levels of coding skills. As Feature Store contains useful metadata fields, such as **Event Time** and **Status**, you can use these times to run *time travel* queries, for instance, to get a historical snapshot of your dataset at a given point in time.

Feature discovery

Once data has been ingested into Feature Store, you can use SageMaker Studio to review and analyze datasets via an intuitive UI component without the need to write any code:

Figure 4.1 – Feature Store dataset discovery via SageMaker Studio UI

Now that we understand the value proposition of Feature Store compared to more general-purpose storage solutions, let's see how it can be used for a typical DL scenario when we want to have tokenized text available next to its original form.

Using Feature Store for inference and training

In this practical example, we will develop skills on how to use SageMaker Feature Store to ingest, process, and consume datasets that contain IMDb reviews. We will take the original dataset that contains the reviews and run a custom BERT tokenizer to convert unstructured text into a set of integer tokens. Then, we will ingest the dataset with the tokenized text feature into Feature Store so that you don't have to tokenize the dataset the next time we want to use it. After that, we will train our model to categorize positive and negative reviews.

We will use SageMaker Feature Store SDK to interact with Feature Store APIs. We will use the HuggingFace Datasets (`https://huggingface.co/docs/datasets/`) and Transformers (`https://huggingface.co/docs/transformers/index`) libraries to tokenize the text and run training and inference. Please make sure that these libraries are installed.

Preparing the data

Follow these steps to prepare the data:

1. The first step is to acquire the initial dataset that contains the IMDb reviews:

    ```
    from datasets import load_dataset
    dataset = load_dataset("imdb")
    ```

2. Then, we must convert the dataset into a pandas DataFrame that is compatible with **Feature Store**. Next, we must cast data types into supported ones using Feature Store. Note that we must also add metadata fields – EventTime and ID. Both are required by Feature Store to support fast retrieval and feature versioning:

    ```
    import pandas as pd
    import time
    dataset_df = dataset['train'].to_pandas()
    current_time_sec = int(round(time.time()))
    dataset_df["EventTime"] = pd.Series([current_time_
    sec]*len(dataset_df), dtype="float64")
    dataset_df["ID"] = dataset_df.index
    dataset_df["text"] = dataset_df["text"].astype('string')
    dataset_df["text"] = dataset_df["text"].str.
    encode("utf8")
    dataset_df["text"] = dataset_df["text"].astype('string')
    ```

3. Now, let's run the downloaded pre-trained tokenizer for the Distilbert model and add a new attribute, tokenized-text, to our dataset. Note that we cast tokenized-text to a string as SageMaker Feature Store doesn't support collection data types such as arrays or maps:

    ```
    from transformers import DistilBertTokenizerFast
    tokenizer = DistilBertTokenizerFast.from_
    pretrained('distilbert-base-uncased')
    dataset_df["tokenized-text"] = tokenizer(dataset_
    df["text"].tolist(), truncation=True, padding=True)
    ["input_ids"]
    dataset_df["tokenized-text"] = dataset_df["tokenized-
    text"].astype('string')
    ```

As a result, we have a pandas DataFrame object that contains the features we are looking to ingest into Feature Store.

Ingesting the data

The next step is to provision Feature Store resources and prepare them for ingestion. Follow these steps:

1. We will start by configuring the feature group and preparing feature definitions. Note that since we stored our dataset in a pandas DataFrame, Feature Store can use this DataFrame to infer feature types:

```
from sagemaker.feature_store.feature_group import
FeatureGroup
imdb_feature_group_name = "imdb-reviews-tokenized"
imdb_feature_group = FeatureGroup(name=imdb_feature_
group_name, sagemaker_session=sagemaker_session)
imdb_feature_group.load_feature_definitions(data_
frame=dataset_df)
```

2. Now that we have prepared the feature group configuration, we are ready to create it. This may take several minutes, so let's add a `Waiter`. Since we are planning to use both online and offline storage, we will set the `enable_online_store` flag to `True`:

```
imdb_feature_group.create(
s3_uri=f"s3://{s3_bucket_name}/{imdb_feature_group_
name}",
    record_identifier_name="ID",
    event_time_feature_name="EventTime",
    role_arn=role,
    enable_online_store=True
)
# Waiter for FeatureGroup creation
def wait_for_feature_group_creation_complete(feature_
group):
    status = feature_group.describe().
get('FeatureGroupStatus')
    print(f'Initial status: {status}')
    while status == 'Creating':
        print(f'Waiting for feature group: {feature_
group.name} to be created ...')
        time.sleep(5)
        status = feature_group.describe().
get('FeatureGroupStatus')
```

```
        if status != 'Created':
            raise SystemExit(f'Failed to create feature group
{feature_group.name}: {status}')
        print(f'FeatureGroup {feature_group.name} was
successfully created.')
    wait_for_feature_group_creation_complete(imdb_feature_
group)
```

3. Once the group is available, we are ready to ingest data. Since we have a full dataset available, we will use a batch ingest API, as shown here:

    ```
    imdb_feature_group.ingest(data_frame=dataset_df, max_
    processes=16, wait=True)
    ```

4. Once the data has been ingested, we can run some analytical queries. For example, we can check if we are dealing with a balanced or imbalanced dataset. As mentioned previously, Feature Store supports querying data using the Amazon Athena SQL engine:

    ```
    athena_query = imdb_feature_group.athena_query()

    imdb_table_name = athena_query.table_name

    result = athena_query.run(f'SELECT "label",
    COUNT("label") as "Count" FROM "sagemaker_
    featurestore"."{imdb_table_name}" group by "label";',
    output_location=f"s3://{s3_bucket_name}/athena_output")

    athena_query.wait()

    print(f"Counting labels in dataset: \n {athena_query.as_
    dataframe()}")
    ```

It will take a moment to run, but in the end, you should get a count of the labels in our dataset.

Using Feature Store for training

Now that we have data available, let's train our binary classification model. Since data in Feature Store is stored in Parquet format (https://parquet.apache.org/) in a designated S3 location, we can directly use Parquet files for training.

To handle Parquet files, we need to make sure that our data reader is aware of the format. For this, we can use the pandas .read_parquet() method. Then, we can convert the pandas DataFrame object into the HuggingFace dataset and select the attributes of interest – tokenized-text and label:

```
df = pd.read_parquet(args.training_dir)
df["input_ids"] = df["tokenized-text"].astype("string")
train_dataset = Dataset.from_pandas(df[["input_ids",
"label"]])
```

Now, we need to convert `tokenized-text` from a string into a list of integers:

```
def string_to_list(example):
    list_of_str = example["input_ids"].strip("][").split(",
")
    example["input_ids"] = [int(el) for el in list_of_str]
    return example
train_dataset = train_dataset.map(string_to_list)
```

The rest of the training script is the same. You can find the full code at https://github.com/
PacktPublishing/Accelerate-Deep-Learning-Workloads-with-Amazon-
SageMaker/blob/main/chapter4/1_sources/train.py.

Now that we've modified the training script, we are ready to run our training job:

1. First, we must get the location of the dataset:

```
train_dataset_uri = imdb_feature_group.describe()
['OfflineStoreConfig']["S3StorageConfig"]
["ResolvedOutputS3Uri"]
```

2. Now, we must pass it to our `Estimator` object:

```
from sagemaker.huggingface.estimator import HuggingFace
estimator = HuggingFace(
    py_version="py36",
    entry_point="train.py",
    source_dir="1_sources",
    pytorch_version="1.7.1",
    transformers_version="4.6.1",
    hyperparameters={
        "model_name":"distilbert-base-uncased",
        "train_batch_size": 16,
        "epochs": 3
        # "max_steps": 100 # to shorten training cycle,
remove in real scenario
    },
    instance_type="ml.p2.xlarge",
    debugger_hook_config=False,
    disable_profiler=True,
```

```
        instance_count=1,
        role=role
    )
    estimator.fit(train_dataset_uri)
```

After some time (depending on how many epochs or steps you use), the model should be trained to classify reviews based on the input text.

Using Feature Store for inference

For inference, we can use the Feature Store runtime client from the Boto3 library to fetch a single record or a batch:

```
import boto3
client = boto3.client('sagemaker-featurestore-runtime')
```

Note that you need to know the unique IDs of the records to retrieve them:

```
response = client.batch_get_record(
    Identifiers=[
        {
            'FeatureGroupName':imdb_feature_group.name,
            'RecordIdentifiersValueAsString': ["0", "1", "2"],
# picking several records to run inference.
            'FeatureNames': [
                'tokenized-text', "label", 'text'
            ]
        },
    ]
)
# preparing the inference payload
labels = []
input_ids = []
texts = []
for record in response["Records"]:
    for feature in record["Record"]:
        if feature["FeatureName"]=="label":
            labels.append(feature["ValueAsString"])
        if feature["FeatureName"]=="tokenized-text":
```

```
            list_of_str = feature["ValueAsString"].strip("][").
split(", ")
            input_ids.append([int(el) for el in list_of_str])
        if feature["FeatureName"]=="text":
            texts.append(feature["ValueAsString"])
```

Now, you can send this request for inference to your deployed model. Refer to the following notebook for an end-to-end example: https://github.com/PacktPublishing/Accelerate-Deep-Learning-Workloads-with-Amazon-SageMaker/blob/main/chapter4/1_Managing_data_in_FeatureStore.ipynb.

In this section, we reviewed the options you can use to store your ML data for inference and training needs. But it's rarely the case that data can be used "as-is." In many scenarios, you need to continuously process data at scale before using it in your ML workloads. SageMaker Processing provides a scalable and flexible mechanism to process your data at scale. Let's take a look.

Processing data at scale

SageMaker Processing allows you to run containerized code in the cloud. This is useful for scenarios such as data pre and post-processing, feature engineering, and model evaluation. SageMaker Processing can be useful for ad hoc workloads as well as recurrent jobs.

As in the case of a training job, Amazon SageMaker provides a managed experience for underlying compute and data infrastructure. You will need to provide a processing job configuration, code, and the container you want to use, but SageMaker will take care of provisioning the instances and deploying the containerized code, as well as running and monitoring the job and its progress. Once your job reaches the terminal state (success or failure), SageMaker will upload the resulting artifacts to the S3 storage and deprovision the cluster.

SageMaker Processing provides two pre-built containers:

- A PySpark container with dependencies to run Spark computations
- A scikit-learn container

When selecting which built-in processing container, note that the PySpark container supports distributed Spark jobs. It allows you to coordinate distributed data processing in a Spark cluster, maintain it globally across the dataset, and visualize processing jobs via the Spark UI. At the same time, the scikit-learn container doesn't support a shared global state, so each processing node runs independently. Limited task coordination can be done by sharding datasets into sub-datasets and processing each sub-dataset independently.

You can also provide a **Bring-Your-Own (BYO)** processing container with virtually any runtime configuration to run SageMaker Processing. This flexibility allows you to easily move your existing processing code so that it can run on SageMaker Processing with minimal effort:

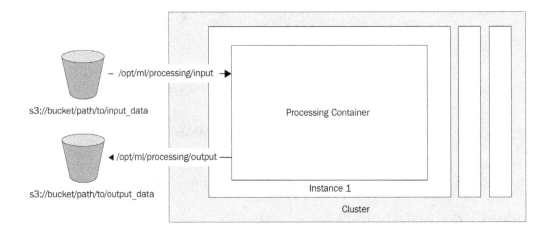

Figure 4.2 – SageMaker Processing node

Let's try to build a container for processing and run a multi-node processing job to augment the image dataset for further training.

Augmenting image data using SageMaker Processing

In this example, we will download the 325 Bird Species dataset from Kaggle (https://www.kaggle.com/gpiosenka/100-bird-species/). Then, we will augment this dataset with modified versions of the images (rotated, cropped, resized) to improve the performance of downstream image classification tasks. For image transformation, we will use the Keras library. Then, we will run our processing job on multiple nodes to speed up our job. Follow these steps:

1. We will start by building a custom processing container. Note that SageMaker runs processing containers using the docker run image_uri command, so we need to specify the entry point in our Dockerfile. We are using the official Python 3.7 container with a basic Debian version:

```
FROM python:3.7-slim-buster
########## Installing packages ##########
RUN pip3 install pandas numpy tensorflow numpy scipy
RUN pip install Pillow
ENV PYTHONUNBUFFERED=TRUE
########## Configure processing scripts ##########
ARG code_dir=/opt/ml/code
```

```
RUN mkdir -p $code_dir
COPY 2_sources $code_dir
WORKDIR $code_dir
ENTRYPOINT ["python3","processing.py"]
```

We will start by building a custom processing container.

2. Now, we need to provide our processing code. We will use keras.utils to load the original dataset into memory and specify the necessary transformations:

```
dataset = keras.utils.image_dataset_from_directory(
    args.data_location,
    labels="inferred",
    label_mode="int",
    class_names=None,
    color_mode="rgb",
    batch_size=args.batch_size,
    image_size=(WIDTH, HEIGHT),
    shuffle=True,
    seed=None,
    validation_split=None,
    subset=None,
    interpolation="bilinear",
    follow_links=False,
    crop_to_aspect_ratio=False,
)
datagen = ImageDataGenerator(
    rotation_range=40,
    width_shift_range=0.2,
    height_shift_range=0.2,
    shear_range=0.2,
    zoom_range=0.2,
    horizontal_flip=True,
    fill_mode="nearest",
)
```

3. Since the Keras generator operates in memory, we need to save the generated images to disk:

```
    for batch_data, batch_labels in dataset.as_numpy_
iterator():
        print(f"Processing batch with index {i} out from
{len(dataset)}")
        for image, label in zip(batch_data, batch_
labels):
            label_name = class_lookup.iloc[label]
["class"]
            image_save_dir = os.path.join(augmented_root_
dir, label_name)
            os.makedirs(image_save_dir, exist_ok=True)
            j = 0
            image = np.expand_dims(image, axis=0)
            # generate 5 new augmented images
            for batch in datagen.flow(
                image,
                batch_size=1,
                save_to_dir=image_save_dir,
                save_prefix="augmented",
                save_format="jpeg",
            ):
                j += 1
                if j > max_augmentations:
                    break
        i += 1
        if args.max_samples is not None:
            if i > args.max_samples:
                break
```

We save the augmented images in a similar directory hierarchy, where labels are defined by directory name.

4. Once we have the BYO container and processing code, we are ready to schedule the processing job. First, we need to instantiate the Processor object with basic job configurations, such as the number and type of instances and container images:

```
from sagemaker.processing import Processor,
ProcessingInput, ProcessingOutput
```

```
lookup_location = "/opt/ml/processing/lookup"
data_location = "/opt/ml/processing/input"
output_location = '/opt/ml/processing/output'
sklearn_processor = Processor(
                    image_uri=image_uri,
                    role=role,
                    instance_count=2,
                    base_job_name="augmentation",
                    sagemaker_session=sess,
                    instance_type="ml.m5.xlarge")
```

To start the job, we must execute the `.run()` method. This method allows us to provide additional configuration parameters. For instance, to distribute tasks evenly, we need to split datasets into chunks. This is easy to do using the `ShardedByKey` distribution type. In this case, SageMaker will attempt to evenly distribute objects between our processing nodes. SageMaker Processing allows you to pass your custom script configuration via the `arguments` collection. You will need to make sure that your processing script can parse these command-line arguments properly:

```
sklearn_processor.run(
    inputs=[
      ProcessingInput(
          source=dataset_uri,
          destination=data_location,
          s3_data_distribution_type="ShardedByS3Key"),
      ProcessingInput(
          source=class_dict_uri,
          destination=lookup_location),],
    outputs=[
      ProcessingOutput(
          source=output_location)],
          arguments = [
              "--data_location", data_location,
              "--lookup_location", lookup_location,
              "--output_location", output_location,
              "--batch_size", "32",
              "--max_samples", "10",
              "--max_augmentations", "5"
              ])
```

For the full processing code, please refer to `https://github.com/PacktPublishing/Accelerate-Deep-Learning-Workloads-with-Amazon-SageMaker/blob/main/chapter4/2_sources/processing.py`.

This example should give you an intuition of how SageMaker Processing can be used for your data processing needs. At the same time, SageMaker Processing is flexible enough to run any arbitrary tasks, such as batch inference, data aggregation and analytics, and others.

In the next section, we will discuss how to optimize data storage and retrieval for large DL datasets.

Optimizing data storage and retrieval

When training **SOTA DL** models, you typically need a large dataset for a model to train. It can be expensive to store and retrieve such large datasets. For instance, the popular computer vision dataset **COCO2017** is approximately 30 GB, while the **Common Crawl** dataset for NLP tasks has a size of hundreds of TB. Dealing with such large datasets requires careful consideration of where to store the dataset and how to retrieve it at inference or training time. In this section, we will discuss some of the optimization strategies you can use when choosing storage and retrieval strategies.

Choosing a storage solution

When choosing an optimal storage solution, you may consider the following factors, among others:

- The cost of storage and data retrieval
- The latency and throughput requirements for data retrieval
- Data partitioning
- How frequently data is refreshed

Let's take a look at the pros and cons of various storage solutions:

- **Amazon S3** provides the cheapest storage solution among those considered. However, you should be aware that Amazon S3 also charges for data transfer and data requests. In scenarios where your dataset consists of a large number of small files, you may incur considerable costs associated with **PUT** and **GET** records. You may consider batching small objects into large objects to reduce this cost. Note that there are additional charges involved when retrieving data stored in another AWS region. It could be reasonable to collocate your workload and data in the same AWS region to avoid these costs. S3 is also generally the slowest storage solution. By default, Amazon SageMaker downloads all objects from S3 before the training begins. This initial download time can take minutes and will add to the general training time. For instance, in the case of the **COCO2017** dataset, it takes ~20 minutes to download it on training nodes from S3. Amazon provides several mechanisms to stream data from S3 and eliminates download time. We will discuss these in this section.

- **Amazon EFS** storage is generally more expensive than Amazon S3. However, unlike Amazon S3, Amazon EFS doesn't have any costs associated with read and write operations. Since EFS provides a filesystem interface, compute nodes can directly mount to the EFS directory that contains the dataset and use it immediately without the need to download the dataset. Amazon EFS provides an easy mechanism to share reusable datasets between workloads or teams.

- **Amazon FSx for Lustre** provides the lowest latency for data retrieval but also the most expensive storage price. Like Amazon EFS, it doesn't require any download time. One of the common use cases for scenarios is to store your data in S3. When you need to run your set of experiments, you can provision FSx for Lustre with synchronization from S3, which seamlessly copies data from S3 to your filesystem. After that, you can run your experiments and use FSx for Lustre as a data source, leveraging the lowest latency for data retrieval. Once experimentation is done, you can de-provision the Lustre filesystem to avoid any additional costs and keep the original data in S3.

- **SageMaker Feature Store** has the most out-of-the-box ML-specific features; however, it has its shortcomings and strong assumptions. Since its offline storage is backed by S3, it has a similar cost structure and latency considerations. Online storage adds additional storage, read, and write costs. SageMaker Feature Store fits well into scenarios when you need to reuse the same dataset for inference and training workloads. Another popular use case for Feature Store is when you need to have audit requirements or run analytical queries against your datasets. Note that since Feature Store supports only a limited amount of data types (for example, it doesn't support any collections), you may need to do type casting when consuming data from Feature Store.

AWS provides a wide range of storage solutions and at times, it may not be obvious which solution to choose. As always, it's important to start by understanding your use case requirements and success criteria (for instance, lowest possible latency, highest throughput, or most cost-optimal solution).

Streaming datasets

Amazon S3 is a popular storage solution for large ML datasets, given its low cost, high durability, convenient API, and integration with other services, such as SageMaker. As we discussed in the previous section, one of the downsides of using S3 to store training datasets is that you need to download the dataset to your training nodes before training can start.

You can choose to use the **ShardedByKey** distribution strategy, which will reduce the amount of data downloaded to each training node. However, that approach only reduces the amount of data that needs to be downloaded to your training nodes. For large datasets (100s+ GB), it solves the problem only partially. You will also need to ensure that your training nodes have enough EBS volume capacity to store data.

An alternative approach to reduce training time is to stream data from Amazon S3 without downloading it upfront. Several implementations of S3 data streaming are provided by Amazon SageMaker:

- Framework-specific streaming implementations, such as `PipeModeDataset` for TensorFlow and Amazon S3 Plugin for PyTorch
- Framework-agnostic FastFile mode

Let's review the benefits of these approaches.

PipeModeDataset for TensorFlow

PipeModeDataset is an open source implementation of the TensorFlow Dataset API that allows to you read SageMaker Pipe mode channels. SageMaker Pipe mode is a mechanism that you can use to access stored on S3 using named pipes. Using `PipeModeDataset`, your training program can read from S3 without managing access to S3 objects. When using `PipeModeDataset`, you need to ensure that you are using a matching version of TensorFlow.

SageMaker Pipe mode is enabled when configuring a SageMaker training job. You can map multiple datasets to a single pipe if you're storing multiple datasets under the same S3 path. Note that SageMaker supports up to 20 pipes. If you need more than 20 pipes, you may consider using Augmented Manifest files, which allow you to explicitly list a set of S3 objects to be streamed. During training, SageMaker will read objects from the manifest file and stream them into the pipe.

`PipeModeDataset` supports the following dataset formats: text line, RecordIO, and TFRecord. If you have a dataset in a different format (for instance, as separate image files) you will have to convert your dataset. Note that the performance of `PipeModeDataset` performance on the number and size of the files. It's generally recommended to keep the file size around 100 to 200 MB for optimal performance.

> **Note**
>
> Since `PipeModeDataset` implements the TensorFlow Dataset API, you can use familiar methods to manipulate your datasets, such as `.apply()`, `.map()`. `PipeModeDataset` also can be passed to TensorFlow Estimator directly.

There are several differences between `PipeModeDataset` and TensorFlow Dataset that you should consider:

- `PipeModeDataset` reads data sequentially in files. SageMaker supports the `ShuffleConfig` (https://docs.aws.amazon.com/sagemaker/latest/APIReference/API_ShuffleConfig.html) parameter, which shuffles the order of the files to read. You can also call the `.shuffle()` method to further shuffle records.
- `PipeModeDataset` supports only three data types, all of which require data to be converted into one of the supported formats.

- PipeModeDataset has limited controls when it comes to manipulating data at training time. For instance, if you need to boost the underrepresented class in your classification dataset, you will need to use a separate pipe to stream samples of the underrepresented file and handle the boosting procedure in your training script.

- PipeModeDataset doesn't support SageMaker Local mode, so it can be tricky to debug your training program. When using SageMaker Pipe mode, you don't have access to the internals of how SageMaker streams your data objects into pipes.

Let's look at how PipeModeDataset can be used. In this example, for training purposes, we will convert the CIFAR-100 dataset into TFRecords and then stream this dataset at training time using PipeModeDataset. We will provide a redacted version for brevity instead of listing the entire example. The full source is available at https://github.com/PacktPublishing/Accelerate-Deep-Learning-Workloads-with-Amazon-SageMaker/blob/main/chapter4/3_Streaming_S3_Data.ipynb. Follow these steps:

1. Let's start by converting our dataset into TFRecord format. In the following code block, there is a method that iterates over a batch of files, converts a pair of images and labels into a TensorFlow Example class, and writes a batch of Example objects into a single TFRecord file:

```
def convert_to_tfrecord(input_files, output_file):
    """Converts a file to TFRecords."""
    print("Generating %s" % output_file)
    with tf.io.TFRecordWriter(output_file) as record_
writer:
        for input_file in input_files:
            data_dict = read_pickle_from_file(input_file)
            data = data_dict[b"data"]
            labels = data_dict[b"fine_labels"]
            num_entries_in_batch = len(labels)
            for i in range(num_entries_in_batch):
                example = tf.train.Example(
                    features=tf.train.Features(
                        feature={
                            "image": _bytes_
feature(data[i].tobytes()),
                            "label": _int64_
feature(labels[i]),
                        }
                    )
```

```
                )
                record_writer.write(example.
SerializeToString())
```

2. Once we have our datasets in TFRecord format, we need to create our training script. It will largely follow a typical TensorFlow training script, with the only difference being that we will use `PipeModeDataset` instead of `TFRecordDataset`. You can use the following code to configure `PipeModeDataset`:

```python
def _input(epochs, batch_size, channel, channel_name):
    mode = args.data_config[channel_name]
["TrainingInputMode"]
    dataset = PipeModeDataset(channel=channel_name,
record_format="TFRecord")
    dataset = dataset.repeat()
    dataset = dataset.prefetch(10)
    dataset = dataset.map(_dataset_parser, num_parallel_
calls=10)
    if channel_name == "train":
        buffer_size = int(NUM_EXAMPLES_PER_EPOCH_FOR_
TRAIN * 0.4) + 3 * batch_size
        dataset = dataset.shuffle(buffer_size=buffer_
size)
    dataset = dataset.batch(batch_size, drop_
remainder=True)
    iterator = tf.compat.v1.data.make_one_shot_
iterator(dataset)
    image_batch, label_batch = iterator.get_next()
    return {INPUT_TENSOR_NAME: image_batch}, label_batch
```

3. When configuring the SageMaker training job, we need to explicitly specify that we want to use Pipe mode:

```python
from sagemaker.tensorflow import TensorFlow
hyperparameters = {"epochs": 10, "batch-size": 256}
estimator = TensorFlow(
    entry_point="train.py",
    source_dir="3_sources",
    metric_definitions=metric_definitions,
    hyperparameters=hyperparameters,
```

```
        role=role,
        framework_version="1.15.2",
        py_version="py3",
        train_instance_count=1,
        input_mode="Pipe",
        train_instance_type="ml.p2.xlarge",
        base_job_name="cifar100-tf",
    )
```

Note that since the CIFAF100 dataset is relatively small, you may be not able to see any considerable decrease in the training start time. However, with bigger datasets such as COCO2017, you can expect the training time to reduce by at least several minutes.

Amazon S3 Plugin for PyTorch

Amazon S3 Plugin for PyTorch allows you to stream data directly from S3 objects with minimal changes to your existing PyTorch training script. Under the hood, S3 Plugin uses `TransferManager` from the AWS SDK for C++ to fetch files from S3 and utilizes S3 multipart download for optimal data throughput and reliability.

S3 Plugin provides two implementations of PyTorch dataset APIs: a map-style `S3Dataset` and an iterable-style `S3IterableDataset`. In the following section, we will discuss when to use one or another.

Map-style S3Dataset

`S3Dataset` represents a mapping of indexes and data records and implements the `__getitem__()` method. It allows you to randomly access data records based on their indices. A map-style dataset works best when each file has a single data record. You can use PyTorch's distributed sampler to further partition the dataset between training nodes.

Here is an example of using `S3Dataset` for images stored on S3:

1. First, we will define the dataset class that inherits from the parent `S3Dataset`. Then, we will define the data processing pipeline using PyTorch functions:

    ```
    from awsio.python.lib.io.s3.s3dataset import S3Dataset
    from torch.utils.data import DataLoader
    from torchvision import transforms
    from PIL import Image
    import io
    class S3ImageSet(S3Dataset):
        def __init__(self, urls, transform=None):
    ```

```
        super().__init__(urls)
        self.transform = transform
    def __getitem__(self, idx):
        img_name, img = super(S3ImageSet, self).__
getitem__(idx)
        # Convert bytes object to image
        img = Image.open(io.BytesIO(img)).convert('RGB')

        # Apply preprocessing functions on data
        if self.transform is not None:
            img = self.transform(img)
        return img
batch_size = 32
preproc = transforms.Compose([
    transforms.ToTensor(),
    transforms.Normalize((0.485, 0.456, 0.406), (0.229,
0.224, 0.225)),
    transforms.Resize((100, 100))
])
```

2. Next, we will create a PyTorch-native `Dataloader` object that can be passed to any training script:

```
# urls can be S3 prefix containing images or list of all
individual S3 images
urls = 's3://path/to/s3_prefix/'
dataset = S3ImageSet(urls, transform=preproc)
dataloader = DataLoader(dataset,
        batch_size=batch_size,
        num_workers=64)
```

Iterable-style S3IterableDataset

`S3IterableDataset` represents iterable objects and implements Python's `__iter__()` method. Generally, you use an iterable-style dataset when random reads (such as in a map-style dataset) are expensive or impossible. You should use an iterable-style dataset when you have a batch of data records stored in a single file object.

When using `S3IterableDataset`, it's important to control your file sizes. If your dataset is represented by a large number of files, accessing each file will come with overhead. In such scenarios, it's recommended to merge data records into larger file objects.

S3IterableDataset doesn't restrict what file types can be used. A full binary blob of the file object is returned, and you are responsible to provide parsing logic. You can shuffle the URLs of file objects by setting the shuffle_urls flag to true. Note that if you need to shuffle records within the same data objects, you can use **ShuffleDataset**, which is provided as part of the S3 PyTorch plugin. ShuffleDataset accumulates data records across multiple file objects and returns a random sample from it.

S3IterableDataset takes care of sharding data between training nodes when running distributed training. You can wrap S3IterableDataset with PyTorch's DataLoader for parallel data loading and pre-processing.

Let's look at an example of how to construct an iterable-style dataset from several TAR archives stored on S3 and apply data transformations:

1. We will start by defining a custom dataset class using PyTorch's native IterableDataset. As part of the class definition, we use S3IterableDataset to fetch data from S3 and data transformations that will be applied to individual data records:

```python
from torch.utils.data import IterableDataset
from awsio.python.lib.io.s3.s3dataset import
S3IterableDataset
from PIL import Image
import io
import numpy as np
from torchvision import transforms
class ImageS3(IterableDataset):
    def __init__(self, urls, shuffle_urls=False,
transform=None):
        self.s3_iter_dataset = S3IterableDataset(urls,
                                    shuffle_urls)
        self.transform = transform
    def data_generator(self):
        try:
            while True:
                label_fname, label_fobj
=         next(self.s3_iter_dataset_iterator)
                image_fname, image_fobj = next(self.s3_
iter_dataset_iterator)
                label = int(label_fobj)
                image_np = Image.open(io.BytesIO(image_
fobj)).convert('RGB')
```

```
                        # Apply torch vision transforms if
        provided
                        if self.transform is not None:
                            image_np = self.transform(image_np)
                        yield image_np, label
                except StopIteration:
                    return
        def __iter__(self):
            self.s3_iter_dataset_iterator = iter(self.s3_
        iter_dataset)
            return self.data_generator()
        def set_epoch(self, epoch):
            self.s3_iter_dataset.set_epoch(epoch)
```

2. Next, we define a transformation to normalize images and then instantiate a dataset instance
    with the ability to stream images from S3:

```
# urls can be a S3 prefix containing all the shards or a
list of S3 paths for all the shards
 urls = ["s3://path/to/file1.tar", "s3://path/to/file2.
tar"]
# Example Torchvision transforms to apply on data
preproc = transforms.Compose([
    transforms.ToTensor(),
    transforms.Normalize((0.485, 0.456, 0.406), (0.229,
0.224, 0.225)),
    transforms.Resize((100, 100))
])
dataset = ImageS3(urls, transform=preproc)
```

Now, let's look at FastFile mode.

FastFile mode

In late 2021, Amazon announced a new approach for streaming data directly from S3 called FastFile
mode. It combines the benefits of streaming data from S3 with the convenience of working with local
files. In **FastFile** mode, each file will appear to your training program as a POSIX filesystem mount.
Hence, it will be indistinguishable from any other local files, such as the ones stored on the mounted
EBS volume.

When reading file objects in FastFile mode, SageMaker retrieves chunks of the file if the file format supports chunking; otherwise, a full file is retrieved. FastFile mode performs optimally if data is read sequentially. Please note that there is an additional overhead on retrieving each file object. So, fewer files will usually result in a lower startup time for your training job.

Compared to the previously discussed framework-specific streaming plugins, FastFile mode has several benefits:

- Avoids any framework-specific implementations for data streaming. You can use your PyTorch or TensorFlow native data utilities and share datasets between frameworks.

- As a result, you have more granular control over data inputs using your framework utilities to perform operations such as shuffling, dynamic boosting, and data processing *on the fly*.

- There are no restrictions on the file format.

- It is easier to debug your training program as you can use SageMaker Local mode to test and debug your program locally first.

To use FastFile mode, you need to supply an appropriate `input_mode` value when configuring your SageMaker `Estimator` object. The following code shows an example of a TensorFlow training job:

```
from sagemaker.tensorflow import TensorFlow
estimator = TensorFlow(
    entry_point="train.py",
    source_dir="3_sources",
    metric_definitions=metric_definitions,
    hyperparameters=hyperparameters,
    role=role,
    framework_version="1.15.2",
    py_version="py3",
    train_instance_count=1,
    input_mode="FastFile",
    train_instance_type="ml.p2.xlarge",
)
```

FastFile mode can be a good starting choice, given its ease of use and versatility. If, for some reason, you are not happy with its performance, you can always consider tuning the configuration of your dataset (file format, file size, data processing pipeline, parallelism, and so on) or reimplement the use of one of the framework-specific implementations. It may also be a good idea to compare FastFile mode's performance of streaming data from S3 using other methods such as Pipe mode and S3 Plugin for PyTorch.

Summary

In this chapter, we reviewed the available storage solutions for storing and managing DL datasets and discussed their pros and cons in detail, along with their usage scenarios. We walked through several examples of how to integrate your SageMaker training scripts with different storage services. Later, we learned about various optimization strategies for storing data and discussed advanced mechanisms for optimizing data retrieval for training tasks. We also looked into SageMaker Processing and how it can be used to scale your data processing efficiently.

This chapter closes the first part of this book, which served as an introduction to using DL models on SageMaker. Now, we will move on to advanced topics. In the next chapter, we will discuss the advanced training capabilities that SageMaker offers.

Part 2:
Building and Training
Deep Learning Models

In this part, we will learn how to train DL models using SageMaker-managed capabilities, outlining available software frameworks to distribute training processes across many nodes, optimizing hardware utilization, and monitoring your training jobs.

This section comprises the following chapters:

- *Chapter 5, Considering Hardware for Deep Learning Training*
- *Chapter 6, Engineering Distributed Training*
- *Chapter 7, Operationalizing Deep Learning Training*

5
Considering Hardware for Deep Learning Training

Training a large **deep learning** (**DL**) model is typically a lengthy and data- and resource-hungry process. Considering an extreme case of the GPT-3 NLP model, it took approximately 34 days to train it from scratch using 1,024 NVIDIA A100 GPUs. While it's unlikely that you will have to train such a large model from scratch, even fine-tuning large DL models on your custom data can take days or even weeks.

Choosing a compute instance type for your specific model is a crucial step that will impact the cost and duration of training. AWS provides a wide spectrum of compute instances for various workload profiles. In this chapter, we will consider the price-performance characteristics of the most suitable instances for DL models, as well as scenarios where you should use one over the other for optimal performance.

Training large models also requires scaling training jobs across multiple GPU devices and compute instances, a process known as distributed training. At a high level, the distributed training process has two phases: the computation phase and the communication phase. During the communication phase, individual devices and nodes exchange individual updates and compute average weight updates. The amount of data that's exchanged is determined by your model size multiplied by its characteristics, such as precision. For large models, it's frequently the case that bottlenecks in your training process will be network throughput and not computations on individual devices. So, as part of the hardware considerations, we will discuss network throughput requirements and the available options, such as AWS **Elastic Fabric Adapter** (**EFA**), to address potential bottlenecks in the communication phase of your training job.

Another way to make your training process more efficient is to optimize your model for the hardware platform in question. When training DL models using frameworks such as TensorFlow and PyTorch, we rely on these frameworks to convert model Python code into instructions to be run on accelerators. However, these computational instructions are generic and do not utilize the specifics of your training loop and model architecture. SageMaker Training Compiler provides a set of capabilities for optimizing your model for specific accelerator devices, thus increasing the training speed and reducing the memory footprint.

In this chapter, we will cover the following topics:

- Selecting optimal compute instances
- Improving network throughput with EFA
- Compiling models for GPU devices with Training Compiler

After reading this chapter, you will be able to select an efficient hardware configuration for your training jobs with optimal price/performance characteristics and perform further optimizations.

Technical requirements

To follow along with the codes in the chapter, you will need the following:

- An AWS account and IAM user with permission to manage Amazon SageMaker resources
- Have a SageMaker Notebook, SageMaker Studio Notebook, or local SageMaker compatible environment established

Selecting optimal compute instances

Amazon SageMaker provides developers with a wide selection of compute instances organized into **instance families**. Each instance family has a set of instance configurations known as *instance types*.

The following list highlights the instance families that are available on SageMaker:

- **ML.M** is a family of standard instances that provides a balanced CPU and memory resource configuration. The more CPU cores you have, the more memory that will be available. This instance family doesn't come with a GPU device.
- **ML.C** is a family of compute-optimized instance designed for compute-bound applications such as data processing or certain **machine learning** (**ML**) algorithms (for instance, support vector machines). This family can be also used for ML inference. It doesn't come with GPU devices.
- **ML.G** is a family based on NVIDIA GPU devices and is primarily used for DL inference workloads. It can be also used for smaller training jobs and other compute-intense workloads.
- **ML.P** is a family that comes with NVIDIA GPU devices and is designed specifically for heavy-duty DL training jobs.

So far, we've only discussed general-purpose instance families that can run any compute operations in principle. In addition to that, there are specialized compute instances (known in the industry as **application-specific integrated circuits** or **ASIC**) designed specifically for DL workloads. At the time of writing, there are several types of ASIC instance families available on SageMaker or as EC2 instances:

- **Inferentia** instances.

- **Tranium** instances, which are only available on EC2 at the time of writing.

- **DL1** instances, which are only available on EC2 at the time of writing. However, SageMaker support has already been announced.

While CPU-based families can be used to run some ML training, it's rarely a good choice for DL model training. Now, let's review the available GPU and ASIC instances in detail.

Reviewing specialized DL hardware

In this chapter, we will focus on two types of hardware used for intensive DL training workloads – GPUs and ASICs – and discuss what makes them suitable for DL training, their characteristics, and their use cases.

If we look at the overall trends in ML and DL, we can observe that the industry is going from more general-purpose compute to more specialized devices.

Initial ML and DL models are trained using CPU devices since CPUs allow you to run almost any type of compute operation. A CPU is also a latency-optimized device when executing a single small compute operation. However, most DL models need to run massive compute operations in parallel (for instance, when multiplying matrices). So, the CPU spends a lot of time executing atomic operations one by one.

GPU devices are designed to solve a different class of problems – running large operations in parallel. You can say that the GPU is a throughput-optimized device as it runs many operations in parallel. Since DL models include large amounts of matrix computations that can be efficiently parallelized, GPUs are significantly more efficient than CPUs.

Advances in GPUs have made a whole new array of DL model architectures possible. For instance, the ground-breaking AlexNet model was trained on the ImageNet dataset in 2012 using GPU devices. The research team implemented convolution and matrix operations to run specifically on a GPU and, thus, achieved a considerable speedup at training time.

To simplify the usage of GPU devices for ML workloads, hardware vendors provide specialized libraries for GPU development. For example, NVIDIA created the CUDA platform – a set of libraries alongside a runtime to execute general-purpose computations on GPU devices. The CuBLAS library (part of CUDA) comes with a wide range of compute operations (such as matrix operations). You can also develop your own operations using the CUTLASS component. This is especially handy for new model architectures. Optimizing compute operations on CUDA also improves training performance.

Recently, a new approach for DL hardware design became popular: ASIC. This is a device designed to do a limited set of operations but perform these operations extremely efficiently. Google's **Tensor Processor Unit** (**TPU**) is an example of an ASIC designed for DL workloads. AWS is also actively working on specialized hardware devices for DL workloads. So far, AWS has launched Inferentia (2018) for inference and Tranium (2021) and DL1 instances (2022) based on Gaudi accelerators for training. Note that the Tranium and DL1 accelerators are only available as EC2 instances at the time of writing. We expect them to be available on SageMaker in the future.

As a result of ASIC's high specialization, it's always a good idea to confirm that a specific DL framework or model architecture is supported by a given ASIC device. Usually, you need to convert your model code into ASIC's instructions. This is usually done automatically by provided compilers. In the case of AWS ASICs, you need to compile your model using the open source Neuron SDK (`https://aws.amazon.com/machine-learning/neuron/`).

When compiling your model, Neuron SDK provides several optimizations, such as batching operations together. It uses ahead-of-time compilation, so the dimensions of the input data batches should be defined as part of the model configuration ahead of time, though note that Neuron SDK also supports a set of defined operators. If your model has unsupported operators (for instance, a custom control flow operation), you will not be able to compile your model at all. Neuron SDK supports the TensorFlow, PyTorch, and MXNet frameworks.

In many cases, choosing an optimal ASIC or GPU device depends on your specific model and training hyperparameters. You can use the industry-standard benchmark known as MLPerf (`https://mlcommons.org/en/training-normal-11/`) for guidance. Leading GPU and ASIC vendors submit the performance details of their hardware accelerators once they've been trained on eight popular DL models. As of December 2021, the NVIDIA A100 GPU demonstrated superior performance on all models among commercially available hardware accelerators. Google's TPUv4 ASIC accelerator improved benchmarks on six models, though at the time of submission, TPUv4 was not commercially available.

Choosing optimal instance types

Your choice of instance family and specific instance type is always driven by your use case requirements. Importantly, you may utilize several instance types and families within the same use case. For instance, you may want to start experimenting with single GPU training while getting your hyperparameters right and performing overall model debugging. Then, you can gradually scale your training to a larger number of nodes or move the training job to an instance type with a more performant accelerator.

You must consider some of the following criteria when selecting an optimal instance type:

- **Model architecture and its size**: This defines the memory requirements for storing the model on a GPU accelerator.
- **Desired training mode**: Here, you must choose whether you want to train the model on a single GPU, multi-GPU, or multi-GPU multi-node.

- **Business priorities**: Here, you must choose whether you want to train your model as fast as possible or as cheap as possible or find an acceptable cost-performance balance.

It's important to keep the following characteristics of instance types in mind when choosing the right one for your particular case:

- **Accelerator architecture**: This influences the performance of computations. For instance, the newest NVIDIA A100 chip delivers ~2.5x performance improvement over the previous generation V100 chip.

- **vCPU cores available**: These will be used in operations such as data loading and processing.

- **Intra- and inter-GPU network throughput**: This defines how quickly data (gradients) can be exchanged between training devices when running multi-GPU and/or multi-node training jobs.

- The price of using the chosen instance type.

In the following subsections, we will outline several typical use cases, ordered from the small and most cost-efficient to the largest and most performant.

The G5 family – cost-efficient training for small and medium models

When experimenting with training small or medium-sized DL models, you may consider G5 instances as cost-efficient yet powerful. They come with up to eight **NVIDIA A10G** accelerators, up to 100 Gbps network bandwidth, and up to 192 vCPUs. The following table shows the specifications for the G5 family:

	Instance Size	GPU	GPU Memory (GiB)	vCPUs	Memory (GiB)	Network Bandwidth (Gbps)
Single-GPU VMs	g5.xlarge	1	24	4	16	Up to 10
	g5.2xlarge	1	24	8	32	Up to 10
	g5.4xlarge	1	24	16	64	Up to 25
	g5.8xlarge	1	24	32	128	25
	g5.16xlarge	1	24	64	256	25
Multi-GPU VMs	g5.12xlarge	4	96	48	192	40
	g5.24xlarge	4	96	96	384	50
	g5.48xlarge	8	192	192	768	100

Figure 5.1 – G5 family specification

If you are looking to run a model on a single GPU device, you should choose a single-GPU VM, depending on other system requirements (network, RAM, vCPUs, and so on). If you would like to run several experiments simultaneously (each using a different GPU device), you should choose a multi-GPU VM. Note that in the case of multi-GPU VMs, individual GPU devices are not connected using a high-speed **NVLink interconnect**. So, if you are looking to run multi-GPU distributed training, the P3 family with NVLink will be more appropriate.

Alternatively, you can also consider the previous generation of G4 instances, which has a lower hourly price (up to 50% of the G5 rate for certain instances). However, according to AWS internal benchmarks, G5 has up to a 40% better price-performance ratio than G4.

The P3 family – high-performance and cost-efficient training

The P3 family offers high performance and cost efficiency for large-scale models. It comes with up to eight **NVIDIA V100** accelerators and unlike the G5 family, it supports the highly efficient NVLink GPU interconnect:

Instance Size	GPUs – Tesla V100	GPU Peer-to-Peer	GPU Memory (GB)	vCPUs	Memory (GB)	Network Bandwidth
p3.2xlarge	1	N/A	16	8	61	Up to 10 Gbps
p3.8xlarge	4	NVLink	64	32	244	10 Gbps
p3.16xlarge	8	NVLink	128	64	488	25 Gbps
p3dn.24xlarge	8	NVLink	256	96	768	100 Gbps

Figure 5.2 – P3 family specification

The p3.2xlarge instance is a good choice for running single-GPU training of complex DL models (assuming you can fit them into memory). If your model doesn't fit into a single-GPU device, you may choose p3.8xlarge or p3.16xlarge, which are multi-node instances. In this case, you will store parts of your model in several GPUs. NVLink interconnect provides high-speed data exchange between GPUs during forward and backward passes.

Another application area for p3.8xlarge and p3.16xlarge is running multi-GPU data parallel training jobs. In this use case, you load the copy of your DL model into each GPU device but use different batches of data to train. NVLink interconnect ensures high-speed gradient exchange and computations at the end of each training iteration between GPU nodes.

The most powerful instance, p3dn.24xlarge, comes with an EFA network device, which provides low latency and consistence communication between nodes. This makes p3dn.24xlarge instances a great choice for large-scale multi-GPU multi-mode training jobs, especially if your training job is network constrained.

The P4 family – highest performance for training

The P4 family is based on NVIDIA A100 GPU accelerators, which beats the MLPerf benchmark among any commercially available accelerators as of December 2021. The P4 family has a single instance, `p4d.24xlarge`, which comes with eight A100 GPU devices, 96 vCPUs, and 1,152 GBs of RAM.

These characteristics make the `p4d.24xlarge` instance ideal for training large SOTA DL models using distributed training approaches. However, when training large models, the amount of data that needs to be exchanged between devices in your training cluster might be higher than your inter-GPU and inter-node network bandwidth, which may lead to slowing your overall training speed and the underutilization of expensive GPU resources. AWS provides several networking capabilities for the `p4d.24xlarge` instance to mitigate this issue:

- Up to 600 GB/s bidirectional bandwidth between GPUs in the same node using NVLink

- Up to 400 GB/s bandwidth between GPUs on different nodes using **GPUDirect RDMA** over EFA

Additionally, `p4d.24xlarge` supports a wide spectrum of precision point types: FP64, FP32, FP16, INT8, BF16, and TF32. If your framework and model support has mixed precision, you may be able to achieve better performance with minimal compromise in terms of model accuracy.

Naturally, `p4d.24xlarge` is more expensive than other instances. However, the price difference between the second-most expensive instance, `p3dn.24xlarge`, is only around ~5%. Given its superior performance, P4 can deliver up to 60% lower costs for training and over 2.5x better DL performance according to internal AWS benchmarks. This makes `p4d.24xlarge` not only the most performant instance for DL training but also the most cost-efficient for large SOTA DL models. You can find detailed performance benchmarks for the P4d instance family in the following article: `https://aws.amazon.com/blogs/compute/amazon-ec2-p4d-instances-deep-dive/`.

Improving network throughput with EFA

When training large DL models, you need to break your large training task into smaller tasks and distribute them across multiple compute devices. Distributed training includes the following key steps:

1. Each device in the training cluster does the following:

    I.   Reads a unique minibatch from the global data batch

    II.   Runs a minibatch through the model and computes loss

    III. Computes the gradients to minimize loss

2. Each device communicates gradients to its peers. Average gradients are computed.

3. Each device updates the model according to the averaged gradients.

To measure the efficiency of distributed training, we can use the scaling factor, which is defined as follows:

$$scaling\ factor = \frac{T_n}{nT}$$

Here, T is the throughput of a single device, n is the number of devices in the training cluster, and nT is the achieved overall throughput of your training cluster. While ideal scaling is rarely achievable (meaning adding more resources proportionally reduces the training time), in many recent benchmarks, it was shown that scaling efficiency as high as 90% is achievable with careful application, hardware, and network optimizations.

To profile your training job for performance bottlenecks, it's important to measure the performance of each step. It was shown that in many instances, the communication phase (*step 2*) is a global bottleneck in the training process (for an example, see *Is Network the Bottleneck of Distributed Training?* At `https://arxiv.org/pdf/2006.10103.pdf`). In this section, we will focus on understanding how to optimize the communication phase.

Several factors define the amount of data that's sent and received on each node:

- First, there's the communication algorithm, which defines how training devices exchange gradient updates with each other. At the time of writing, the most popular approach is called Ring-AllReduce. This algorithm allows you to efficiently communicate gradient updates between each training device. Each of the N nodes communicates with two of its peers $2 * (N - 1)$ times. The overall amount of information that's sent in a single iteration by each training device is $\frac{2 * D * (N - 1)}{N} \approx 2 * D$ for large N, where D is the size of the gradient updates. This can be seen in the following diagram:

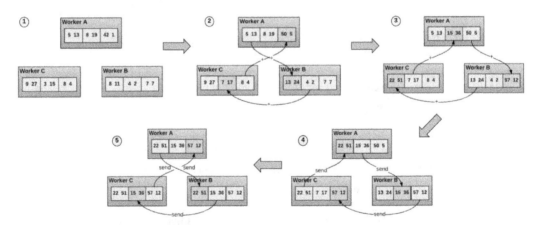

Figure 5.3 – Ring-AllReduce communication algorithm

- Second, there's the size of the model and its precision (D in the preceding formula).

For instance, if we use the Ring-AllReduce algorithm to train the BERT model (which contains approximately 340 million parameters) with half-precision, each training device will send and receive approximately 650 MB of data during a single iteration. Communication needs to happen quickly. The slowdown of an individual device will cause an overall slowdown in the training process.

Introducing EFA

Amazon EFA is a network device that provides lower and more consistent latency than traditional TCP transport. EFA was designed specifically for high-performance and ML use cases where inter-instance communication is critical for distributed jobs.

EFA provides the following benefits:

- OS bypass functionally, which allows DL applications to communicate directly with the network interface hardware to provide low latency and reliable transport functionality.

- Support for high-performance message protocols such as **MPI** and **NCCL**. For DL use cases, we are specifically interested in the NVIDIA NCCL library, which provides high-performance communication routines for GPU devices.

Using EFA allows you to significantly increase training job performance. According to AWS benchmarks, using EFA allows you to train BERT 130% faster on 32 instances of ml.p4dl.24xlarge compared to the default **Elastic Network Adapter (ENA)**.

There is no additional cost to using EFA on SageMaker. EFA is available for the ml.p3dn.24xlarge, ml.p4d.24xlarge, and ml.c5n.18xlarge SageMaker instances.

Using EFA with custom training containers

SageMaker provides seamless integration with EFA devices. If you are using TensorFlow or PyTorch DL containers with supported training instances, EFA will be enabled automatically.

If you choose to use a custom container, you will need to install the necessary EFA packages, as well as the MPI and NCCL libraries, in that container. The following steps show how to do it in your Dockerfile:

1. First, you must define the versions of the MPI, NCCL, EFA, and OFI libraries you will be using, as follows:

    ```
    ARG OPEN_MPI_PATH=/opt/amazon/openmpi/
    ENV NCCL_VERSION=2.7.8
    ENV EFA_VERSION=1.11.2
    ENV BRANCH_OFI=1.1.1
    ```

2. Then, you must download and execute the EFA driver installer:

```
RUN cd $HOME \
   && curl -O https://s3-us-west-2.amazonaws.com/aws-efa-
installer/aws-efa-installer-${EFA_VERSION}.tar.gz \
   && tar -xf aws-efa-installer-${EFA_VERSION}.tar.gz \
   && cd aws-efa-installer \
   && ./efa_installer.sh -y --skip-kmod -g \
ENV PATH="$OPEN_MPI_PATH/bin:$PATH"
ENV LD_LIBRARY_PATH="$OPEN_MPI_PATH/lib/:$LD_LIBRARY_
PATH"
```

3. Now, you must clone and build the NCCL library from the public NVIDIA repository:

```
RUN cd $HOME \
   && git clone https://github.com/NVIDIA/nccl.git -b
v${NCCL_VERSION}-1 \
   && cd nccl \
   && make -j64 src.build BUILDDIR=/usr/local
```

4. Next, you must install the AWS OFI NCCL plugin, which allows you to use the EFA networking module with NCCL applications:

```
RUN apt-get update && apt-get install -y autoconf
RUN cd $HOME \
   && git clone https://github.com/aws/aws-ofi-nccl.git -b
v${BRANCH_OFI} \
   && cd aws-ofi-nccl \
   && ./autogen.sh \
   && ./configure --with-libfabric=/opt/amazon/efa \
      --with-mpi=/opt/amazon/openmpi \
      --with-cuda=/usr/local/cuda \
      --with-nccl=/usr/local --prefix=/usr/local \
   && make && make install
```

5. Finally, you must install NCCL tests and execute them to check the correctness and performance of NCCL operations:

```
RUN cd $HOME \
   && git clone https://github.com/NVIDIA/nccl-tests \
   && cd nccl-tests \
```

```
          && make MPI=1 MPI_HOME=/opt/amazon/openmpi CUDA_HOME=/
       usr/local/cuda NCCL_HOME=/usr/local
```

In this section, we discussed the network between devices in distributed training and its implications for overall training efficiency. Since the network frequently becomes a global bottleneck for your training, we shared an intuition on how you can size your network bandwidth based on your cluster configuration and model parameters. Then, we reviewed the EFA network device from AWS, which improves network bandwidth and efficiency. Since EFA comes at no additional cost or any drawbacks for users, it's advisable to use it when possible.

Compiling models for GPU devices with Training Compiler

SageMaker Training Compiler is a capability that allows you to automatically optimize NLP DL models to run on GPU instances. For supported model architectures and frameworks, no code changes are required in your training scripts. You will only need to enable Training Compiler in your SageMaker training job configuration. Training Compiler can both reduce training speed time and memory requirements without this having any impact on model accuracy. For instance, according to AWS benchmarks, the training time and cost for the RoBERTa-based model are reduced by 30% when using Training Compiler.

Let's review how SageMaker Training Compiler works under the hood and how to use it in training jobs.

Introducing the XLA optimization library

Accelerated Linear Algebra (**XLA**) is a domain-specific compiler that accelerates model training and execution with little to no changes in model code. At the time of writing, XLA is supported for the TensorFlow and PyTorch frameworks. SageMaker Training Compiler abstracts interactions with the XLA library and uses them to optimize training jobs running on SageMaker. SageMaker Training Compiler supports both single-GPU and distributed training jobs.

When you're training your model without XLA, all operations are executed individually. Let's say your model has two sequential operations: matrix multiplication and matrix addition. Without XLA, your framework execution engine will send these two operations (known as *kernels*) one by one to the GPU device. When running with XLA, it will compile two operations into a single kernel launch by fusing the addition and multiplication operations. Fused operations must be executed entirely on GPU registers and only joined results should be streamed to end users. Removing redundant memory operations is one of the key optimization features of the XLA compiler.

Another notable difference between the XLA compiler and others is that unlike your regular CUDA operations, which are executed immediately (known as *eager* execution), XLA tensors operations are "lazy." First, the XLA compiler constructs the graph of fused operations and keeps tensors as placeholders in this execution graph. Only when the results of operations are needed will the compute operations be performed. By deferring execution, XLA finds opportunities to fuse operations in your model's computational graph.

Using SageMaker Training Compiler

SageMaker Training Compiler is tested on a wide range of NLP models, as well as on popular CV models for image classification and object detection for both PyTorch and TensorFlow implementations. As we expect this list to grow over time, please consult the following page for the latest set of supported models: `https://docs.aws.amazon.com/sagemaker/latest/dg/training-compiler-support.html`. This page also provides suggested training and model configurations, such as instance type, precision (mixed or not), and batch size.

SageMaker Training Compiler can also be used for models that have not been officially tested. When using Training Compiler with untested models, keep the following in mind:

- You may need to modify your training script, such as by setting a proper XLA device, using XLA-compatible optimizers, data loaders, and XLA training loop semantics.

- You may need to do a hyperparameter search (specifically, batch size and learning rate) to find the optimal configuration for your training job. This is because SageMaker Training Compiler changes the memory footprint of your model.

- Training Compiler is only available for a subset of SageMaker Deep Learning Containers. Refer to the following page for the latest containers with Training Compiler support: `https://github.com/aws/deep-learning-containers/blob/master/available_images.md`.

When benchmarking the results of your custom models with and without Training Compiler enabled, keep in mind that it takes some time for SageMaker to compile your model, which adds to the overall training time. Hence, it may not be practical to use Training Compiler for short-running training jobs (such as fine-tuning a task on a small dataset). Also, it's important to get your batch size right. Typically, you can expect Training Compiler to reduce the memory print of your model so that you can increase the maximum batch size. With increased batch size, you will need to scale your learning rate proportionally. Please note that the memory requirements for a given model may not always be reduced. In this case, you won't be able to increase your batch size. Using Training Compiler for untested models requires experimentation to achieve optimal results.

Using Training Compiler

To use Training Compiler for one of the tested models, you will need to enable it explicitly as part of your training job configuration. Follow these steps:

1. Start by importing the `TrainingCompilerConfig` object. Note that it's available in PythonSDK > 2.7.x:

    ```
    from sagemaker.huggingface import HuggingFace,
    TrainingCompilerConfig
    ```

The `TrainingCompilerConfig` object supports the following arguments:

- enabled (bool): Optional. This is a switch that enables SageMaker Training Compiler. The default is `True`.

- debug (bool): Optional. This specifies whether detailed logs for debugging are dumped. This comes with a potential performance slowdown. The default is `False`.

2. Next, you need to configure the necessary hyperparameters for SageMaker Training Compiler:

```
hyperparameters = {
    "epochs": 5,
    "train_batch_size": 24,
    "model_name": "bert-base-cased",
}
# Scale the learning rate by batch size, as original LR
was using batch size of 32
hyperparameters["learning_rate"] = float("5e-5") / 32 *
hyperparameters["train_batch_size"]
```

3. Next, you must configure the `HuggingFace` training job, as you did previously, with the only exception that you must explicitly pass `TrainingCompilerObject` in the default enabled state as part of the training configuration:

```
sm_training_compiler_estimator = HuggingFace(
    entry_point="train.py",
    instance_type="ml.p3.2xlarge",
    instance_count=1,
    role=role,
    py_version="py38",
    transformers_version="4.11.0",
    pytorch_version="1.9.0",
    compiler_config=TrainingCompilerConfig(),
    hyperparameters=hyperparameters,
    disable_profiler=True,
    debugger_hook_config=False,
)
```

> **Note**
>
> It's recommended that you disable the SageMaker Profile and SageMaker Debugger capabilities for the optimal performance of Training Compiler. Note the appropriate settings in our training job.

Once the training job has started, you must ensure that the model was compiled. For this, you should expect to see the following message in the training job logs, which indicates that Training Compiler worked as expected:

```
Found configuration for Training Compiler
Configuring SM Training Compiler...
```

Now, let's summarize this chapter.

Summary

In this chapter, we focused on the hardware aspects of engineering DL distributed training. We reviewed the available SageMaker compute instances and focused on instance families with GPU devices. After that, we discussed different DL use cases and how to select optimal compute instances for them. Then, we reviewed the network requirements for distributed training and learned how Amazon EFA can help you avoid network bottlenecks when running large-scale training jobs. We also reviewed how models can be optimized to run on GPU devices using SageMaker Training Compiler and gained practical experience in using this feature.

In the next chapter, *Chapter 6, Engineering Distributed Training*, we will continue this discussion of distributed training. We will focus on how to select the most appropriate type of distributed training for your use case, DL framework, and model architecture and then develop practical experience in these areas.

6
Engineering Distributed Training

In the previous chapter, we discussed how to select optimal hardware for the **Deep Learning** (DL) training job and optimize your model for the target hardware platform. In this chapter, we will consider, in depth, how to design efficient distributed training on Amazon SageMaker given your particular use case and model architecture.

There are two specific problems that distributed training aims to address. The first problem is how to reduce the training time of large models by distributing training tasks across multiple compute devices. Another problem arises when we need to train large models that cannot fit into the memory of a single GPU device. This problem is especially relevant for NLP tasks where it's shown that very large models have more expressive power and, hence, better performance on a wide range of NLP tasks. For instance, the latest open source SOTA language model, called BLOOM, was trained for ~3.5 months on a compute cluster with 384 GPU accelerators (NVIDIA A100). Model weights alone are around 329 GB, and a checkpoint with model weights and optimizer states is 2.3 TB. For more details, please refer to the model card at `https://huggingface.co/bigscience/bloom`.

Two approaches have emerged to address these problems; the first is **Data parallel** distributed training to speed up training time by simultaneously distributing tasks. The second is **Model parallel** distributed training to distribute large models between several GPUs and, hence, allow you to use models that cannot fit into the memory of an individual GPU device.

As you probably already guessed, large models that do not fit a single GPU device also require considerable time to train. So, inevitably, model parallelism will need to be combined with data parallelism to make the training time acceptable. The combination of data parallelism and model parallelism is known as **hybrid parallelism**. In this chapter, we will discuss these three types of parallelism.

While understanding distributed training approaches is essential, you also need to understand the available implementations for your DL framework and model architecture. SageMaker provides proprietary libraries for distributed training: **SageMaker Distributed Data Parallel** (SDDP) and **SageMaker Distributed Model Parallel** (SDMP). We will review their benefits and gain practical experience in how to use them in this chapter. Additionally, we will discuss other popular open source alternatives for distributed training for both the TensorFlow and PyTorch frameworks and how to use them on the SageMaker platform.

In this chapter, we will cover the following topics:

- Engineering data parallel training
- Engineering model parallel and hybrid training
- Optimizing distributed training jobs

By the end of this chapter, you will have a good understanding of distributed training and will have gained practical experience of how to implement various types of distributed training on Amazon SageMaker.

Technical requirements

In this chapter, we will provide code walk-through samples, so you can develop practical skills. The full code examples are available at `https://github.com/PacktPublishing/Accelerate-Deep-Learning-Workloads-with-Amazon-SageMaker/blob/main/chapter6/`.

To follow along with this code, you will need to have the following:

- An AWS account and IAM user with the permissions to manage Amazon SageMaker resources.
- A SageMaker Notebook, SageMaker Studio Notebook, or local SageMaker-compatible environment established.
- Access to GPU training instances in your AWS account. Each example in this chapter will provide a recommended instance type to use. It's possible that you will need to increase your compute quota for *SageMaker Training Job* to have GPU instances enabled. In that case, please follow the instructions at `https://docs.aws.amazon.com/sagemaker/latest/dg/regions-quotas.html`.

Engineering data parallel training

First, let's outline some important terminology that we'll use throughout this chapter:

- **Training process**, **trainer**, or **worker** – These terms are used interchangeably to identify an independent training process in a compute cluster. For example, a distributed DL training process usually runs on a single GPU device.
- **Training node**, **server**, or **host** – These terms define the server in the training cluster. The server can have one or several GPU devices, which means that one or several training processes can run on the same server.

- **World size** – This is the number of independent training processes running in the training cluster. Typically, the world size is equal to the number of GPU devices that are available in your training cluster.

- **Rank (also global rank)** – This is a unique zero-based ID of training processes running in your training cluster. For instance, if you have 4 training processes, they will have the ranks of 0, 1, 2, and 3.

- **Local rank** – This is a unique zero-based ID of training processes running within a single node. For example, if you have two training nodes with two GPU devices each, then the local ranks will be 0 and 1, and the global ranks will be 0, 1, 2, and 3.

- **Communication backend** or **Collective communication** – These terms define the mechanism and protocol for training processes to communicate and coordinate computations with each other. Some popular backends are **NVIDIA NCCL**, **Gloo**, and **Message passing interface (MPI)**.

- **Collective operation** – This is a specific operation performed between the processes of a training cluster, such as the `allreduce` operation, to aggregate and average tensors or **broadcast** to send the tensor from one training process to other processes in your cluster. Typically, communication backends provide the implementation of collective operations.

Now that we understand the basic terminology of distributed training, let's review data parallelism in depth.

Data parallel distributed training is useful when you are looking to reduce the training time of your model across multiple training devices. Each individual training process has a copy of the global model but trains it on a unique slice of data in parallel with others (hence *data parallelism*). At the end of the training step, each training process exchanges with other learned gradient updates. Then, the gradient updates are averaged and distributed back to all training processes so that they can update their individual model copies. *Figure 6.1* illustrates how data batches are distributed in a data-parallel two-node two-GPU cluster:

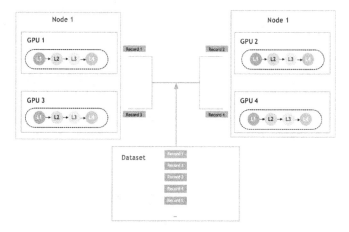

Figure 6.1 – An overview of data parallelism

When engineering your data parallel training job, you need to be aware of several key design choices to debug and optimize your training job, such as the following:

- How the coordination happens between processes

- How individual compute processes communicate with each other

- How compute processes are distributed in the training cluster

In the following section, we will discuss these design options.

Coordination patterns – Parameter Server versus Allreduce

There are two ways to coordinate compute processes in distributed clusters: using a **dedicated centralized coordinator** and using **peer-to-peer coordination** where each node communicates with one or many peers in a cluster directly. In the context of data parallel training, a centralized coordination pattern is called **Parameter Server** where the parameter server process coordinates the distribution of gradient updates and maintains a global model copy. The peer-to-peer pattern is called **Allreduce** that goes by the name of the peer-to-peer algorithm to distribute gradient updates between the training processes. In *Figure 6.2*, you can see the difference between the two coordination patterns:

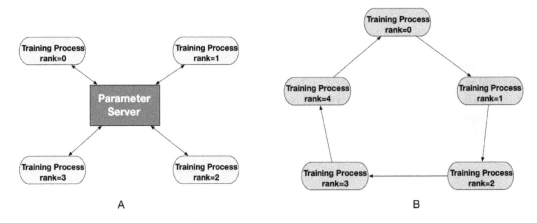

Figure 6.2 – The Parameter Server (A) and Allreduce (B) coordination patterns

Parameter Server is responsible for coordinating training processes in the cluster, namely the following:

- Allocating a unique set of data records for each training process

- Receiving gradients from each individual training process

- Aggregating gradients and updating the model weights accordingly

- Sending the updated model back to the training processes

Parameter Server stores a master copy of model weights. For larger DL models, it's possible that you might not be able to store the full model on Parameter Server. Additionally, Parameter Server can become a network and computation bottleneck. In that case, you might introduce multiple parameter servers that will store a subset of model parameters to reduce the network and memory requirements. Multiple parameter servers allow you to scale your distributed training for large models; however, it introduces additional complexities when coordinating model updates between the training processes and parameter servers and might still lead to network congestion. Finding an optimal configuration between the training processes and parameter servers can be a daunting task with a considerable trial-and-error effort required to find the optimal configuration.

The **Allreduce** algorithm employs peer-to-peer communication when each training process exchanges gradient updates with only two neighbors. A training process with a rank of i calculates gradients for the unique data micro-batch, receives gradients from process i-1, summarizes the received gradients with its own calculated gradients, and then sends the aggregated gradients to node i+1. In total, each process will communicate with its peers $2 \times (N - 1)$ times:

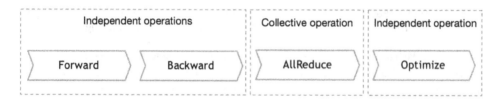

Figure 6.3 – The sequence of compute operations in the Allreduce algorithm

The Allreduce algorithm is considered bandwidth-efficient with constant communication costs and avoids having communication bottlenecks such as in the case of Parameter Server. Additionally, it has less complexity in operating compared to the Parameter Server approach (specifically, in the case of multiple parameter server instances). Therefore, many recent research papers and implementations are based on the Allreduce algorithm and its modifications. The most popular implementations of the Allreduce algorithm are Horovod, TensorFlow Mirror Strategy, and PyTorch **Distributed Data Parallel (DDP)**. AWS utilizes the modified Allreduce algorithm in the SDDP library, too. Later in this chapter, we will develop a distributed training job on SageMaker using the previously mentioned Allreduce implementations.

Communication types – sync versus async

There are two types of communication in distributed training jobs: **synchronous (sync)** and **asynchronous (async)**.

Sync communication implies that each training process will perform its computations synchronously with other processes in the cluster. For instance, in the case of the synchronous Allreduce algorithm, each training process will wait for other processes to complete their backward and forward passes before starting to exchange their gradients. This leads to situations where the cluster performance on each training step is defined by the performance of the slowest training process and might result in waiting for time (waste) for other training processes. However, the benefits of sync communication include more stable training convergence. Different implementations of the Allreduce algorithm also provide optimizations to reduce waiting time.

In **async communication**, each node acts independently. It sends gradient updates to other processes or centralized parameter servers and proceeds with the next training iteration without waiting for results from peers. This approach allows you to minimize the waiting time and maximize the throughput of each training process. The disadvantage of this approach is that the training process can be slow to converge and unstable due to increased stochasticity.

In practice, it's important to balance the system throughout and training converge. For this reason, sync communication is used in most implementations of distributed training with a number of optimizations to increase training throughput.

Training process layouts in a cluster

There are several ways to organize training processes in your training cluster depending on your model size/architecture and training requirements (such as the desired duration of training):

- **Single node with multiple GPUs** – This allows you to keep you to distributed training inside a single server and, hence, uses a fast inter-GPU NVLink network. This layout can be a great choice for smaller training jobs. However, even the most performant p4d.24xlarge instance only has 8 GPU devices, which limits how much you can scale your training job on a single node.

- **Multiple nodes with a single GPU** – This implies that all coordination between the processes happens over network communication, which can frequently be a global training bottleneck. Hence, this layout is suboptimal for most training scenarios.

- **Multiple nodes with multiple GPUs** – This allows you to scale your training job to 10s and 100s of individual training processes. When choosing this layout, you need to pay attention to the network throughput between training nodes since it can become a global bottleneck. SageMaker instances such as *p4d* and *p3dn* provide improved network capabilities to address this issue.

Now that we have the initial intuition of data parallelism, let's gain some practical experience and build data parallel distributed training jobs for the TensorFlow and PyTorch frameworks. We will use both native data parallelism implementations and DL frameworks, as well as the popular framework-agnostic Horovod library. Then, we will learn how to use AWS's proprietary SageMaker Data Parallel library and review its benefits compared to open source implementations of data parallelism.

Engineering TensorFlow data parallel training

When designing distributed training jobs for the TensorFlow framework, you have several implementations of data parallelism available:

- The native data parallel implementation (known as "strategies")
- The Horovod implementation for TensorFlow

Let's review the pros and cons of these implementations.

Using native TensorFlow strategies

TensorFlow 2 significantly expanded the number of distribution strategies compared to TensorFlow 1. Note that since TensorFlow 2 has several APIs for training, some APIs have limited support for distributed strategies. Please refer to *Figure 6.4* for the support matrix:

Training API	Mirrored Strategy	TPU Strategy	Multi Worker Mirrored Strategy (MWMS)	Central Storage Strategy	Parameter Server Strategy
Keras Model. fit	Supported	Supported	Supported	Experimental support	Experimental support
Custom training loop	Supported	Supported	Supported	Experimental support	Experimental support
Estimator API	Limited Support	Not supported	Limited Support	Limited Support	Limited Support

Figure 6.4 – TensorFlow 2 distributed strategies

Parameter Server Strategy and **Central Storage Strategy** are marked as **Experimental support**, which means that they are currently in active development. It's generally advised not to use experimental features in production workloads. So, we will not consider them in the scope of this book.

> **Note**
>
> While the Amazon SageMaker documentation states that it supports TensorFlow Parameter Server, this claim is misleading. SageMaker supports TensorFlow 1 Parameter Server, which is obsolete and should not be used in new development. SageMaker does not directly support the TensorFlow 2 native strategies out of the box, though it can support them with a few code changes, as shown next.

TPU Strategy is designed to work with Google TPU devices and, hence, is not supported by Amazon SageMaker. Therefore, in this section, we will focus on **Mirrored Strategy** and MWMS.

Both strategies implement the sync Allreduce algorithm for GPU devices. As their names suggest, the Multi Worker strategy supports distributing training tasks across multiple training nodes. For *intra-node communication*, you might choose either the *NCCL backend* or the *native RING communication* backend. In the case of both strategies, full model copies (known as *MirroredVariables*) are stored on each training process and updated synchronously after each training step. Let's review an example of how to implement **MWMS** on the SageMaker platform.

As a test task, we will choose everyone's favorite MNIST dataset and train a small computer vision model to solve a classification task. We will use the convenient **Keras API** to build and train the model and evaluate the results. An example notebook with more details is available at `https://github.com/PacktPublishing/Accelerate-Deep-Learning-Workloads-with-Amazon-SageMaker/blob/main/chapter6/1_distributed_training_TF.ipynb`.

We will start by reviewing which modifications are required to enable MWMS.

Cluster configuration and setup

MWMS is not natively supported by Amazon SageMaker, so we need to correctly configure the MWMS environment in SageMaker. TensorFlow2 uses an environment variable called `tf_config` to represent the cluster configuration. This configuration is then used to start the training processes. You can read about how to build the `'TF_CONFIG'` variable at `https://www.tensorflow.org/guide/distributed_training#TF_CONFIG`. In the following code block, we use the `'_build_tf_config()'` method to set up this variable. Note that we are using the `'SM_HOSTS'` and `'SM_CURRENT_HOST'` SageMaker environment variables for it:

```
Def _build_tf_config():
    hosts = json.loads(os.getenv("SM_HOSTS"))
    current_host = os.getenv("SM_CURRENT_HOST")
    workers = hosts
    def host_addresses(hosts, port=7777):
        return ["{}:{}".format(host, port) for host in hosts]
    tf_config = {"cluster": {}, "task": {}}
    tf_config["cluster"]["worker"] = host_addresses(workers)
    tf_config["task"] = {"index": workers.index(current_host),
"type": "worker"}
    os.environ["TF_CONFIG"] = json.dumps(tf_config)
```

In this example, by default, we use two `p2.xlarge` instances with a total world size of just two training processes. So, `_build_tf_config()` will produce the following `'TF_CONFIG'` variable in the rank=0 node:

```
{
    "cluster":
```

```
    {
            "worker":  ["algo-1:7777", "algo-2:7777"] },
            "task": {"index": 0, "type": "worker"
    }
}
```

Once the TF config has been correctly set, TF2 should be able to start training processes on all nodes and utilize all available GPU devices for it. This is a default setting, but you can provide a list of specific GPU devices to use, too.

To complete the cluster setup, we also need to make sure that the NCCL backend has been configured (please see the `_set_nccl_environment()` method) and that all nodes in the cluster can communicate with each other (please see the `_dns_lookup()` method). Note that these methods are required because TensorFlow 2 strategies are not officially supported by SageMaker. For supported data-parallel implementations, SageMaker provides these utilities out of the box and runs them as part of the training cluster initiation.

Using MWMS

To use MWMS, we will start by initiating a strategy object as follows. Please note that, here, we explicitly set the communication backend to AUTO, which means that TF2 will identify which backend to use. You can also define a specific backend manually. NCCL and the custom RING backends are available for GPU devices:

```
strategy = tf.distribute.MultiWorkerMirroredStrategy(
    communication_options=tf.distribute.experimental.
CommunicationOptions(
        implementation=tf.distribute.experimental.
CollectiveCommunication.AUTO
    )
)
```

Once the strategy has been correctly initiated, you can confirm your cluster configuration by properly checking `strategy.num_replicas_in_sync`, which will return your world size. It should match the number of GPUs per node multiplied by the number of nodes.

In this example, we are using the Keras API, which fully supports MWMS and, thus, simplifies our training script. For instance, to create model copies on all workers, you just need to initiate your Keras model within `strategy.scope`, as demonstrated in the following code block:

```
with strategy.scope():
        multi_worker_model = build_and_compile_cnn_model()
```

Additionally, MWMS automatically shards your dataset based on the world size. You only need to set up a proper global batch size, as shown in the following code block. Note that automatic sharding can be turned on if some custom sharding logic is needed:

```
global_batch_size = args.batch_size_per_device * _get_world_
size()
multi_worker_dataset = mnist_dataset(global_batch_size)
```

The rest of the training script is like your single-process Keras training script. As you can see, using MWMS is quite straightforward, and TF2 does a good job at abstracting complexities from developers, but at the same time, gives you the flexibility to adjust the default settings if needed.

Running a SageMaker job

So far, we have discussed how to update the training script to run in a data parallel way. In the source directory, you will also see the `mnist_setup.py` script to download and configure the MNIST dataset. Now we are ready to run data-parallel training on SageMaker.

In the following code block, we define the TF version (2.8), the Python version (3.9), the instance type, and the number of instances. Additionally, we pass several training hyperparameters. Since the MNIST dataset has been downloaded from the internet as part of our training script, no data is passed to the `estimator_ms.fit()` method:

```
from sagemaker.tensorflow import TensorFlow
ps_instance_type = 'ml.p2.xlarge'
ps_instance_count = 2
hyperparameters = {'epochs': 4, 'batch-size-per-device' : 16,
'steps-per-epoch': 100}
estimator_ms = TensorFlow(
                    source_dir='1_sources',
                    entry_point='train_ms.py',
                    role=role,
                    framework_version='2.8',
                    py_version='py39',
                    disable_profiler=True,
                    debugger_hook_config=False,
                    hyperparameters=hyperparameters,
                    instance_count=ps_instance_count,
                    instance_type=ps_instance_type,
                    )
estimator_ms.fit()
```

The training job should complete within 10–12 minutes using the default settings. Feel free to experiment with the number of nodes in the cluster and instance types and observe any changes in `'TF_CONFIG'`, the training speed, and convergence.

In the next section, we will learn about an open source alternative for data parallel – the Horovod framework.

Using the Horovod framework

The Horovod framework provides implementations of synchronous data parallelism for the most popular DL frameworks such as TensorFlow 1 and TensorFlow 2 (including Keras), PyTorch, and Apache MXNet. One of the benefits of Horovod is that it requires minimal modification of your training scripts to distribute training tasks, which is compatible with various cluster layouts. Horovod supports several communication backends: Gloo and Open MPI for CPU-based training and NCCL to run on NVIDIA GPU devices.

Horovod comes with a number of features to address the conceptual limitations of the Allreduce algorithm, which we discussed earlier. To decrease waiting times during the `allreduce` computation and to increase the utilization of training devices, Horovod introduces a concept called **Tensor Fusion**, which allows you to interleave communication and computations. This mechanism attempts to batch all the gradients ready for reduce operations together into a single reduction operation. Another notable feature that improves performance in certain scenarios is called **Hierarchical Operations**. This attempts to group operations (such as hierarchical `allreduce` and `allgather`) into a hierarchy and, thus, achieve better overall performance. Additionally, Horovod provides an **Autotune** utility to tune the performance of training jobs by tweaking the training parameters. Note that running an Autotune job is not intended for production usage.

Now, let's review how to use Horovod for TensorFlow 2 on SageMaker. Please note that Horovod is natively supported for both the TensorFlow and PyTorch frameworks. In this chapter, we will only review the Horovod implementation for TensorFlow 2 since the PyTorch variant will be very similar. We will solve the same MNIST classification problem that we did earlier.

Configuring the Horovod cluster

Unlike with MWMS, we don't have to configure and set up a training cluster in the training script since Horovod is supported by SageMaker. The Horovod cluster configuration is done on the level of the TensorFlow Estimator API via the `distribution` object, as shown in the following code block:

```
distribution = {"mpi": {"enabled": True, "custom_mpi_options":
"-verbose --NCCL_DEBUG=INFO", "processes_per_host": 1}}
```

Note the `processes_per_host` parameter, which should match the number of GPUs in the chosen instance type. Additionally, you can set `custom_mpi_options` as needed, which SageMaker will pass to the **mpirun** run utility. You can view the list of supported MPI options at `https://www.open-mpi.org/doc/v4.0/man1/mpirun.1.php`.

Developing the training script

You can find the full training script at `https://github.com/PacktPublishing/Accelerate-Deep-Learning-Workloads-with-Amazon-SageMaker/blob/main/chapter6/1_sources/train_hvd.py`. Let's perform the following steps:

1. We start by initiating Horovod in the training script via the `_initiate_hvd()` method. We also need to associate the Horovod training processes with the available GPU devices (one device per process):

```
def _initiate_hvd():
    hvd.init()
    gpus = tf.config.experimental.list_physical_
devices("GPU")
    for gpu in gpus:
        tf.config.experimental.set_memory_growth(gpu,
True)
    if gpus:
tf.config.experimental.set_visible_devices(gpus[hvd.
local_rank()], "GPU")
```

2. Next, we need to shard our dataset based on the world size, so each process can get a slice of data based on its global rank. For this, we use the `shard` method of the TensorFlow dataset instance. Note that we are getting local and global ranks of the given training process using the Horovod properties of `size()` and `rank()`:

```
train_dataset = train_dataset.shard(hvd.size(), hvd.
rank())
```

3. Then, we use the `DistributedOptimizer` Horovod wrapper to enable the distributed gradient update. Note that we are wrapping an instance of the native TF2 optimizer:

```
optimizer = tf.keras.optimizers.SGD(learning_rate=0.001 *
hvd.size())
optimizer = hvd.DistributedOptimizer(optimizer)
```

4. Lastly, we use special Horovod callbacks, which will be used by Keras in the training loop:

- `hvd.callbacks.BroadcastGlobalVariablesCallback(0)` to distribute initial variables from the `rank=0` process to other training processes in the cluster

- `hvd.callbacks.MetricAverageCallback()` to calculate the global average of metrics across all training processes

5. These callbacks are then passed to the `model.fit()` method, as follows:

```
hvd_model.fit(
    shareded_by_rank_dataset,
    epochs=args.epochs,
    steps_per_epoch=args.steps_per_epoch // hvd.
size(),
    callbacks=callbacks,
)
```

These are the minimal additions to your training script that allow you to use Horovod.

Running the SageMaker job

The SageMaker training job configuration is like the MWMS example, but we will add the `distribution` parameter, which allows us to set the MPI parameters and defines how many processes will be started per host:

```
from sagemaker.tensorflow import TensorFlow
ps_instance_type = 'ml.p2.xlarge'
ps_instance_count = 2
distribution = {"mpi": {"enabled": True, "custom_mpi_options":
"-verbose --NCCL_DEBUG=INFO", "processes_per_host": 1}}
hyperparameters = {'epochs': 4, 'batch-size-per-device' : 16,
'steps-per-epoch': 100}
estimator_hvd = TensorFlow(
                    source_dir='1_sources',
                    entry_point='train_hvd.py',
                    role=role,
                    framework_version='2.8',
                    py_version='py39',
                    disable_profiler=True,
                    debugger_hook_config=False,
                    hyperparameters=hyperparameters,
                    instance_count=ps_instance_count,
                    instance_type=ps_instance_type,
                    distribution=distribution
                    )
estimator_hvd.fit()
```

Here, we implemented minimal viable examples of data parallel training jobs using TensorFlow 2 MWMS and TensorFlow 2 Horovod. Now, you should have some practical experience in developing baseline training jobs. There are more knobs and capabilities in both Allreduce implementations, which we encourage you to explore and try in your real-life use cases. The choice of specific implementations (MWMS or Horovod) in many instances is use case specific without a clear-cut winner. The benefits of Horovod are that it supports several DL frameworks and its maturity (specifically its troubleshooting and optimization utilities). On the other hand, TensorFlow 2 strategies provide native integration with various TensorFlow APIs and different approaches, with many of them currently in experimental mode.

In the next section, we will move on to the PyTorch framework and review its native data parallel implementation.

Engineering PyTorch data parallel training

PyTorch provides a native implementation of data parallelism called **DDP**. DDP implements a synchronous Allreduce algorithm that can be scaled for multiple devices and multiple nodes. It supports both CPU and GPU training devices. To use DDP, you need to spawn multiple processes (one process per training device) on each node. PyTorch provides a special launch utility, called `torch.distributed.run`, to simplify and coordinate the processes launch. Similarly to Horovod, PyTorch DDP supports NCCL, Gloo, and the MPI communication backends. Additionally, PyTorch DDP natively supports **mixed precision** and **Automatic Mixed Precision** (**AMP**), which allows you to train your model with half-precision and minimal impact on model accuracy and training convergence. The benefits of AMP include the speeding up of computations and the reduction of a memory footprint.

While SageMaker doesn't support PyTorch DDP natively, it's possible to run DDP training jobs on SageMaker. Let's review the implementation example.

We take the pretrained CV Resnet18 model and then fine-tune it to classify ants and bees. We use data parallel to distribute tasks between two `p2.xlarge` instances with a single GPU device each. Feel free to change or modify the number and type of instances in the training cluster and observe how this changes the training speed.

Note that this is small-scale training and will not be indicative of training efficiency in real-life tasks.

Next, we will highlight key code constructs. A notebook and other code assets are available at `https://github.com/PacktPublishing/Accelerate-Deep-Learning-Workloads-with-Amazon-SageMaker/blob/main/chapter6/2_distributed_training_PyTorch.ipynb`.

Launching training processes

Amazon SageMaker has no out-of-the-box support for PyTorch DDP training. Specifically, it doesn't know how to start distributed DDP processes in the training cluster. Therefore, we need to develop a launching utility to perform this function. This utility is quite simple and can also be reused for any other DDP-based training jobs.

In the launcher script, we will use a DDP module, `torch.distributed.run`, which simplifies the spawning of training processes in a cluster. As part of the launcher script, we need to collect information about the training world, specifically, the number of nodes and GPU devices in the cluster as well as identify the node that will act as the master coordinator. Then, `torch.distributed.run` will spawn multiple training processes. Please refer to *Figure 6.5* for a visual illustration:

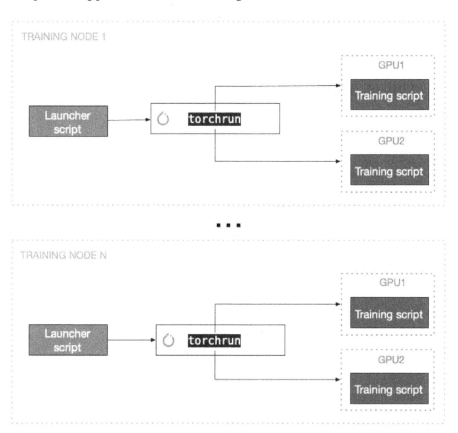

Figure 6.5 – Launching PyTorch DDP training on N nodes with two GPUs

Let's highlight several key areas in our launcher script:

1. First, we need to collect information about the SageMaker training cluster. For this, we use the environmental variables set by SageMaker automatically:

```
nodes = json.loads(os.getenv("SM_HOSTS"))
nnodes = len(nodes)
node_rank = nodes.index(os.getenv("SM_CURRENT_HOST"))
nproc_per_node = os.getenv("SM_NUM_GPUS", 1)
```

2. Next, we need to form the command line to start `torch.distributed.run`:

```
cmd = [
    sys.executable,
    "-m",
    "torch.distributed.run",
    f"--nproc_per_node={nproc_per_node}",
    f"--nnodes={str(nnodes)}",
    f"--node_rank={node_rank}",
    f"--rdzv_id={os.getenv('SAGEMAKER_JOB_NAME')}",
    "--rdzv_backend=c10d",
    f"--rdzv_endpoint={nodes[0]}:{RDZV_PORT}",
    distr_args.train_script,
]
# Adding training hyperparameters which will then be
passed in training script
cmd.extend(training_hyperparameters)
```

Note that we are adding `training hyperparameters` "as is" at the end of the command line. These arguments are not handled by the launcher but by the training script to configure training.

3. Lastly, we use Python's `subprocess.Popen` to start the `torch.distributed.run` utility as a module:

```
process = subprocess.Popen(cmd, env=os.environ)
process.wait()
if process.returncode != 0:
    raise subprocess.
CalledProcessError(returncode=process.returncode,
cmd=cmd)
```

Note that we are copying the environment variables to subprocesses to preserve all the SageMaker variables. If the spawned process returns nonzero code (an indication of error), we will then raise an exception to propagate the error code to the SageMaker control plane.

In summary, our launcher utility is responsible for collecting training cluster configuration and then starting `torch.distributed.run` on each node. The utility then takes care of starting multiple training processes per node.

Adopting the training script for DDP

To use DDP, we need to make minimal changes to our training script:

1. First, we initialize the training process and add it to the DDP process group:

```
dist.init_process_group(
    backend="nccl",
    rank=int(os.getenv("RANK", 0)),
    world_size=int(os.getenv("WORLD_SIZE", 1)),
)
```

   Since we have GPU-based instances, we use the NCCL communication backend. Also, we utilize the environment variables set by the `torch.distributed.run` module: world size and global rank.

2. Next, we need to identify which GPU device will store the model and run computations. We use the LOCAL_RANK variable set by `torch.distributed.run` during the process spawn:

```
torch.cuda.set_device(os.getenv("LOCAL_RANK"))
device = torch.device("cuda")
model = model.to(device)
```

3. Then, we wrap our regular PyTorch model with a special DDP implementation. This implementation allows us to work with the PyTorch model as if it is a regular, locally stored model. Under the hood, the DDP module implements gradient synchronization between training processes in the process group. Also, observe that we are scaling down the global batch size provided by the user based on the world size:

```
model = DDP(model)
args.batch_size //= dist.get_world_size()
args.batch_size = max(args.batch_size, 1)
```

4. The last step we need to do is to modify the training data loader so that each training process gets a unique slice of data during the training step. For this, we use `DistributedSampler`, which samples data records based on the total number of processes, and process the global rank:

```
    train_sampler = torch.utils.data.distributed.
DistributedSampler(
        image_datasets["train"], num_replicas=args.world_
size, rank=args.rank
    )
    train_loader = torch.utils.data.DataLoader(
```

```
        image_datasets["train"],
        batch_size=args.batch_size,
        shuffle=False,
        num_workers=0,
        pin_memory=True,
        sampler=train_sampler,
    )
```

The rest of the training script is similar to *non-distributed training*. As you can see, the amount of modification in the training script to make it compatible with PyTorch DDP is minimal.

Running a SageMaker training job

Once the launcher and training scripts are ready, we can start the SageMaker training job. Note that we identify the launcher script as an entry_point parameter. A reference to the training script is provided along with the training hyperparameters in the hyperparameter object:

```
from sagemaker.pytorch import PyTorch
ps_instance_type = 'ml.p3.2xlarge'
ps_instance_count = 2
hyperparameters = {
  'train-script': 'train_ddp.py',
  'epochs': 25,
  }
estimator_ms = PyTorch(
                    source_dir='2_sources',
                    entry_point='launcher.py',
                    role=role,
                    framework_version='1.9',
                    py_version='py38',
                    disable_profiler=True,
                    debugger_hook_config=False,
                    hyperparameters=hyperparameters,
                    instance_count=ps_instance_count,
                    instance_type=ps_instance_type,
                    )
estimator_ms.fit(inputs={"train":f"{data_url}/train",
"val":f"{data_url}/val"})
```

The training job should complete within 8–9 minutes. Feel free to review the debug messages in the training job logs. Additionally, you can experiment with other parameters such as the instance type and size, the number of epochs, the batch size, and more.

In this section, we learned how to use native data parallel implementation in the PyTorch framework. In the next section, we will cover SageMaker's proprietary data parallel implementation.

Engineering SageMaker's DDP jobs

The SDDP library provides a proprietary implementation of data parallelism with native integration with other SageMaker capabilities. SDDP is packaged in SageMaker DL containers and supports both the TensorFlow 2 and PyTorch frameworks.

SDDP utilized MPI (like Horovod) to manage processes in the training cluster. Under the hood, SDDP uses the **mpirun** utility to start training in the training cluster. SDDP is only available for GPU-based instances: `ml.p3.16xlarge`, `ml.p3dn.24xlarge`, and `ml.p4d.24xlarge`. SDDP provides an API very similar to Horovod and PyTorch DDP, which makes it easy to switch from open source implementations to it.

SDDP implements a modified Allreduce algorithm with a number of optimizations to improve the overall training performance and, specifically, waiting time during the `allreduce` operation. As discussed earlier, in the synchronous Allreduce algorithm, typically, the distributed `allreduce` operation is a bottleneck and becomes even less efficient with the scaling out of the training cluster. Please view *Figure 6.6*:

Figure 6.6 – Allreduce times with a cluster increase

To increase training efficiencies, specifically, in a large cluster, SDDP introduces several novel optimizations:

- SDDP utilizes GPU and CPU devices during training, so GPU devices perform forward and backward passes, and CPU devices perform gradient averaging and communication with other training processes during the `allreduce` stage. This approach allows you to run compute operations and `allreduce` in parallel and, hence, maximize utilizations.

- SDDP supports **FusionBuffers** to balance data sent over the network during `allreduce` (such as Horovod's Tensor Fusion feature).

As a result, AWS claims that SDDP provides near linear scaling of training throughput with an increase in the training cluster size. AWS published the following benchmarks to demonstrate the optimization gains of SDDP compared to native PyTorch DDP: for 8 node clusters of `p3dn.24xl`, SSDP outperforms PyTorch DDP by 41% when training the BERT model and by 13% when training the MaskRCNN model. Please refer to this article for more details: `https://docs.aws.amazon.com/sagemaker/latest/dg/data-parallel-intro.html`.

When engineering an SDDP training job, keep the following aspects in mind:

- SDDP relies on the CPU device to perform the `allreduce` operation. Most framework data loaders use CPU, too. So, make sure that you control your CPU usage to avoid overutilization. In *Chapter 7, Operationalizing Deep Learning Training*, we will discuss tools that you can use to control your resource utilization such as SageMaker Debugger. Alternatively, you can move data loading operations to GPU. However, in this case, you will have less available GPU memory to load the model and run its forward and backward passes.

- SDDP might not have significant or any benefits when used in small clusters or on a single node, as it was designed to specifically address the bottlenecks of large training clusters.

Let's review an example of an SDDP-based training job. For this, we will reuse the previous PyTorch DDP and make minimal modifications to switch from PyTorch DDP to the SDDP library.

As a training task, we use the same binary classification CV as in the PyTorch DDP sample. Since SDDP is natively supported by SageMaker, we don't need to develop any custom launcher utilities. SDDP uses the `mpirun` utility to spawn training processes in our cluster. You can use the `distribution` parameter to enable data-parallel execution and provide any `mpi` options, as follows:

```
distribution = {
    "smdistributed": {
        "dataparallel": {
            "enabled": True,
            "custom_mpi_options": "-verbose -x NCCL_
DEBUG=VERSION"
        }
    }
}
```

Now, let's move on to adopting the training script.

Adopting the training script

SDDP's starting version 1.4.0 is an integrated PyTorch DDP package that we used in the previous example as a specific backend option. This significantly reduces the changes needed to use SDDP. In fact, if you already have a DDP-enabled training script, you will only need to add an import of the `torch_sddp` package and use the `smddp` communication backend when initializing the process group, as follows:

```
import smdistributed.dataparallel.torch.torch_smddp
import torch.distributed as dist
dist.init_process_group(backend='smddp')
```

Keep in mind that SDDP v1.4 is only available with the latest PyTorch v10 DL containers. For earlier versions, the SDDP API is slightly different. For more details, please refer to the official API documentation at https://sagemaker.readthedocs.io/en/stable/api/training/distributed.html#the-sagemaker-distributed-data-parallel-library.

Running the SDDP SageMaker training job

Starting the SDDP job requires you to provide a special `distribution` object with the configuration of data parallelism. Another thing to keep in mind is that SDDP is only available for a limited set of multi-GPU instance types: `ml.p3.16xlarge`, `ml.p3dn.24xlarge`, and `ml.p4d.24xlarge`. Take a look at the following:

```
from sagemaker.pytorch import PyTorch
instance_type = 'ml.p3.16xlarge'
instance_count = 2
distribution = {
    "smdistributed": {
        "dataparallel": {
            "enabled": True,
            "custom_mpi_options": "-verbose -x NCCL_
DEBUG=VERSION"
        }
    }
}
sm_dp_estimator = PyTorch(
            entry_point="train_sm_dp.py",
            source_dir='3_sources',
            role=role,
            instance_type=instance_type,
```

```
        sagemaker_session=sagemaker_session,
        framework_version='1.10',
        py_version='py38',
        instance_count=2,
        hyperparameters={
            "batch-size":64,
            "epochs":25,
        },
        disable_profiler=True,
        debugger_hook_config=False,
        distribution=distribution,
        base_job_name="SM-DP",
    )
```

Note that since we are using a small dataset, this training sample won't be indicative of any performance efficiencies of SDDP compared to the open source data parallel frameworks.

Summarizing data parallelism

So far, we have discussed how to speed up the training of DL models, which can fit into the memory of an individual device. We discussed and developed training scripts using native implementations as part of the DL frameworks, open source, and proprietary cross-framework Allreduce implementations (Horovod and SageMaker SDDP, respectively). However, we didn't attempt to benchmark the training efficiencies of the given implementation. While each use case is unique, the general recommendation would be to consider SDDP as a first choice when you are dealing with large-scale and lengthy training processes involving large clusters. If you have a medium- or small-scale training job, you still might consider using framework-native data-parallel implementations. In such cases, the SDDP performance benefits can be negligible.

In the next section, we will discuss how to optimally train models that cannot fit into single GPU memory using model parallelism.

Engineering model parallel training jobs

In model parallelism, a single copy of the model is distributed across two or more training devices to avoid the memory limitations of a single GPU device. A simple method of model parallelism is to explicitly assign layers of the model onto different devices. In this case, forward pass computations will be performed on the GPU device storing the first set of layers. Then, the results will be transferred to the GPU device storing the next set of layers, and so on. The handoff between layers will happen in reverse order during the backward pass. This type of model parallelism is known as **naïve model parallelism** or **vertical model parallelism** because we split the model vertically between devices.

However, this type of model parallelism is inefficient, as each GPU device will wait for a significant amount of time for other devices to complete their computations. A more efficient way to organize model parallelism is called **Pipeline Parallelism**. This splits a single data batch into a number of micro-batches and tries to minimize the waiting time by overlapping the computing gradients for different **micro-batches**. See a comparison of naïve model parallelism and pipeline parallelism in *Figure 6.7*:

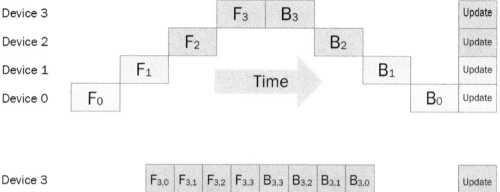

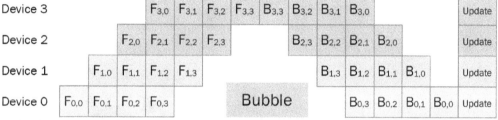

Figure 6 .7 – Naïve model parallelism and pipeline model parallelism

---

Source of the figure

```
https://ai.googleblog.com/2019/03/introducing-gpipe-open-source-
library.html
```

Implementing pipeline parallelism has several challenges, as you will likely need to reimplement your training script to assign parts of the model to different devices and reflect the new computation flow in your training loop. Also, you will need to decide how to optimally place your model layers on devices within the same node and across nodes. Additionally, pipeline parallel doesn't support conditional flows and requires each layer to take a tensor as input and produce a tensor output. You will also need to reimplement pipeline parallelism for each new model architecture. Later in this section, we'll see how the SMDP library addresses these challenges.

Splitting the model vertically is one way to minimize memory footprint. Another parallelization approach is called **Tensor Parallelism**. Each tensor (data inputs and layer outputs) is split across multiple devices and processed in parallel. Then, the individual results are aggregated. Tensor parallelism is possible as many compute operations can be represented as matrix operations, which can be split along the X or Y axes. Refer to *Figure 6.8* for a visual representation of how tensors can be split. Tensor parallelism is also known as **horizontal parallelism**:

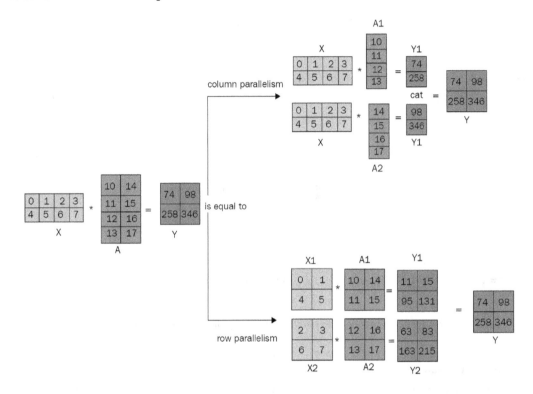

Figure 6.8 – Row-wise and column-wise tensor parallelism

Source of the figure

https://github.com/huggingface/transformers/blob/main/docs/
source/en/perf_train_gpu_many.mdx

Pipeline and tensor model parallelism can be combined. Moreover, data parallelism can be added to achieve even further parallelization and a better training speed. The combination of data parallelism and model parallelism is known as **hybrid parallelism**. This approach is used to train most of the current large SOTA NLP models such as T5 or GPT3. Refer to *Figure 6.9*, which illustrates a combination of pipeline parallelism and data parallelism:

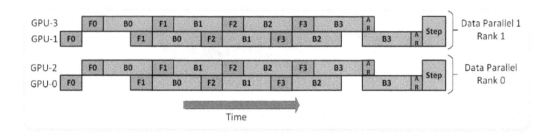

Figure 6.9 – Combining pipeline parallelism and data parallelism

Now that we have refreshed our understanding of key model parallel approaches, let's review the SDMP library – the SageMaker proprietary implementation of model parallelism.

Engineering training with SDMP

SDMP is a feature-rich library that implements various types of model parallelism and hybrid parallelism and is optimized for the SageMaker infrastructure. It supports the TensorFlow and PyTorch frameworks and allows you to automatically partition models between devices with minimal code changes to your training script. Like SDDP, SDMP uses MPI to coordinate tasks in the training cluster, performing forward and backward computations on GPU devices and communication tasks on CPU devices.

SDMP has a few notable features to simplify the development of model parallel training jobs and optimize hardware utilization at training time:

- SDMP supports arbitrary model architecture and requires minimal code changes to your training script. It doesn't have any accuracy penalties.

- **Automated model splitting** partitions your model between devices in the training cluster. You can choose to optimize for speed and memory utilization. Additionally, SDMP supports manual model splitting (however, in practice, this is rarely a good approach).

- **Interleaved pipeline** is an improvement of simple model pipelining and allows you to minimize the amount of time processing micro-batches by prioritizing backward operations whenever possible:

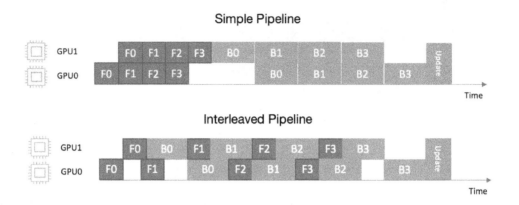

Figure 6.10 – A comparison of simple and interleaved pipelines

---

Source of the figure

```
https://docs.aws.amazon.com/sagemaker/latest/dg/model-parallel-
core-features.html
```

While SDMP officially supports both TensorFlow 2 and PyTorch, certain optimizations are only available for PyTorch. This extended support for PyTorch includes the following:

- **Optimizer state sharding** allows you to split not only the model but also the optimizer state between training devices in data parallel groups. This further reduces the memory footprint of individual devices during training. Note that optimizer state sharding adds an aggregation step (when the global optimizer state is reconstructed from individual shards), which will result in additional latency.

- **Tensor parallelism** in addition to pipeline and data parallelism. Tensor parallelism can be specifically useful for large layers that cannot fit into a single GPU device, such as embeddings.

- **Activation checkpointing** and **activation offloading** are two other techniques that further minimize the training memory footprint in exchange for some additional compute time to reconstruct the training state.

As using these advanced optimization features comes with a memory-compute trade-off, it's generally advised that you only use them for large models (that is, billions of parameters).

Now, let's develop a hybrid parallel job using the SDMP library. We will reuse the previous PyTorch example with CV models.

> **Note**
>
> This example has an educational purpose only. Usually CV models (such as Resnet18) can fit into a single GPU, and in this case, model parallelism is not required. However, smaller models are easy to manage and quick to train for demo purposes.

Configuring model and hybrid parallelism

First, let's understand how our training will be executed and how we can configure parallelism. For this, we will use the distribution object of the SageMaker training job. It has two key components: `model parallel` and `mpi`.

SageMaker relies on the `mpi` utility to run distributed computations. In the following code snippet, we set it to run 8 training processes. Here, `processes_per_host` defines how many training processes will be run per host, which includes both processes running model parallelism, data parallelism, or tensor parallelism. In most cases, the number of processes should match the number of available GPUs in the node.

The `Modelparallel` object defines the configuration of the SDMP library. Then, in the code snippet, we set 2-way model parallelism (the `partitions` parameter is set to 2). Also, we enable data parallelism by setting the `ddp` parameter to `True`. When data parallelism has been enabled, SDMP will automatically infer the data parallel size based on the number of training processes and the model parallelism size. Another important parameter is `auto_partition`, so SDMP automatically partitions the model between GPU devices.

In the following code block, we configure our training job to run on 2 instances with a total of 16 GPUs in the training cluster. Our `distribution` object defines 2-way model parallelism. Since the total number of training processes is 16, SDMP will automatically infer 8-way data parallelism. In other words, we split our model between 2 GPU devices, and have a total of 8 copies of the model:

```
smd_mp_estimator = PyTorch(
# ... other job parameters are reduced for brevity
instance_count=2,
instance_type= 'ml.p3.16xlarge',
distribution={
                "modelparallel": {
                    "enabled":True,
                    "parameters": {
                        "microbatches": 8,
                        "placement_strategy": "cluster",
                        "pipeline": "interleaved",
                        "optimize": "speed",
```

```
                                "partitions": 2,
                                "auto_partition": True,
                                "ddp": True,
                            }
                        }
                    },
                "mpi": {
                        "enabled": True,
                        "processes_per_host": 8,
                        "custom_mpi_options": mpioptions
                }
```

Please note that you need to align the configuration of hybrid parallelism with your cluster layout (the number of nodes and GPU devices). SageMaker Python SDK provides upfront validation of the hybrid parallelism configuration; however, this doesn't guarantee that all your GPU devices will be used during the training process. It's a good idea to add debug messages to your training scripts to ensure that all GPU devices are properly utilized.

Adopting the training scripts

One of the benefits of SDMP is that it requires minimal changes to your training script. This is achieved by using the Python decorator to define computations that need to be run in a model parallel or hybrid fashion. Additionally, SDMP provides an API like other distributed libraries such as Horovod or PyTorch DDP. In the following code block, we only highlight the key parts. The full source is available at https://github.com/PacktPublishing/Accelerate-Deep-Learning-Workloads-with-Amazon-SageMaker/tree/main/chapter6/4_sources:

1. We start by importing and initializing the SDMP library:

    ```
    import smdistributed.modelparallel.torch as smp
    smp.init()
    ```

2. Once the library has been initialized, we can use the SDMP API to check that our hybrid parallelism has been correctly configured. For this, you can run the following debug statement as part of your training script:

    ```
    logger.debug(
    f"Hello from global rank {smp.rank()}. "
        f"Local rank {smp.local_rank()} and local size
    {smp.local_size()}. "
        f"List of ranks where current model is stored {smp.
    get_mp_group()}. "
    ```

```
        f"List of ranks with different replicas of the same
model {smp.get_dp_group()}. "
        f"Current MP rank {smp.mp_rank()} and MP size is
{smp.mp_size()}. "
          f"Current DP rank {smp.dp_rank()} and DP size is
{smp.dp_size()}."
        )
```

3. The output will be produced in each training process. Let's review the output from global rank 0. Here, the message prefix in brackets is provided by the MPP utility, marking the unique MPI process, and algo-1 is a reference to the hostname. From the debug message, you can confirm that we have configured 2-way parallelism and 8-way data parallelism. Additionally, we can observe GPU assignments for the data parallel and model parallel groups:

```
[1,mpirank:0,algo-1]:INFO:__main__:Hello from global
rank 0. Local rank 0 and local size 8. List of ranks
where current model is stored [0, 1]. List of ranks with
different replicas of the same model [0, 2, 4, 6, 8, 10,
12, 14]. Current MP rank 0 and MP size is 2. Current DP
rank 0 and DP size is 8.
```

4. SDMP manages the assignment of model partitions to the GPU device, and you don't have to explicitly move the model to a specific device (in a regular PyTorch script, you need to move the model explicitly by calling the model.to(device) method). In each training script, you need to choose a GPU device based on the SMDP local rank:

```
torch.cuda.set_device(smp.local_rank())
device = torch.device("cuda")
```

5. Next, we need to wrap the PyTorch model and optimizers in SDMP implementations. This is needed to establish communication between the model parallel and data parallel groups.

6. Once wrapped, you will need to use SDMP-wrapped versions of the model and optimizer in your training script. Note that you still need to move your input tensors (for instance, data records and labels) to this device using the PyTorch input_tensor.to(device) method:

```
model = smp.DistributedModel(model)
optimizer = smp.DistributedOptimizer(optimizer)
```

7. After that, we need to configure our data loaders. SDMP doesn't have any specific requirements for data loaders, except that you need to ensure batch size consistency. It's recommended that you use the drop_last=True flag to enforce it. This is because, internally, SDMP breaks down the batch into a set of micro-batches to implement pipelining. Hence, we need to make

sure that the batch size is always divisible by the micro-batch size. Note that, in the following code block, we are using the SDMP API to configure a distributed sampler for data parallelism:

```
dataloaders_dict = {}
train_sampler = torch.utils.data.distributed.
DistributedSampler(
        image_datasets["train"], num_replicas=sdmp_args.
dp_size, rank=sdmp_args.dp_rank)
        dataloaders_dict["train"] = torch.utils.data.
DataLoader(
        image_datasets["train"],
        batch_size=args.batch_size,
        shuffle=False,
        num_workers=0,
        pin_memory=True,
        sampler=train_sampler,
        drop_last=True,
    )
    dataloaders_dict["val"] = torch.utils.data.
DataLoader(
        image_datasets["val"],
        batch_size=args.batch_size,
        shuffle=False,
        drop_last=True,
    )
```

8. Once we have our model, optimizer, and data loaders configured, we are ready to write our training and validation loops. To implement model parallelism, SDMP provides a `@smp.step` decorator. Any function decorated with `@smp.set` splits executes internal computations in a pipelined manner. In other words, it splits the batch into a set of micro-batches and coordinates the computation between partitions of models across GPU devices. Here, the training and test computations are decorated with `@smp.step`. Note that the training step contains both forward and backward passes, so SDMP can compute gradients on all partitions. We only have the forward pass in the test step:

```
@smp.step
def train_step(model, data, target, criterion):
    output = model(data)
    loss = criterion(output, target)
```

```
      model.backward(loss)  #  instead of PyTorch loss.
  backward()
      return output, loss
  @smp.step
  def test_step(model, data, target, criterion):
      output = model(data)
      loss = criterion(output, target)
      return output, loss
```

Note another difference: when calculating loss, we used the `model.backward(loss)` SDMP method. So, SDMP can correctly compute gradient values across model partitions.

9. We use decorated training and test steps in the outer training loop as follows. The training loop construct is like a typical PyTorch training loop with one difference. Since SDMP implements pipelining over micro-batches, the loss values will be calculated for micro-batches, too (that is, the `loss_mb` variable). Hence, to calculate the average loss across the full batch, we call the `reduce_mean()` method. Note that all variables returned by the `@smp.step` decorated function are instances of the class that provides a convenient API to act across mini-batches (such as the `.reduce_mean()` or `.concat()` methods):

```
for epoch in range(num_epochs):
        for phase in ["train", "val"]:
            if phase == "train":
                model.train()  # Set model to training
mode
            else:
                model.eval()  # Set model to evaluate
mode
            for inputs, labels in dataloaders[phase]:
                inputs = inputs.to(device)
                labels = labels.to(device)
                optimizer.zero_grad()
                with torch.set_grad_enabled(phase ==
"train"):
                    if phase == "train":
                        outputs, loss_mb = train_
step(model, inputs, labels, criterion)
                        loss = loss_mb.reduce_mean()
                        optimizer.step()
                    else:
```

```
                              outputs, loss_mb = test_
    step(model, inputs, labels, criterion)
                              loss = loss_mb.reduce_mean()
```

10. Once training is done, we need to save our distributed model. For this, SMDP provides the smp.
    save() method, which supports saving both the model and optimizer states in pickle format.
    You can choose whether you want to persist model partitions or not by using the partial
    flag. If partial saving is enabled, then the model partitions are saved separately along with their
    model parallel ranks. In the following code block, we save a single model checkpoint. Note
    that we are saving the model in a single process based on the rank filter to avoid any conflicts:

```
    if smp.dp_rank() == 0:
        model_file_path = os.path.join(
            os.environ["SM_MODEL_DIR"], f"finetuned-
    {args.model_name}-checkpoint.pt"
        )
        model_dict = model.state_dict()   # save the full
    model
        opt_dict = optimizer.state_dict()   # save the
    full optimizer state
        smp.save(
            {"model_state_dict": model_dict, "optimizer_
    state_dict": opt_dict},
            model_file_path,
            partial=False,
        )
```

11. Once our testing is complete, SageMaker will upload the model and optimizer checkpoints to
    the S3 location. You can use this model for inference as follows:

```
    model_state = torch.load('finetuned-resnet-checkpoint.
    pt')['model_state_dict']
    model_ft = models.resnet18(pretrained=False)
    num_ftrs = model_ft.fc.in_features
    model_ft.fc = nn.Linear(num_ftrs, num_classes)
    model_ft.load_state_dict(model_state)
    outputs = model_ft(inputs)
```

These are the minimal changes that are required in your training script to make it compatible with the SDMP library to implement model or hybrid parallelism. We encourage you to experiment with various SDMP configuration parameters (please refer to the `distribution` object from the previous section) to develop good intuition, specifically the following:

- Change the number of model *partitions*. Our implementation has 2 partitions; you might try to set 1 or 4 partitions and see how this changes the data parallel and model parallel groups.

- Change the number of *micro-batches* and *batch size* to see how it impacts training speed. In production scenarios, you will likely need to explore an upper memory limit for batch size and micro-batches to improve training efficiency.

- See how the type of *pipeline implementation* – interleaved or simple – impacts the training speed.

Additional considerations

We used relatively simple and small models such as Resnet to demonstrate how to implement hybrid parallelism. However, the implementation of more complex models such as GPT-n will require additional considerations. The following sections detail them.

Tensor parallelism

Tensor parallelism is only available in the PyTorch version of the SDMP library. Tensor parallelism makes sense to use for scenarios when a parameter layer consumes a considerable amount of GPU memory (such as embedding tables). When using tensor parallelism, you need to make sure that SDMP supports the modules of your model. SDMP provides distributed implementations of common modules such as `nn.Linear`, `nn.Embedding`, and more. If a specific module is not supported, first, you will need to implement a tensor-parallelizable version of it. Please refer to the SDMP API documentation for details: `https://sagemaker.readthedocs.io/en/stable/api/training/smp_versions/latest/smd_model_parallel_pytorch_tensor_parallel.html`.

Reference implementations

AWS provides a few example scripts to train popular large models such as GPT2, GPT-J, and BERT using the SDMP library. See the official GitHub repository at `https://github.com/aws/amazon-sagemaker-examples/tree/main/training/distributed_training/pytorch/model_parallel`.

You can also find the reference configuration of SDMP at `https://docs.aws.amazon.com/sagemaker/latest/dg/model-parallel-best-practices.html`.

So far, we have covered different ways to distribute your training job and looked at sample implementations. In the next section, we will cover some parameters to improve the efficiency of your distributed training job.

Optimizing distributed training jobs

In many cases, optimizing your large-scale distributed training jobs requires a lot of trial and error and is very specific to the runtime environment, hardware stack, model architecture, and other parameters. But there are several key knobs that might help to optimize your training speed and overall efficiency.

Cluster layout and computation affinity

When running distributed training jobs, especially model parallel or hybrid parallel, it's always a good idea to understand how different types of computation are aligned with your cluster layout.

Let's consider a situation when we need to run model parallel training in the cluster of two nodes with two GPU devices each. The total training processes count is 4 with global ranks ranging from 0 to 3 and local ranks being 0 and 1. We assume that the model copy and gradients can fit into two devices. In this case, we need to ensure that each model will be stored within each node: one model copy will be placed on ranks 0 and 1 (local ranks 0 and 1), and another on ranks 2 and 3 (local ranks 0 and 1). This will ensure that communication between layers of the model will happen over faster inter-GPU connections and won't, typically, traverse slower intra-node networks.

To address this situation, SDMP provides a special parameter called `placement_strategy`, which allows you to control the training process's affinity to your hardware.

Communication backend

In this chapter, we covered some of the most popular communication backends, such as NCCL, Gloo, and MPI. The following list is a rule of thumb when choosing which backend to use given your specific case:

- **Message passing interface** (**MPI**) is a communication standard in distributed computations that comes with a number of backend implementations, such as Open-MPI, MVAPICH2, and more. MPI backends also support inter-GPU operations on CUDA tensors. However, MPI is rarely an optimal choice for your training job if you have other options.

- **Gloo** backends come with wide support for point-to-point and collective computations between CPU devices as well as collective computations between GPU devices. Gloo can be a good choice for initial debugging on CPU devices. However, you should usually prefer NCCL when using GPU devices for training.

- **NCCL** backends are provided by NVIDIA and are optimal for training jobs on NVIDIA GPUs.

- **Custom** backends can be provided as part of the DL framework. For instance, TensorFlow 2 provides a custom **RING** backend.

> **Note**
>
> When working with a newer SOTA model, make sure that the communication backend of your choice supports the collective and point-to-point operations required by your model architecture.

Training hyperparameters

There are many training hyperparameters that can impact your training efficiencies. While we don't intend to cover all of them, we have listed some hyperparameters that you can tweak in your optimization efforts:

- Use **AMP** to reduce memory requirements and speed up training with minimal impact on accuracy and training convergence. AMP is a popular technique that is used to combine single (FP32) and half-precision (FP16) tensors during the forward, backward, and update steps. Note that you will likely need to have a large batch size in order to have meaningful improvements with AMP.

- Use **hardware-optimized data types** (such as TF32, BF32, and BF16) to speed up training. These data types are optimized for specific DL computations and provide speed up compared to the common FP32 and FP16 types. Note that to use these types, you need to ensure that your framework, model architecture, and hardware support it.

- Optimize your **global batch size** to speed up training. As you scale out your training cluster, make sure that you are updating your global batch size accordingly. Typically, the upper limit of local batch size is defined by available GPU memory (you will likely see a *CUDA OOM* error if the local batch size cannot fit into memory). Keep in mind that increasing the batch size beyond a certain threshold might not increase the global training throughput either. You can find some additional materials and benchmarks in the *NVIDIA* guide at `https://docs.nvidia.com/deeplearning/performance/dl-performance-fully-connected/index.html#batch-size`. Another thing to keep in mind is that you might need to proportionally increase the learning rate with an increase in the batch size.

- Use **fused optimizers** (such as the FusedAdam optimizer) to speed up weight updates using the operation fusion – combining multiple operations into one. Make sure that you confirm that your DL framework and hardware support fused optimizers.

These are several common parameters that might improve the efficiency of your training jobs. Note that, in many real-life use cases, you might have model- or task-specific tuning parameters.

Summary

In this chapter, we focused on how to engineer large-scale data parallel, model parallel, and hybrid distributed training jobs. We discussed which type of parallelism to choose based on your specific use case and model architecture. Then, we reviewed several popular approaches of how to organize distributed training – such as the Parameter Server and Allreduce algorithms – along with various performance considerations to tune distributed training jobs. You will now be able to select the correct type of distributed training, technical stack, and approach to debug and tune training job performance. Then, we reviewed several examples of distributed training jobs in Amazon SageMaker using the popular open source and proprietary libraries SDDP and SMDP.

Running large-scale training jobs requires not only initial engineering efforts but also the well-established operational management of your training jobs. In many cases, the training job can run for days and weeks, or you will need to periodically retrain your models on new data. As each long-running DL training job requires considerable compute resources and associated time and cost resources, we want to make sure that our training is efficient. For instance, we need to control in real time whether our model is converging during training. Otherwise, we might want to stop earlier and avoid wasting compute resources and time. In the next chapter, we will focus on setting up an operational stack for your DL training jobs.

7
Operationalizing Deep Learning Training

In *Chapter 1*, *Introducing Deep Learning with Amazon SageMaker*, we discussed how SageMaker integrates with CloudWatch Logs and Metrics to provide visibility into your training process by collecting training logs and metrics. However, **deep learning (DL)** training jobs are prone to multiple types of specific issues related to model architecture and training configuration. Specialized tools are required to monitor, detect, and react to these issues. Since many training jobs run for hours and days on large amounts of compute instances, the cost of errors is high.

When running DL training jobs, you need to be aware of two types of issues:

- Issues with model and training configuration, which prevent the model from efficient learning during training. Examples of such issues include vanishing and exploding gradients, overfitting and underfitting, not decreasing loss, and others. The process of finding such errors is known as **debugging**.
- Suboptimal model and training configuration, which doesn't allow you to fully utilize available hardware resources. For instance, let's say that the batch size is smaller than the optimal value and the GPU resources are underutilized. This leads to a slower than possible training speed. We call the process of finding such issues **profiling**.

In this chapter, we will review the available open source and SageMaker capabilities for training, debugging, and profiling. We will start with the popular open source tool for training monitoring and debugging called **TensorBoard** and review how it can be integrated with SageMaker's training infrastructure. Then, we will compare it to the proprietary **SageMaker Debugger**, which provides advanced capabilities to help you automatically detect various types of issues and manage your training job accordingly. You will develop practical experience in using both tools.

Another type of problem you typically need to solve when operationalizing your DL models is establishing an efficient way to find optimal combinations of model hyperparameters. This process is known as **hyperparameter tuning**. It is especially relevant in the initial stages of model development and adoption when you need to establish a production-ready model baseline. SageMaker provides an automated way to tune your model using a feature called **Automatic Model Tuning**.

Finally, we will discuss how to reduce the cost of your training job and model tuning jobs by using **EC2 Spot Instances**.

In this chapter, we will cover the following topics:

- Debugging training jobs
- Profiling your DL training
- Hyperparameter optimization
- Using EC2 Spot Instances

After reading this chapter, you will be able to establish profiling and debugging procedures for your large-scale DL training to minimize unnecessary costs and time to train. You will also know how to organize hyperparameter tuning and optimize it for cost using Spot Instances.

Technical requirements

In this chapter, we will provide code samples so that you can develop practical skills. The full code examples are available here: `https://github.com/PacktPublishing/Accelerate-Deep-Learning-Workloads-with-Amazon-SageMaker/blob/main/chapter7/`.

To follow along with this code, you will need the following:

- An AWS account and IAM user with permission to manage Amazon SageMaker resources.
- Have a SageMaker notebook, SageMaker Studio notebook, or local SageMaker compatible environment established.
- Access to GPU training instances in your AWS account. Each example in this chapter will provide recommended instance types to use. You may need to increase your compute quota for **SageMaker Training Job** to have GPU instances enabled. In this case, please follow the instructions at `https://docs.aws.amazon.com/sagemaker/latest/dg/regions-quotas.html`.
- You must install the required Python libraries by running `pip install -r requirements.txt`. The file that contains the required libraries is located at the root of `chapter7`.

Debugging training jobs

To effectively monitor and debug DL training jobs, we need to have access to the following information:

- Scalar values such as accuracy and loss, which we use to measure the quality of the training process

- Tensor values such as weights, biases, and gradients, which represent the internal state of the model and its optimizers

Both TensorBoard and SageMaker Debugger allow you to collect tensors and scalars, so both can be used to debug the model and training processes. However, unlike TensorBoard, which is primarily used for training visualizations, SageMaker Debugger provides functionality to react to changes in model states in near-real time. For example, it allows us to stop training jobs earlier if training loss hasn't decreased for a certain period.

In this section, we will dive deep into how to use TensorBoard and SageMaker Debugger. We will review the features of both solutions in detail and then develop practical experiences of using both solutions to debug your training script.

Please note that we will use the same examples for both debugging and profiling tasks.

Using TensorBoard with SageMaker

TensorBoard is an open source tool developed originally for the TensorFlow framework, but it is now available for other DL frameworks, including PyTorch. TensorBoard supports the following features for visualizing and inspecting the training process:

- Tracking scalar values (loss, accuracy, and others) over time.
- Capturing tensors such as weights, biases, and gradients and how they change over time. This can be useful for visualizing weights and biases and verifying that they are changing expectedly.
- Experiment tracking via a dashboard of hyperparameters.
- Projecting high-dimensional embeddings to a lower-dimensionality space.
- Capturing images, audio, and text data.

Additionally, TensorBoard comes with native profiling capabilities for TensorFlow programs. Profiling is also available for PyTorch via an add-on.

Debugging PyTorch training

Let's review how TensorBoard can help you to get insights into your training process and debug it using a practical example. We will use a pre-trained ResNet model from the PyTorch model zoo and train it to recognize two classes: bees and ants.

We provide code highlights in this section. The full training code is available here: https://github. com/PacktPublishing/Accelerate-Deep-Learning-Workloads-with-Amazon- SageMaker/blob/main/chapter7/1_TensorBoard_PyTorch.ipynb.

Modifying the training script

To use TensorBoard, we need to make minimal changes to our training script. Follow these steps:

1. First, we must import and initialize TensorBoard's `SummaryWriter` object. Here, we are using the S3 location to write TensorBoard summaries:

    ```
    from torch.utils.tensorboard import SummaryWriter
    tb_writer = SummaryWriter(args.tb_s3_url)
    ```

2. Next, we must capture some training artifacts that won't change during training – in our case, the model graph. Note that we need to execute the model's forward path on the sample data to do so:

    ```
    sample_inputs, _ = next(iter(dataloaders_dict["val"]))
    tb_writer.add_graph(model, sample_inputs, verbose=False,
    use_strict_trace=False)
    ```

3. In our training loop, we capture the scalars and tensors that we wish to inspect. We use the epoch number as the time dimension. Let's say that in our case, we wish to capture the following data:

    *   How accuracy and loss change every epoch for training and validation datasets

    *   Distribution of gradients and weights on the first convolutional and last fully connected layers during the training phase

    *   The training hyperparameters and how they impact performance

    To capture these parameters, we must add the following code to our training loop:

    ```
    tb_writer.add_histogram("conv1.weight", model.conv1.
    weight, epoch)
    tb_writer.add_histogram("conv1.weight_grad", model.conv1.
    weight.grad, epoch)
    tb_writer.add_histogram("fc.weight", model.fc.weight,
    epoch)
    tb_writer.add_histogram("fc.weight_grad", model.
    fc.weight.grad, epoch)
    tb_writer.add_scalar(f"Loss/{phase}", epoch_loss, epoch)
    tb_writer.add_scalar(f"Accuracy/{phase}", epoch_accuracy,
    epoch)
    tb_writer.add_hparams(hparam_dict=vars(args), metric_
    dict={
                            f"hparam/loss_{phase}": epoch_loss,
                            f"hparam/accuracy_{phase}": epoch_
    accuracy})
    ```

Now, let's review our training job configuration with debugging enabled.

Monitoring the training process

To start the SageMaker training job, we need to provide the S3 location where TensorBoard summaries will be written. We can do this by setting the `tb-s3-url` hyperparameter, as shown here:

```
instance_type = 'ml.p2.xlarge'
instance_count = 1
job_name = "pytorch-tb-profiling-12"
tb_debug_path = f"s3://{bucket}/tensorboard/{job_name}"
estimator = PyTorch(
            entry_point="train_resnet_tb.py",
            source_dir='1_sources',
            role=role,
            instance_type=instance_type,
            sagemaker_session=sagemaker_session,
            image_uri="763104351884.dkr.ecr.us-east-1.amazonaws.
com/pytorch-training:1.10.2-gpu-py38-cu113-ubuntu20.04-
sagemaker",
            instance_count=instance_count,
            hyperparameters={
                "batch-size":64,
                "num-epochs":10,
                "input-size" : 224,
                "feature-extract":False,
                "tb-s3-url": tb_debug_path,
                "num-data-workers": 4
            },
            disable_profiler=True,
            debugger_hook_config=False,
            base_job_name=job_name,
    )
```

Once the training job has started, you can start your TensorBoard locally by running the following command in the terminal:

```
tensorboard --logdir ${tb_debug_path}
```

Note the following when using TensorBoard in cloud development environments:

- If you are using a SageMaker notebook instance, then TensorBoard will be available here: `https://YOUR_NOTEBOOK_DOMAIN/proxy/6006/`

- If you are using SageMaker Studio, then TensorBoard will available here: `https://<YOUR_STUDIO_DOMAIN>/jupyter/default/proxy/6006/`

The TensorBoard data will be updated in near-real time as the training job progresses. Let's review our training process in TensorBoard:

- On the **Scalar** and **Time Series** tabs, you can find changes in scalar values over time. We use the epoch index as an indicator of time. *Figure 7.1* shows the training and validation accuracies at every epoch:

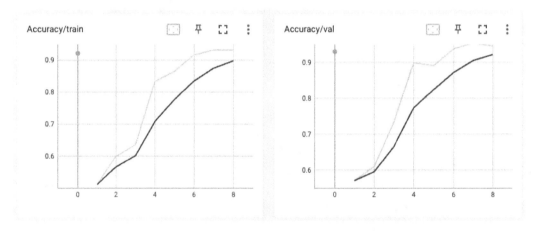

Figure 7.1 – Accuracies over time in TensorBoard

- On the **Graph** tab, you can see visual representations of the model and how data flows from inputs to outputs.

- The **Histogram** and **Distributions** tabs visualize tensor distributions over time (for instance, the distribution of weights or gradients changes over epochs). For example, in *Figure 7.2*, we can see how gradient distribution on the last fully connected layer is becoming increasingly concentrated around 0, which indicates that our model is learning and, hence, the absolute gradient values are decreasing:

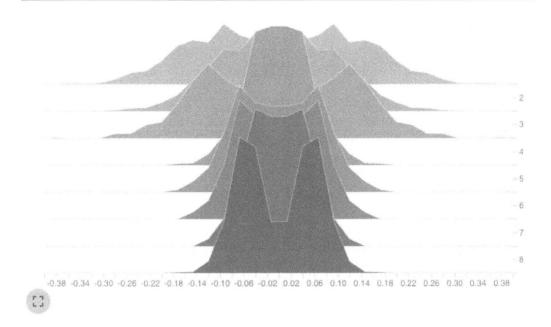

Figure 7.2 – Histogram of model weights in TensorBoard

- The **HParam** tab allows us to capture and compare hyperparameters side by side. This can be useful for tracking experiments during hyperparameter searches to identify optimal model and training job configuration.

Now that we understand how to use TensorBoard to visualize the training process, let's see how we can use TensorBoard to profile our training job.

Profiling PyTorch training

TensorBoard provides out-of-the-box profiling capabilities for TensorFlow programs (including Keras). To profile PyTorch programs in TensorBoard, you can use the open source **torch_tb_profiler** plugin.

When profiling the training process, we are usually interested in the following:

- How efficiently we utilize our resources (GPU and CPU) over time
- What operations (DL operators, data loading, memory transfer, and so on) utilize what resources
- In the case of distributed training, how efficient the communication is between nodes and individual training devices
- How to improve the overall resource utilization and increase training efficiency

Both the TensorFlow and PyTorch plugins for TensorBoard provide such capabilities for profiling. Let's review how profiling works for the same task we did for debugging.

Modifying the training script

To profile applications using `torch_tb_profiler`, we need to make minimal modifications to our training code. Specifically, we need to wrap our training loop with the plugin context manager, as shown in the following code block:

```
with torch.profiler.profile(
    schedule=torch.profiler.schedule(wait=1, warmup=1,
active=3, repeat=5),
    on_trace_ready=torch.profiler.tensorboard_trace_handler(
        os.path.join(os.environ["SM_OUTPUT_DATA_DIR"], "tb_
profiler")
    ),
    record_shapes=True,
    profile_memory=True,
    with_stack=True,
) as prof:
    for _, (inputs, labels) in enumerate(dataloaders[phase]):
        # The rest of training loop without changes
```

The parameters of the context manager that are passed at initialization time define what profiling data must be gathered and at what intervals. At the time of writing this book, the `torch_db_profiler` plugin doesn't support writing to the S3 location. Hence, we must write the profiling data to the local output directory stored in the `"SM_OUTPUT_DATA_DIR"` environment variable. After training is done, SageMaker automatically archives and stores the content of this directory to the S3 location.

Using TensorBoard Profiler

To review the output of TensorBoard Profiler, we need to download the data to the local environment:

1. We will start by getting a path to the profiler data. For this, we can use the training job estimator instance:

```
tb_profiler_path = f"{estimator.latest_training_job.
describe()['OutputDataConfig']['S3OutputPath']}
{estimator.latest_training_job.describe()
['TrainingJobName']}/output/output.tar.gz"
```

2. Then, in your notebook or terminal window, you can run the following commands to unarchive the profiler data and start TensorBoard:

```
aws s3 cp ${ tb_profiler_path} .
mkdir profiler_output
```

```
tar -xf output.tar.gz -C profiler_output
tensorboard --logdir ./profiler_output
```

Upon starting TensorBoard, you should be automatically redirected to the profiler summary. From there, you have access to several views that contain profiling information:

- The **Overview** tab provides a general summary of the device(s) used for training, their utilization over time, and the breakdown of operations. In our case, for example, the majority of the time is spent performing kernels that comprise forward and backward model passes. This is generally a good indicator that we utilize our GPU resources on the training model:

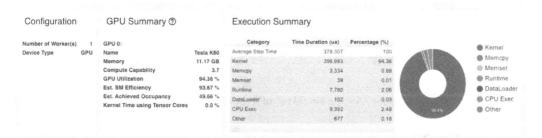

Figure 7.3 – The Overview tab of TensorBoard Profiler

- The **Operators** tab gives you an idea of how much time specific operators consume (such as convolution or batch normalization). In the following screenshot, we can see, for instance, that the backward pass on convolution layers takes most of the GPU time:

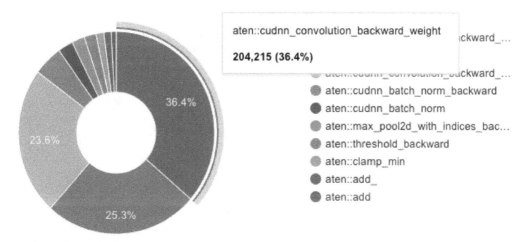

Figure 7.4 – The Operators tab of TensorBoard Profiler

- The **Kernel** tab breaks down the time spent performing on specific GPU kernels. For instance, in the following diagram, you can see that various **Single-Precision General Matrix Multiply (SGEMM)** kernels take most of the time:

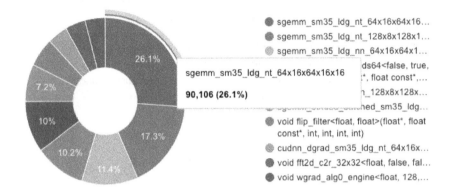

Figure 7.5 – The Kernel tab of TensorBoard Profiler

- The **Trace** tab shows the timeline of the profiled operators and GPU kernels, as well as the handoff between CPU and GPU devices (for instance, transferring data inputs from CPU to GPU):

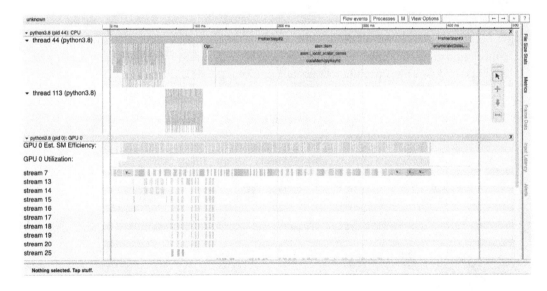

Figure 7.6 – The Trace tab of TensorBoard Profiler

- The **Memory** tab provides memory utilization over time for a given device. In the following chart, for instance, you can see allocated memory (that is, memory used to store tensors) and total reserved memory:

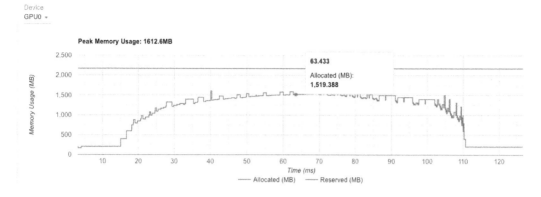

Figure 7.7 – The Memory tab of TensorBoard Profiler

As you can see, TensorBoard is a great tool for monitoring, debugging, and profiling your training script. TensorBoard, when used with plugins, supports both TensorFlow and PyTorch frameworks. However, one of the drawbacks of TensorBoard is that it doesn't provide any ways to react to suboptimal conditions, such as underutilization of GPU devices or slow or no convergences of your model during training. To stop training jobs earlier when such conditions happen, you will need to further instrumentalize your code via callbacks and custom logic.

SageMaker Debugger addresses these limitations by providing a generic mechanism to detect common training problems and take mitigation actions.

Monitoring training with SageMaker Debugger

SageMaker Debugger is a comprehensive SageMaker capability that allows you to automatically monitor, debug, and profile DL training jobs running on SageMaker. SageMaker Debugger provides you with insights into your DL training by capturing the internal state of your training loop and instances metrics in near-real time. Debugger also allows you to automatically detect common issues happening during training and take appropriate actions when issues are detected. This allows you to automatically find issues in complex DL training jobs earlier and react accordingly. Additionally, SageMaker Debugger supports writing custom rules for scenarios not covered by built-in rules.

SageMaker has several key components:

- The open source smedebug library (https://github.com/awslabs/sagemaker-debugger), which integrates with DL frameworks and Linux instances to persist debugging and profiling data to Amazon S3, as well as to retrieve and analyze it once the training job has been started

- The SageMaker Python SDK, which allows you to configure the smedebug library with no or minimal code changes in your training script

- Automatically provisioned processing jobs to validate output tensors and profiling data against rules

SageMaker Debugger supports TensorFlow, PyTorch, and MXNet DL frameworks. The `smedebug` library is installed by default in SageMaker DL containers, so you can start using SageMaker Debugger without having to make any modifications to your training script. You can also install the `smdebug` library in a custom Docker container and use all the features of SageMaker Debugger.

> **Note**
> Please note that there are minor differences in the `smedebug` APIs for different DL frameworks.

The `smedebug` library provides a rich API for configuring, saving, and analyzing captured tensors. It uses a `hook` object to capture tensors and scalars by injecting them into the training process. `hook` allows you to group tensors and scalars into logical tensor **collections** for analysis. You can define parameters on how often to save a given collection and which tensors to include in the collection when configuring your SageMaker training job. SageMaker Debugger saves default collections without any additional configuration. Note that default collections and their configurations depend on the DL framework. Debugger *rules* define which errors we want to monitor and *actions* we want to perform once the rule has been triggered. When the rule has been defined, SageMaker Debugger automatically creates a separate processing job to run rule validation on stored tensors and trigger actions once the rule is violated. SageMaker Debugger provides multiple built-in rules that address most of the common issues, such as vanishing gradients. You can also define your own custom rule. Note that using Debugger built-in rules is free of charge, while if you choose to use a custom Debugger rule, you will pay the cost of processing jobs and tensor storage. The `Trial` object allows you to query the stored tensors of a given training job for further analysis. You can run tensor queries in real time without waiting for the training job to be fully complete. SageMaker Debugger also supports emitting TensorBoard-compatible summary logs for easy visualization of output tensors and scalars.

Using SageMaker Debugger

Let's apply these concepts to a practical task. We will instrumentalize the ResNet model and fine-tune it for a binary classification task. The full code is available here: `https://github.com/PacktPublishing/Accelerate-Deep-Learning-Workloads-with-Amazon-SageMaker/blob/main/chapter7/2_SMDebugger_PyTorch.ipynb`.

Code instrumentalization

The `smedebug` library requires minimal changes to capture tensors and scalars. First, you need to initiate the `hook` object outside of your training loop, as well as after model and optimizer initialization:

```
...
model = initialize_resnet_model(
```

```
    NUM_CLASSES, feature_extract=False, use_pretrained=True
)
model.to(torch.device("cuda"))
optimizer = optim.SGD(params_to_update, lr=0.001, momentum=0.9)
criterion = nn.CrossEntropyLoss()
exp_lr_scheduler = lr_scheduler.StepLR(optimizer, step_size=7,
gamma=0.1)
hook = smd.Hook.create_from_json_file()
hook.register_hook(model)
hook.register_loss(criterion)
...
```

Note that we are using .create_from_json_file() to create our hook object. This method instantiates hook based on the hook configuration you provide in the SageMaker training object. Since we are adding both the model and criterion objects to hook, we should expect to see both model parameters (weights, biases, and others), as well as loss scalar.

Inside our training loop, the only modification we need to make is to differentiate between the training and validation phases by switching between smedebug.modes.Train and smedebug. modes.Eval. This will allow smedebug to segregate the tensors that are captured in the training and evaluation phases:

```
for epoch in range(1, args.num_epochs + 1):
    for phase in ["train", "val"]:
        if phase == "train":
            model.train()  # Set model to training mode
            if hook:
                hook.set_mode(modes.TRAIN)
        else:
            model.eval()  # Set model to evaluate mode
            if hook:
                hook.set_mode(modes.EVAL)

        running_corrects = 0
        running_loss = 0.0
        step_counter = 0
        epoch_start = time.time()

        for _, (inputs, labels) in enumerate(
        dataloaders[phase]):
        # inside training loop
...
```

Now, let's review how to configure `hook`, rules, actions, and tensor collections when running a SageMaker training job.

Training job configuration

As part of the SageMaker Python SDK, AWS provides the `sagemaker.debugger` library for Debugger configuration. Let's take a look:

1. We will start by importing some Debugger entities:

    ```
    from sagemaker.debugger import (
        Rule,
        DebuggerHookConfig,
        TensorBoardOutputConfig,
        CollectionConfig,
        rule_configs,
        ProfilerRule
    )
    ```

2. Then, we must define automatic actions and a set of rules. Here, we are using Debugger's built-in rules to detect some common DL training issues. Note that we can assign different actions to different rules. In our case, we want to stop our training job immediately when the rule is triggered:

    ```
    actions = rule_configs.ActionList(
        rule_configs.StopTraining())
    rules = [
        Rule.sagemaker(rule_configs.vanishing_gradient(),
    actions=actions),
        Rule.sagemaker(rule_configs.overfit(),
    actions=actions),
        Rule.sagemaker(rule_configs.overtraining(),
    actions=actions),
        Rule.sagemaker(rule_configs.poor_weight_
    initialization(), actions=actions),
    ]
    ```

3. Next, we must configure the collection of tensors and how they will be persisted. Here, we will define that we want to persist the weights and losses collection. For weights, we will also save a histogram that can be further visualized in TensorBoard. We will also set a saving interval for the training and evaluation phases:

    ```
    collection_configs=[
            CollectionConfig(
                name="weights",
    ```

```
                parameters={
                    "save_histogram": "True"
                    }
                ),
            CollectionConfig(name="losses"),
        ]
    hook_config = DebuggerHookConfig(
        hook_parameters={"train.save_interval": "1", "eval.
    save_interval": "1"},
        collection_configs=collection_configs
    )
```

4. Now, we are ready to pass these objects to the SageMaker Estimator object:

```
    tb_debug_path = f"s3://{bucket}/tensorboard/{job_name}"
    tensorboard_output_config = TensorBoardOutputConfig(
        s3_output_path=tb_debug_path
    )
    debug_estimator = PyTorch(
                entry_point="train_resnet_sm.py",
                source_dir='2_sources',
                role=role,
                instance_type=instance_type,
                sagemaker_session=sagemaker_session,
                image_uri=image_uri,
                instance_count=instance_count,
                disable_profiler=True,
                rules=rules,
                debugger_hook_config=hook_config,
                tensorboard_output_config=tensorboard_output_
    config,
                base_job_name=job_name,
            )
```

Now, we are ready to start training the job using the fit() method. In the next section, we will learn how to retrieve and analyze SageMaker Debugger outputs.

Reviewing the Debugger results

SageMaker Debugger provides functionality to retrieve and analyze collected tensors from training jobs as part of the smedebug library. In the following steps, we will highlight some key APIs:

1. In the following code block, we are creating a new trial object using the S3 path where the tensors were persisted:

    ```
    import smdebug.pytorch as smd
    tensors_path = debug_estimator.latest_job_debugger_
    artifacts_path()
    trial = smd.create_trial(tensors_path)
    ```

2. Now, let's output all the available tensors by running the following command:

    ```
    print(f"Persisted tensors: {trial.tensor_names()}")
    ```

3. You should be able to see multiple collections with many tensors, including biases, weights, losses, and gradients. Let's access specific numeric values. Running the following command will return a list of associated scalar values:

    ```
    print(f"Loss values {trial.tensor('CrossEntropyLoss_
    output_0').values()}")
    ```

4. Using a simple plotting function (refer to the sources for its implementation), we can visualize loss for the training and evaluation phases. Running the following command will result in a 2D loss chart. Similarly, you can access and process tensors:

    ```
    plot_tensor(trial, "CrossEntropyLoss_output_0")
    ```

The following figure visualizes the training and validation losses:

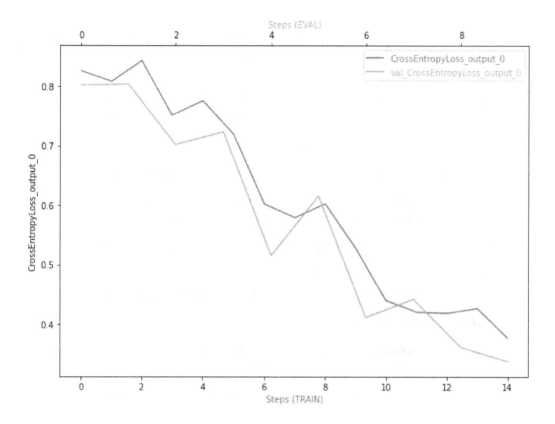

Figure 7.8 – Training and validation losses

5. Now, let's review if any rules were triggered during our training:

```
for s in debug_estimator.latest_training_job.rule_job_
summary():
    print(f"Rule: {s['RuleConfigurationName']}",
          f"status: {s['RuleEvaluationStatus']}")
```

This outputs all configured rules; their statuses are as follows:

```
Rule: VanishingGradient, status: NoIssuesFound
Rule: Overfit, status: NoIssuesFound
Rule: Overtraining, status: NoIssuesFound
Rule: PoorWeightInitialization, status: NoIssuesFound
```

As we can see, in our case, no rules were triggered, and our job was completed. You can experiment with rule settings. For instance, you can reset weights on one of the model layers. This will result in triggering the `PoorWeightInitiailization` rule and the training process being stopped.

6. Lastly, let's visually inspect the saved tensors using TensorBoard. For this, we simply need to start TensorBoard using the S3 path we supplied to the `Estimator` object earlier:

```
! tensorboard --logdir  {tb_debug_path}
```

Feel free to explore TensorBoard on your own. You should expect to find histograms of weights.

In this section, we reviewed SageMaker Debugger's key capabilities and learned how to use them. You may have already observed some benefits of SageMaker Debugger over TensorBoard:

- Zero or minimal effort in instrumentalizing your code for SageMaker Debugger

- A rich API to process and analyze output tensors

- A large number of built-in rules and actions with the ability to create custom rules and actions

- TensorBoard functionality is supported out of the box

With these capabilities, SageMaker Debugger allows you to improve the quality of your training jobs, accelerate experimentation, and reduce unnecessary costs.

Additionally, SageMaker Debugger provides profiling capabilities. We'll review them next.

Profiling your DL training

SageMaker Debugger allows you to collect various types of advanced metrics from your training instances. Once these metrics have been collected, SageMaker generates detailed metrics visualizations, detects resource bottlenecks, and provides recommendations on how instance utilization can be improved.

SageMaker Debugger collects two types of metrics:

- **System metrics**: These are the resource utilization metrics of training instances such as CPU, GPU, network, and I/O.

- **Framework metrics**: These are collected at the DL framework level. This includes metrics collected by native framework profiles (such as PyTorch profiler or TensorFlow Profiler), data loader metrics, and Python profiling metrics.

As in the case of debugging, you can define rules that will be automatically evaluated against collected metrics. If a rule is triggered, you can define one or several actions that will be taken. For example, you can send an email if the training job has GPU utilization below a certain threshold.

It's time to profile our training code with SageMaker Debugger. You can find the full code in the *Profiling DL Training* section at https://github.com/PacktPublishing/Accelerate-Deep-Learning-Workloads-with-Amazon-SageMaker/blob/main/chapter7/2_SMDebugger_PyTorch.ipynb.

Configuring the training job for profiling

We will start by defining what system and framework metrics we want to collect. For instance, we can provide a custom configuration for the framework, data loader, and Python. Note that system profiling is enabled by default:

```
from sagemaker.debugger import (ProfilerConfig,
                                FrameworkProfile,
                                DetailedProfilingConfig,
                                DataloaderProfilingConfig,
                                PythonProfilingConfig,
                                PythonProfiler, cProfileTimer)
profiler_config=ProfilerConfig(
    system_monitor_interval_millis=500,
    framework_profile_params=FrameworkProfile(
        detailed_profiling_config=DetailedProfilingConfig(
            start_step=2,
            num_steps=1),
        dataloader_profiling_config=DataloaderProfilingConfig(
            start_step=2,
            num_steps=1),
        python_profiling_config=PythonProfilingConfig(
            start_step=2,
            num_steps=1,
            python_profiler=PythonProfiler.CPROFILE,
            cprofile_timer=cProfileTimer.TOTAL_TIME)))
```

Then, we must provide the profiling config to the SageMaker training job configuration:

```
profiler_estimator = PyTorch(
        entry_point="train_resnet_sm.py",
        source_dir='2_sources',
        role=role,
        instance_type='ml.p2.xlarge',
```

```
                sagemaker_session=sagemaker_session,
                image_uri=image_uri,
                instance_count=instance_count,
                hyperparameters={
                    "num-data-workers":8,
                },
                disable_profiler=False,
                profiler_config=profiler_config,
                rules=rules,
            #   debugger_hook_config=hook_config,
            #   tensorboard_output_config=tensorboard_output_config,
                base_job_name=job_name,
        )
```

Note that we set num-data-workers to 8, while ml.p2.xlarge has only 4 CPU cores. Usually, it's recommended to have the number of data workers equal to the number of CPUs. Let's see if SageMaker Debugger will be able to detect this suboptimal configuration.

Reviewing profiling outcomes

You can start monitoring profiling outcomes in near-real time. We will use the semdebug.profiler API to process profiling outputs:

```
training_job_name = profiler_estimator.latest_training_job.
job_name
region = "us-east-1"
tj = TrainingJob(training_job_name, region)
tj.wait_for_sys_profiling_data_to_be_available()
```

Once the data is available, we can retrieve and visualize it. Running the following code will chart the CPU, GPU, and GPU memory utilization from system metrics:

```
from smdebug.profiler.analysis.notebook_utils.timeline_charts
import TimelineCharts
system_metrics_reader = tj.get_systems_metrics_reader()
system_metrics_reader.refresh_event_file_list()
view_timeline_charts = TimelineCharts(
    system_metrics_reader,
    framework_metrics_reader=None,
```

```
      select_dimensions=["CPU", "GPU"],
      select_events=["total"],
)
```

Similarly, you can visualize other collected metrics. SageMaker Debugger also generates a detailed profiling report that aggregates all visualizations, insights, and recommendations in one place. Once your training job has finished, you can download the profile report and all collected data by running the following command in your terminal:

```
aws s3 cp s3://<JOB_BUCKET>/<JOB_NAME>/rule-output ./
--recursive
```

Once all the assets have been downloaded, open the profiler-report.html file in your browser and review the generated information. Alternatively, you can open profiler-report.ipynb, which provides the same insights in the form of an executable Jupyter notebook.

The report covers the following aspects:

- System usage statistics

- Framework metrics summary

- Summary of rules and their status

- Training loop analysis and recommendations for optimizations

Note that, in the *Dataloading analysis* section, you should see a recommendation to decrease the number of data workers according to our expectations.

As you can see, SageMaker Debugger provides extensive profiling capabilities, including a recommendation to improve and automate rule validation with minimal development efforts. Similar to other Debugger capabilities, profiling is free of charge, so long as you are using built-in rules.

Hyperparameter optimization

A SageMaker Automatic Model Tuning job allows you to run multiple training jobs with a unique combination of hyperparameters in parallel. In other words, a single tuning job creates multiple SageMaker training jobs. Hyperparameter tuning allows you to speed up your model development and optimization by trying many combinations of hyperparameters in parallel and iteratively moving toward more optimal combinations. However, it doesn't guarantee that your model performance will always improve. For instance, if the chosen model architecture is not optimal for the task at hand or your dataset is too small for the chosen model, you are unlikely to see any improvements when running hyperparameter optimizations.

When designing for your tuning job, you need to consider several key parameters of your tuning job, as follows:

- **Search algorithm** (or **strategy**): This defines how SageMaker chooses the next combination of hyperparameters.

- **Hyperparameters with ranges**: The SageMaker search algorithm will pick hyperparameter values within user-defined ranges.

- **Objective metric**: This will be used to compare a combination of hyperparameters and define the best candidate. SageMaker doesn't restrict you from choosing any arbitrary target metric.

SageMaker supports two search strategies: **Bayesian** and **Random**. Random search selects the next combination of hyperparameters randomly within defined ranges. While it's a simple strategy, it is considered a relatively efficient one. Because the next hyperparameter combination doesn't depend on previously tried or currently running combinations, you can have a large number of training jobs running in parallel. Bayesian search selects the next combination of hyperparameters based on the outcomes of previous training jobs. Under the hood, SageMaker trains a regression model for this, which takes the results of previous jobs as input (hyperparameters and resulting target metrics) and outputs the candidate hyperparameter combination. Note that the Bayesian model may not converge. In such cases, it makes sense to review identified hyperparameter ranges.

Choosing hyperparameters and their ranges significantly impacts your tuning job performance. SageMaker supports several types of hyperparameters – categorical, continuous, and integer. You can combine different types of hyperparameters. For instance, the following code defines the model architecture as a categorical hyperparameter, the learning rate scheduler step is defined as an integer parameter, and the learning rate is defined as a continuous parameter (in other words, a float type):

```
hyperparameter_ranges = {
"model_type" : sagemaker.tuner.CategoricalParameter(["resnet",
"vgg16", "densenet"]}]),
"learning_rate" : sagemaker.tuner.
ContinuousParameter(0.0001,0.1, scaling_type="Logarithmic"),
"lr_scheduler_step_size" : sagemaker.tuner.
IntegerParameter(10,100, scaling_type="Linear"),
}
```

Note that for numeric hyperparameters, we also define **Scaling Type**, which defines the scale of parameters when the search algorithm selects the next value of hyperparameters. In our case, we choose the `"Logarithmic"` scaling type for the learning rate parameter since its range spans multiple orders of magnitude. For the scheduler step size, we choose the `"Linear"` scaling type since its range is narrow.

You also need to define the objective metric for your hyperparameter tuning job. The objective metric is defined similarly to other metrics via a Regex pattern. Note that you need to ensure that your training script outputs your objective metric in the `stdout`/`stderr` streams. Follow these steps:

1. In the following code, we are defining four metrics that will be captured by SageMaker and then choosing `val_accuracy` as our objective metric to optimize for:

```
metric_definitions = [
    {"Name": "train_loss",
     "Regex": "Train Loss = (.*?);"},
    {"Name": "val_loss",
     "Regex": "Val Loss=(.*?);"},
    {"Name": "train_accuracy",
     "Regex": "Train Accuracy = (.*?);"},
    {"Name": "val_accuracy",
     "Regex": "Val Accuracy = (.*?);"},]
objective_metric_name = "val_accuracy"
```

2. Next, we must define the parameters of the training job. Note that the hyperparameters that are provided as part of the training job configuration will be static and won't be changed as part of the tuning job:

```
estimator = PyTorch(
            entry_point="train_script.py",
            role=role,
            instance_type=instance_type,
            sagemaker_session=sagemaker_session,
            image_uri=image_uri,
            instance_count=instance_count,
            hyperparameters={
                "batch-size":64,
                "num-epochs":5,
            })
```

3. Then, we must combine our objective metric, metric definitions, and hyperparameter ranges in the `HyperParameterTuner` object, which will orchestrate the creation of child training jobs and track the overall status of your tuning. Additionally, we must provide the total max number of training jobs and the number of concurrent training jobs. These parameters will have an impact on how quickly the tuning job will run and its total cost:

```
tuner = sagemaker.tuner.HyperparameterTuner(
        estimator,
```

```
        objective_metric_name,
        hyperparameter_ranges,
        metric_definitions,
        objective_type="Maximize",
        max_jobs=200,
        max_parallel_jobs=10)
```

Also, pay attention to the objective_type parameter, which defines whether the tuning job will try to maximize or minimize the objective metric. Since we chose accuracy as our objective metric, we want to maximize it.

4. Once the tuner object has been instantiated, you can use the .fit() method to start training:

```
    tuner.fit({"train":train_data_location, "val":val_data_
    location})
```

5. Once the job is completed, you can analyze the outcomes of the tuning job. For this, you can navigate to the AWS console and inspect them visually. Alternatively, you can export tuner job results and statistics to a pandas DataFrame for further analysis, as shown here:

```
    tuner = sagemaker.HyperparameterTuningJobAnalytics(tuning_
    job_name)
    tuner_results = tuner.dataframe()
```

Using this method, you can perform more advanced analytics, such as defining the correlation between various hyperparameters and objective metrics. This type of analysis, for instance, may uncover cases where your hyperparameter ranges need to be modified to further improve the target metric.

Using EC2 Spot Instances

Running large training and model tuning jobs can be very expensive. One approach to minimize costs is to use EC2 Spot Instances from a pool of unused compute resources in a chosen AWS region. Thus, Spot Instances are considerably cheaper than regular on-demand instances (up to 90%). However, Spot Instances can be stopped with short notice if the spot capacity of the chosen instance type is exhausted in a given AWS region.

SageMaker simplifies the provisioning of Spot Instances for training jobs and fully handles interruption and training job restarts when the spot capacity is available again. When the training job is interrupted and then restarted, we want to continue our training process rather than starting from scratch. To support this, your training script needs to be modified so that it can save and restart the training job.

To support spot training, your training script needs the following modifications:

- When loading the model for the first time, check if there is a model copy already available in the /opt/ml/checkpoints path. If the checkpointed model is available, this means that we trained this model previously. To continue training, we need to load the checkpointed model and proceed with training. If the checkpointed model is not available, we proceed with regular model loading:

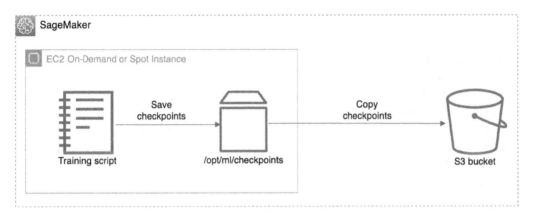

Figure 7.9 – Uploading the checkpoint artifacts to S3 storage

- In your training script, you need to specify the checkpoint handler (refer to the DL framework documentation for this) and store your model checkpoints in the designated directory – that is, /opt/ml/checkpoints. In the case of Spot Instance interruption, SageMaker will automatically copy the content of this directory to S3. When the Spot Instance is available again, SageMaker will copy your checkpoints from S3 back to the /opt/ml/checkpoints directory:

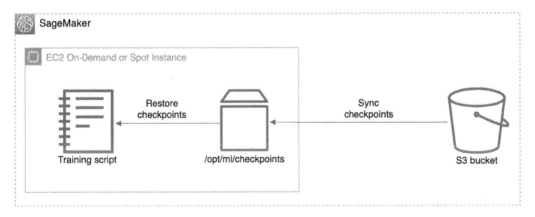

Figure 7.10 – Restoring the checkpoint artifacts from S3 storage

When using Spot Instances, please be aware that using spot training may result in longer and unpredictable training times. Each Spot Instance interruption will result in additional startup time during restart. The amount of available spot capacity depends on the instance type and AWS region. GPU-based instance types in certain AWS regions may have very limited spot capacity. Note that spot capacity constantly fluctuates. You can use the **Amazon Spot Instance advisor** feature to determine available spot capacity for different EC2 instances, the chance of interruption, and cost savings compared to regular on-demand instances.

Summary

This chapter concludes *Part 2* of this book. In this and the two previous chapters, we discussed how to build and optimize large-scale training jobs. First, we reviewed the available specialized hardware for DL training and how to choose optimal instance types. Then, we discussed how to engineer distributed training using open source and Amazon proprietary solutions. In this chapter, we discussed how to efficiently operationalize your model training. We reviewed different issues that may occur during training and how to detect and mitigate them. We also discussed how to manage and optimize hyperparameter tuning.

In *Part 3*, *Serving Deep Learning Models*, we will dive deep into DL inference on Amazon SageMaker. We will discuss what hardware is available for inference and how to engineer your inference server. Then, we will review the operational aspects of model serving. In the next chapter, *Chapter 8*, *Considering Hardware for Inference*, we will review the available hardware accelerators suitable for inference workloads, discuss selection criteria, and explain how you can optimize your model for inference on specific hardware accelerators using model compilers and SageMaker Neo.

Part 3: Serving Deep Learning Models

In this chapter, we will focus on hosting trained models on Amazon SageMaker. We will review available software and hardware options and provide recommendations on what to choose and when.

This section comprises the following chapters:

- *Chapter 8, Considering Hardware for Inference*
- *Chapter 9, Implementing Model Servers*
- *Chapter 10, Operationalizing Inference Workloads*

8

Considering Hardware
for Inference

In *Part 3, Serving Deep Learning Models* of this book, we will focus on how to develop, optimize, and operationalize inference workloads for **deep learning** (**DL**) models. Just like training, DL inference is computationally intensive and requires an understanding of specific types of hardware built for inference, model optimization techniques, and specialized software servers to manage model deployment and handle inference traffic. Amazon SageMaker provides a wide range of capabilities to address these aspects.

In this chapter, we will discuss hardware options and model optimization for model serving. We will review the available hardware accelerators that are suitable for DL inference and discuss how to select one. Amazon SageMaker offers multiple NVIDIA GPU accelerators and a proprietary chip built for DL inference – **AWS Inferentia**. SageMaker also allows you to access accelerator capacity using its **Elastic Inference** capability. As each inference use case is unique and comes with its own set of business requirements, we will propose a set of selection criteria that can be used when evaluating the optimal hardware accelerator for inference.

Another important aspect when building your DL inference workload is understanding how to optimize a specific model architecture for inference on the target hardware accelerator. This process is known as model compilation. We will review the popular optimizer and runtime environment known as NVIDIA **TensorRT**, which delivers optimal latency and throughput for models running on NVIDIA GPU accelerators. Then, we will discuss **Neuron SDK**, which optimizes models to run on AWS Inferentia chips. We will also discuss **SageMaker Neo** – a managed model compilation service that allows you to compile models for a wide range of data center and edge hardware accelerators. Note that you won't cover any edge or embedded platforms in this book.

In this chapter, we will cover the following topics:

- Selecting hardware accelerators in AWS Cloud
- Compiling models for inference

After reading this chapter, you will be able to select an efficient hardware configuration for your inference workloads with optimal price/performance characteristics and perform further optimizations.

Technical requirements

In this chapter, we will provide code samples so that you can develop practical skills. The full code examples are available here: `https://github.com/PacktPublishing/Accelerate-Deep-Learning-Workloads-with-Amazon-SageMaker/blob/main/chapter8/`.

To follow along with this code, you will need the following:

- An AWS account and IAM user with permission to manage Amazon SageMaker resources.

- Have a SageMaker notebook, SageMaker Studio notebook, or local SageMaker compatible environment established.

- Access to GPU training instances in your AWS account. Each example in this chapter will provide recommended instance types to use. You may need to increase your compute quota for **SageMaker Training Job** to have GPU instances enabled. In this case, please follow the instructions at `https://docs.aws.amazon.com/sagemaker/latest/dg/regions-quotas.html`.

- You must install the required Python libraries by running `pip install -r requirements.txt`. The file that contains the required libraries can be found in the `chapter8` directory.

- In this chapter, we will provide examples of compiling models for inference, which requires access to specific accelerator types. If you intend to follow these code samples, please provision a SageMaker notebook instance or SageMaker Studio notebook with the target accelerator.

Selecting hardware accelerators in AWS Cloud

AWS Cloud and Amazon SageMaker provide a range of hardware accelerators that are suitable for inference workloads. Choosing a hardware platform often requires multiple experiments to be performed with various accelerators and serving parameters. Let's look at some key selection criteria that can be useful during the evaluation process.

Latency-throughput trade-offs

Inference latency defines how quickly your model can return inference outcomes to the end user, and we want to minimize latency to improve user experience. Inference throughput defines how many inference requests can be processed simultaneously, and we want to maximize it to guarantee that as many inference requests as possible are served. In software engineering, it's common to discuss latency-throughput trade-offs as it's usually impractical to minimize latency and maximize throughput at the same time, so you need to find a balance between these characteristics.

It's common to set target latency and throughput SLAs as part of the business requirements of your specific use case. Finding an acceptable latency-throughput trade-off requires benchmarking with different accelerators and model/server parameters against target SLAs.

For instance, when running a real-time inference endpoint, usually, you are concerned with the latency SLA as it will have a direct impact on your end users. You may start by finding the hardware and model configuration with the latency within the target SLA number, and then scale it to reach the desired throughput. In the case of batch inference, overall system throughput is usually more important than latency. We want to maximize throughput to guarantee that our hardware resources are utilized efficiently.

Cost

The cost of running the inference workload is another important parameter that influences which hardware you use and your latency and throughput SLAs. While AWS and SageMaker offer one of the most powerful GPU accelerators on the market, their cost may be prohibitively high for your specific use case. Hence, it's often the case that you may need to adjust your latency and throughput SLAs to make your DL inference application economically viable.

Supported frameworks and operators

Running inference workloads is computationally intensive as it requires calculating a model forward pass on a single or batch of inputs. Each forward pass consists of a sequence of individual compute tasks. A type of computing task is known as an operator. Some examples of common DL operators include matrix multiplication, convolution, and average pooling.

Operators supported by DL frameworks can always run on CPU devices. However, CPU, as we discussed in *Chapter 5*, *Considering Hardware for Training*, is not the most efficient DL accelerator. Therefore, running inference using a CPU results in higher latency compared to specialized accelerators such as GPUs and ASIC chips.

NVIDIA GPU accelerators support a wide range of operators via the CUDA toolkit. In certain cases, you may need to implement a new operator for your specific model architecture. The CUDA toolkit provides a programming API for such custom operator development.

ASIC accelerators such as AWS Inferentia provide support for a finite list of operators and frameworks. In cases where a specific operator is not supported, this operator will be executed on the CPU device. This allows you to run many model architectures on specialized accelerators, but on the other hand, it will likely result in increased inference latency due to overall slowness of CPU execution and the necessary handoff between the ASIC and CPU accelerators of the tensors during the model's forward pass.

Hence, when choosing your target hardware accelerator, you need to understand which DL frameworks and operators are supported.

In *Chapter 5*, *Considering Hardware for Deep Learning Training*, we provided an overview of the available hardware accelerators for DL on the Amazon SageMaker platform. In the following sections, we will highlight some accelerators and compute instances recommended for inference workloads.

G4 instance family – best price and performance ratio for inference

The G4 instances feature NVIDIA T4 Tensor Core GPUs with 16 GB of memory. This accelerator is designed by NVIDIA for inference in the cloud and data centers. It supports FP32, FP16, INT8, and INT4 precision types. G4 should be considered as the default option for running DL inference workloads since it combines performance characteristics relevant for inference workloads and lower cost compared to the more powerful P3 family.

For further performance optimizations, you can compile your model using the NVIDIA TensorRT optimizer. We will discuss the TensorRT optimizer in detail in the next section.

P3 instance family – performant and expensive for inference

A P3 instance with NVIDIA V100 accelerators is primarily designed for large-scale training. Compared to G4, the P3 family has up to 32 GB of GPU memory and larger network bandwidth (both inter-GPU and inter-node). P3 also supports the F64, FP32, FP16, and INT8 precision types.

Many of P3's characteristics are very desirable for large-scale distributed training, but they are less relevant for inference. For instance, you rarely need to have a double precision type; rather, you want to reduce precision during inference to minimize latency. Higher network bandwidth (specifically inter-node) is also less relevant for inference workloads since it's rare to distribute your model across nodes at serving time.

So, while the P3 family is more performant than G4, it costs more and has minimal benefits for inference workloads. One scenario where you may want to use P3 instead of G4 is when you're running inference for large models. In this case, the `P3dn.24xlarge` instance can provide you with 8 V100 GPUs with 32 GB each.

> **Important note**
> Not that here, we are only considering accelerators that are available as part of SageMaker. Some instance families (such as the G5 and P4 families) are only available as part of the Amazon EC2 service. We expect these instances to be supported by Amazon SageMaker in the future.

AWS Inferentia

AWS Inferentia is a purpose-built ASIC accelerator for DL inference workloads. According to AWS, it offers the lowest inference cost in the cloud. Each Inferentia chip consists of four NeuronCores, which are high-performance matrix-multiply engines. NeuronCores are optimized for operations on small batch sizes to guarantee the lowest possible inference latency. Inferentia supports the FP16, BF16, and

INT8 precision types. The **Inf1 instance family** comes with a range of Inferentia accelerators: from 1 to up to 16. Public AWS benchmarks claim that Inferentia chips can deliver considerable price and latency/throughput improvements compared to G4 instance alternatives. For instance, the BERT model running BERT inference can achieve 12 times higher throughput than a `g4dn.xlarge` alternative, while costing 70% less to run.

To run inference on an Inferentia instance, you need to compile the model using AWS Neuron SDK (`https://github.com/aws/aws-neuron-sdk/`). Neuron SDK supports TensorFlow, PyTorch, and MXNet DL frameworks. We will discuss model compilation and optimization with Neuron SDK in the next section.

AWS Inferentia offers a performant and cost-efficient inference accelerator. Additionally, you can further optimize your models using Neuron SDK. Note that you need to consider whether the given model architecture and its operators are supported by Neuron SDK. Unsupported operators will be executed on the CPU device, which will result in additional latency. This may or may not be acceptable based on your target SLAs.

Amazon Elastic Inference

Elastic Inference (EI) is a capability that allows you to attach user-defined accelerator capacity to regular CPU instances. EI was designed specifically for inference use cases. Accelerator capacity is available via an attached network interface. EI supports TensorFlow, MXNet, and PyTorch frameworks and the ONNX model format. To be able to use EI, you need to load your models in a special EI-enabled version of DL frameworks. The modified versions of DL frameworks automatically detect the presence of EI accelerators and execute operators over the network interface. The following diagram illustrates this:

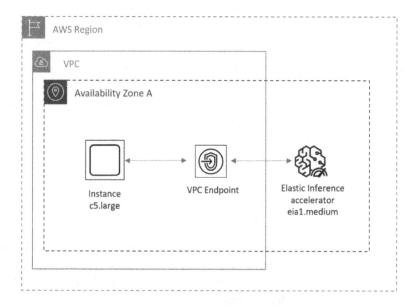

Figure 8.1 – Accessing the EI GPU capacity via a network interface

EI has several accelerator types available. You can select one based on the amount of required accelerator memory or anticipated throughput (in TFLOPS). EI provides low cost and high flexibility when it comes to instance configuration. Unlike dedicated GPU instances with restricted configurations, you can mix and match CPU instances and EI to achieve acceptable SLAs for inference latency and throughput while keeping the overall cost low:

Accelerator Type	FP32 Throughput (TFLOPS)	FP16 Throughput (TFLOPS)	Memory (GB)
eia2.medium	1	8	2
eia2.large	2	16	4
eia2.xlarge	4	32	8

Figure 8.2 – EI performance characteristics

When selecting EI, you need to keep several caveats in mind:

- By design, EI accelerators always introduce additional latency due to network transfer. EI accelerators may underperform on models with complex control flows.

- The EI-enabled DL frameworks are lagging considerably behind the latest open source versions. Also, you may experience compatibility issues trying to run the latest model architectures on EI.

- EI provides relatively low GPU memory (compared to the latest generations of GPU instances), which may restrict the types of models you can run on it.

Like GPU instances and Inferentia, EI supports model compilation and optimization. You can use a SageMaker Neo optimizer job for TensorFlow models, which uses the **TF-TRT** library for TensorRT. Optimized models typically have better latency-throughput characteristics but may take up large GPU memory at inference time. This may lead to potential **out-of-memory** (**OOM**) issues.

EI can be a useful option in your toolbox when selecting a DL accelerator, especially when you are looking for a highly flexible and cost-efficient solution and are running more compact and less demanding model architectures. However, if you are looking for high-performant inference for demanding models, you should consider Inferentia and G4 instances first.

Compiling models for inference

To achieve optimal inference performance on the given accelerator hardware, you usually need to compile your model for this accelerator. The compilation process includes various computational optimizations, such as layer and tensor fusion, precision calibration, and discarding unused parameters.

In this section, we will review the optimizers that perform compilation for previously discussed inference accelerators: NVIDIA TensorRT for NVIDIA GPU accelerators and Neuron SDK compiler for AWS Inferentia. After that, we will review a managed compilation service called SageMaker Neo, which supports multiple cloud and edge hardware accelerators.

We will start by looking at the TensorRT compiler for NVIDIA GPU accelerators.

Using TensorRT

NVIDIA TensorRT is a compiler and inference runtime built for the CUDA ecosystem. According to NVIDIA benchmarks, it can improve model performance up to six times compared to an uncompiled model version on the same hardware accelerator. TensorRT supports TensorFlow and PyTorch frameworks, as well as the cross-framework ONNX model format. TensorRT is integrated with the NVIDIA Triton model server to manage model deployment and serve inference requests. TensorRT provides both C++ and Python runtime environments. The C++ runtime can be especially useful for inference at the edge and embedded devices that may not have a Python runtime configured:

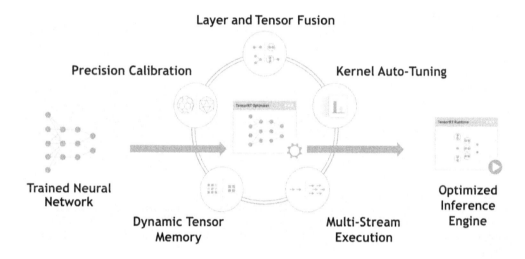

Figure 8.3 – Accessing EI GPU capacity via a network interface

TensorRT provides several key optimization mechanisms when compiling models (refer to *Figure 8.3*):

- **Precision Calibration** converts weights and activations into INT8 precision type without impacting accuracy to maximize model throughput

- **Layer and Tensor Fusion** combines multiple layers and tensor operators into a single computation to optimize memory utilization and latency

- **Kernel Auto-Tuning** selects optimal data layers and algorithms for the given hardware accelerator

- **Dynamic Tensor Memory** allows you to efficiently reuse the memory that's been allocated for tensors

- **Multi-Stream Execution** allows you to process multiple inputs in parallel

Most of these optimizations happen automatically without user input. At compile time, you need to set the following parameters:

- **Precision mode** defines the precision type that the model parameters will be converted into. TensorRT allows you to reduce precision without or with minimal impact on accuracy. A lower precision allows you to reduce the memory footprint, which, in turn, speeds up memory-bound operations.

- **Input batch size** sets how many sample inputs are expected in a single inference request. Increasing the batch size usually increases the overall system throughput. However, a larger batch size requires more available memory and may also increase inference request latency.

- **Max memory size** defines how much GPU memory is available for the model at inference time.

It's recommended to experiment with various combinations of these parameters to achieve optimal performance, given your available resources and latency-throughput SLAs.

Depending on the DL framework model, the compilation path to the TensorRT format is different. For TensorFlow, you can use the **TensorFlow-TensorRT** (**TRT**) integration library (`https://github.com/tensorflow/tensorrt`). For PyTorch, you need to convert the model into TorchScript format using the PyTorch JIT compiler. Then, you can use Torch-TensorRT integration (`https://github.com/pytorch/TensorRT`) to compile the model into TensorRT format. Then, the compiled model can be served using the model server of your choice. In *Chapter 9*, *Implementing Model Servers*, we will develop an inference application for the TensorRT compiled model using the NVIDIA Triton model server.

Let's review an example of how to compile the PyTorch ResNet50 model using TensorRT and then benchmark it against an uncompiled model. To compile the model using TensorRT, you need to have access to the environment that contains the target NVIDIA GPU. In the case of Amazon SageMaker, you can use a SageMaker notebook instance with the NVIDIA GPU accelerator. It's recommended to use the official NVIDIA PyTorch container that comes with all the dependencies preconfigured.

> **Important note**
>
> Note that Amazon SageMaker Studio notebooks don't allow you to run Docker containers. Hence, in this example, we will use a SageMaker notebook instance. Choose a notebook instance with the same GPU accelerator as the intended inference cluster.

Follow the next steps to compile PyTorch model for TensorRT runtime:

1. Start a SageMaker notebook instance with the NVIDIA GPU accelerator. For example, you can use the `ml.p3.2xlarge` notebook instance.

2. Once your notebook has been fully provisioned, open the JupyterLab service via the respective link in the AWS Console.

3. In your JupyterLab environment, open a **Terminal** session and run the following commands to copy the source code for model compilation:

```
cd ~/SageMaker
git clone https://github.com/PacktPublishing/Accelerate-
Deep-Learning-Workloads-with-Amazon-SageMaker
```

4. In the same Terminal session, run the following commands to download the NVIDIA PyTorch container with TensorRT configured:

```
docker pull nvcr.io/nvidia/pytorch:22.06-py3
docker run --gpus all --ipc=host --ulimit memlock=-1
--ulimit stack=67108864 -it --rm -v ~/SageMaker/
Accelerate-Deep-Learning-Workloads-with-Amazon-SageMaker/
chapter8/1_src:/workspace/tensorrt_benchmark nvcr.io/
nvidia/pytorch:22.06-py3
```

5. A new Terminal session will open in the PyTorch container. Run the following commands to download the test images and start benchmarking:

```
cd tensorrt_benchmark/
bash data_download.sh
python benchmarking_resnet50.py
```

The benchmarking script should take several minutes to complete. You will be able to get inference results for the uncompiled ResNet50 model and the compiled model with FP32 precision and with FP16 precision. As you can see from the following summary, there is a latency improvement of more than five times in the FP16 model compared to the uncompiled model with the same accuracy:

- *Uncompiled ResNet50 model*: Average batch time: 102.17 ms

- *Compiled ResNet50 model with FP32 precision*: Average batch time: 70.79 ms

- *ResNet50 model with FP16 precision*: Average batch time: 17.26 ms

Let's review the compilation and inference part of the benchmarking script to familiarize ourselves with the PyTorch TensorRT API:

1. First, we will load the regular, uncompiled ResNet50 model from PyTorch Hub:

```
import torch
resnet50_model = torch.hub.load("pytorch/vision:v0.10.0",
"resnet50", pretrained=True)
resnet50_model.eval()
```

2. To compile the model, we can use the `torch_tensorrt` integration API. In the following example, we are compiling the model into a TorchScript module, optimized for the TensorRT engine:

```
import torch_tensorrt
trt_model_fp32 = torch_tensorrt.compile(model, inputs =
[torch_tensorrt.Input((128, 3, 224, 224), dtype=torch.
float32)],
    enabled_precisions = torch.float32,
    workspace_size = 1 << 22
)
```

3. Now, you can save and load the compiled model as a regular TorchScript program:

```
trt_model_fp32.save('resnet50_fp32.pt')
loaded = torch.jit.load('resnet50_fp32.pt')
```

In this section, you learned how to manually compile a PyTorch model for NVIDIA GPU accelerators using TensorRT and reviewed the latency improvements of the compiled model.

If you are interested in compiling TensorFlow models, you can use a similar approach. Note that you would need to use the official NVIDIA TensorFlow container instead. For a code example for this, you can refer to the official TensorFlow tutorial at `https://blog.tensorflow.org/2021/01/leveraging-tensorflow-tensorrt-integration.html`.

As you can see, the overall compilation process is manual. Later in this chapter, we will review SageMaker Neo, which allows us to compile TensorFlow and PyTorch models for NVIDIA GPU accelerators with minimal manual effort.

Using Neuron SDK

AWS Neuron SDK allows you to compile your DL models for AWS Inferentia instances. It provides several parameters to help you optimize your inference program based on the available Inferentia chips and your latency and throughput SLAs. Neuron SDK supports TensorFlow, PyTorch, and MXNet frameworks. Neuron SDK is an ahead-of-time compiler, so you must explicitly provide the batch size at compilation time. It also includes a runtime environment in which we load the model and get predictions at inference time. Note that the compiled model by Neuron SDK can only be used on AWS Inferentia chips.

Neuron SDK supports a wide but finite set of operators. AWS tested Neuron SDK on the following popular model architectures:

- *NLP models from the HuggingFace Transformer library*: **BERT, distilBERT, XLM-BERT, Robert, BioBERT, MarianMT, Pegasus, and Bart**
- *Computer vision models*: **Resnet, Renext, VGG, Yolo v3/v4/v5, SSD**

Neuron SDK also supports generic model layers such as a fully connected layer or embeddings lookup. If your model architecture uses supported operators, you will be able to fully utilize Neuron SDK optimizations. You can refer to the list of supported operators for specific DL frameworks in the official Neuron SDK documentation at `https://awsdocs-neuron.readthedocs-hosted.com/en/latest/index.html`.

When compiling your model using Neuron SDK, keep the following caveats in mind:

- If a specific operator is not supported, its execution will be performed on the CPU accelerator. This will lead to slower performance.
- The control flows in your model may not be fully supported.
- If you expect variable batch size, you will need to implement **dynamic batching**.
- If you expect a variable input size (for example, the variable size of input images), you should consider implementing padding or bucketing.

Now, let's discuss the available Neuron SDK optimizations.

FP32 Autocasting

Whenever possible, Neuron SDK converts your model into the BF16 precision type to reduce the memory footprint and improve latency-throughput characteristics.

Batching inference inputs

Batching refers to combining multiple inference inputs into a single batch. In this regard, it's the same as batching during model training. In the case of an inference workload, batching influences your throughput. Like TensorRT, Neuron SDK requires you to define the target batch size at compilation time. The Inferentia accelerator is specifically optimized for running inference on smaller batch sizes. This is achieved through combining latency-sensitive operations (such as reading weights from memory) for the whole inference batch, thus achieving better latency-throughput characteristics than performing the same operations on each inference input. The following diagram illustrates this concept:

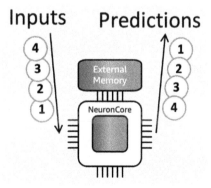

Figure 8.4 – Batched inference with single memory retrieval

Dynamic batching is a feature of Neuron SDK that allows you to slice the input tensors so that they match the batch size that's used at compilation time. Please note that dynamic batching is available for several eligible model architectures.

NeuronCore pipelining

Each Inferentia accelerator consists of four **NeuronCores**. Pipelining allows you to shard a model across multiple NeuronCores, caching the model parameters in on-chip memory. This allows you to process network operators with locally cached data faster and avoid accessing external memory. According to AWS, internal benchmark pipelines usually allow us to achieve the highest hardware utilization without batching. The following diagram shows an example of pipelining:

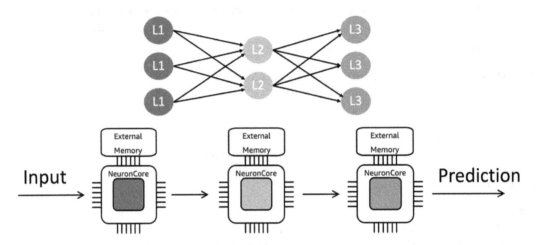

Figure 8.5 – Pipelining model across three NeuronCores

In the following example, we will compile and benchmark the ResNet50 model on an AWS Inferentia instance. At the time of writing, Amazon SageMaker doesn't support managed notebook instances. Hence, we used the Amazon EC2 `inf1.xlarge` instance with a **Deep Learning AMI GPU PyTorch 1.11.0 (Ubuntu 20.04)** image. While provisioning the instance's configuration, make sure that you download and save the SSH key. To be able to access the Jupyter notebook from your browser, please make sure that your EC2 instance allows TCP traffic on port 8888. For this, you will need to set up your instance security group like so:

Inbound rules (4)

Q Filter security group rules

	Name ▽	Security group rule... ▽	IP version ▽	Type ▽	Protocol ▽	Port range ▽	Source
☐	jupyter-rule	sgr-07f3e02a98383b2d0	IPv4	Custom TCP	TCP	8888	0.0.0.0/0
☐	–	sgr-08fb228ebf920237b	IPv4	HTTP	TCP	80	0.0.0.0/0
☐	–	sgr-00462cf887501080d	IPv4	SSH	TCP	22	0.0.0.0/0
☐	–	sgr-046da588e60003e...	IPv4	HTTPS	TCP	443	0.0.0.0/0

Figure 8.6 – Security group configuration to allow Jupyter traffic

Before we can start compiling Neuron SDK, we need to install Neuron SDK and its dependencies on the EC2 instance. Follow these steps:

1. First, you will need to SSH to your instance using the following commands:

    ```
    chmod 400 <your_ssh_key>
    ssh -i <your_ssh_key>ubuntu@<your_instance_public_DNS>
    ```

    Once you have logged into the EC2 instance, please follow the instructions at https://awsdocs-neuron.readthedocs-hosted.com/en/latest/neuron-intro/pytorch-setup/pytorch-install.html to install Neuron PyTorch on your Ubuntu OS. Note that installation may take around 5 minutes to complete.

2. Once the installation has finished, clone the sources and start the Jupyter server application:

    ```
    git clone https://github.com/PacktPublishing/Accelerate-Deep-Learning-Workloads-with-Amazon-SageMaker
    cd Accelerate-Deep-Learning-Workloads-with-Amazon-SageMaker/chapter8/
    jupyter notebook --ip=0.0.0.0
    ```

3. After that, you can open <your_instance_public_DNS>:8888/tree to access the Jupyter notebook for this example. Note that the first time you do this, you will need to copy the security token that was returned by jupyter notebook... previously.

Once the setup is done, we can compile and benchmark the models on the AWS Inferentia accelerator. The full code is available here: https://github.com/PacktPublishing/Accelerate-Deep-Learning-Workloads-with-Amazon-SageMaker/blob/main/chapter8/2_Neuron_SDK_compilation.ipynb. Follow these steps:

1. In the opened Jupyter notebook, change the kernel to **Python (Neuron PyTorch)**, which we configured previously.

2. Next, we must import the required libraries, including `torch_neuron`, and download the ResNet50 model:

```
import torch
from torchvision import models, transforms, datasets
import torch_neuron
image = torch.zeros([1, 3, 224, 224], dtype=torch.
float32)
model = models.resnet50(pretrained=True)
model.eval()
```

3. Then, we must analyze the model operators to identify if any model operators are not supported by Inferentia/Neuron SDK. Since the ResNet50 model is supported, the output of this command should confirm that all the model operators are supported:

```
torch.neuron.analyze_model(model, example_inputs=[image])
```

4. Now, we are ready to compile by running the following command. You will see the compilation statistics and status in the output:

```
model_neuron = torch.neuron.trace(model, example_
inputs=[image])
```

5. Since Neuron SDK compiles into a TorchScript program, saving and loading the model is similar to what you would do in regular PyTorch:

```
model_neuron.save("resnet50_neuron.pt")
model_neuron = torch.jit.load('resnet50_neuron.pt')
```

6. Now, let's benchmark the compiled model with batching or pipelining. For this, we will prepare preprocessing and benchmark methods to form an inference batch and **measure latency (ms)** and **throughput (samples/s)**:

```
model_neuron_parallel = torch.neuron.DataParallel(model_
neuron)
num_neuron_cores = 4
image = preprocess(batch_size=batch_size, num_neuron_
cores=num_neuron_cores)
benchmark(model_neuron_parallel, image)
```

The benchmark results should be similar to the following:

```
Input image shape is [4, 3, 224, 224]
Avg. Throughput: 551, Max Throughput: 562
```

```
Latency P50: 7
Latency P90: 7
Latency P95: 7
Latency P99: 7
```

7. Next, we will recompile the model with batching enabled (by setting `batch_size` to 5 samples per NeuronCore):

```
batch_size = 5
image = torch.zeros([batch_size, 3, 224, 224],
dtype=torch.float32)
model_neuron = torch.neuron.trace(model, example_
inputs=[image])
model_neuron.save("resnet50_neuron_b{}.pt".format(batch_
size))
```

8. After rerunning the benchmark, please note that while latency is decreased, the overall throughput has increased, as shown here:

```
Batch_size = 5
model_neuron = torch.jit.load("resnet50_neuron_b{}.pt".
format(batch_size))
model_neuron_parallel = torch.neuron.DataParallel(model_
neuron)
image = preprocess(batch_size=batch_size, num_neuron_
cores=num_neuron_cores)
benchmark(model_neuron_parallel, image)
```

The benchmark's output should look as follows:

```
Input image shape is [20, 3, 224, 224]
Avg. Throughput: 979, Max Throughput: 998
Latency P50: 20
Latency P90: 21
Latency P95: 21
Latency P99: 24
```

9. Lastly, let's compile and benchmark the model with pipelining enabled. We will start by tracing the original model with the `neuroncore-pipeline-cores` parameter:

```
neuron_pipeline_model = torch.neuron.trace(model,
                                    example_
```

```
            inputs=[image],

                                                verbose=1,

                                                compiler_args
        = ['--neuroncore-pipeline-cores', str(num_neuron_cores)])
```

10. Then, we will rerun the benchmark on this new model:

```
    image = preprocess(batch_size=batch_size, num_neuron_
    cores=num_neuron_cores)
    benchmark(neuron_pipeline_model, image)
```

The output of this benchmarking will be as follows:

```
    Input image shape is [20, 3, 224, 224]
    Avg. Throughput: 271, Max Throughput: 274
    Latency P50: 73
    Latency P90: 74
    Latency P95: 74
    Latency P99: 79
```

Note that the resulting latency and throughput of the pipeline model are lower than the model without batching and with batching. One reason for this is that in our benchmark test, we run inference requests sequentially. To leverage the pipeline model better, we would need to create several parallel inference requests.

Using SageMaker Neo

SageMaker Neo allows you to compile and optimize DL models for a wide range of target hardware platforms. It supports PyTorch, TensorFlow, MXNet, and ONNX models for hardware platforms such as Ambarella, ARM, Intel, NVIDIA. NXP, Qualcomm, Texas Instruments, and Xilinx. SageMaker Neo also supports deployment for cloud instances, as well as edge devices.

Under the hood, SageMaker Neo converts your trained model from a framework-specific representation into an intermediate framework-agnostic representation. Then, it applies automatic optimizations and generates binary code for the optimized operations. Once the model has been compiled, you can deploy it to the target instance type it using the SageMaker Inference service. Neo also provides a runtime for each target platform that loads and executes the compiled model. An overview of SageMaker Neo is shown in the following diagram:

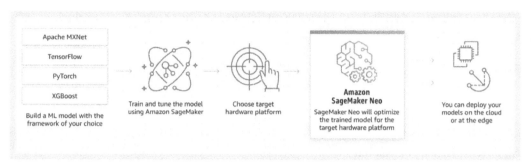

Figure 8.7 – SageMaker Neo overview

SageMaker Neo enables users to significantly reduce any additional development or setup work. However, it also comes with certain limitations that may or may not be suitable for your specific use case:

- SageMaker Neo primarily supports computer vision models such as **Image Classification**, **Object Detection**, and **Semantic Segmentation**. It doesn't support, for example, NLP model architectures.

- SageMaker Neo supports various DL frameworks but they are several major versions behind. So, if you are looking to use the latest model architecture and/or the latest framework version features, you will have to consider other compilation options (for instance, manually compiling using TensorRT). For the latest details on SageMaker Neo support, refer to https://docs. aws.amazon.com/sagemaker/latest/dg/neo-supported-cloud.html.

- SageMaker Neo supports a set of cloud instances. At the time of writing, it supports compilation for ml.c5, ml.c4, ml.m5, ml.m4, ml.p3, ml.p2, and ml.inf1 instances.

- SageMaker Neo sets specific requirements on the inference request format, (specifically, around the shape of the input).

These are key limitations you need to keep in mind when considering using SageMaker Neo. In many cases, SageMaker Neo can be a convenient and efficient way to compile your DL models if your model architecture, framework version, and target hardware accelerators are supported.

Let's review how to compile a TensorFlow model using SageMaker Neo. In this example, we will train the ResNet50 model, compile it for several hardware platforms, and deploy inference endpoints of optimized models. We will highlight the key aspects. The full source code is available here: https:// github.com/PacktPublishing/Accelerate-Deep-Learning-Workloads-with-Amazon-SageMaker/blob/main/chapter8/3_SageMaker_Neo_TF.ipynb.

Developing a training and inference script

In the previous chapters, we mentioned that SageMaker must implement specific methods to be able to train models and run inference on SageMaker. Depending on the DL framework and target hardware platform, the required API will be slightly different. Refer to the official documentation for details: https://docs.aws.amazon.com/sagemaker/latest/dg/neo-deployment-hosting-services-prerequisites.html.

To serve TensorFlow models, we implemented the simple `serving_input_fn()` method, which passes inputs to the model and returns predictions:

```
def serving_input_fn():
    inputs = {"x": tf.placeholder(tf.float32, [None, 784])}
    return tf.estimator.export.ServingInputReceiver(inputs,
inputs)
```

Next, we schedule our compilation job.

Running compilation jobs and deployment

To start compilation jobs, we must train our model using the SageMaker Python SDK from `sagemaker.tensorflow` and then import TensorFlow:

```
mnist_estimator = TensorFlow(entry_point='mnist.py',
                             source_dir="3_src",
                             role=role,
                             instance_count=1,
                             instance_type='ml.p3.2xlarge',
                             framework_version='1.15.0',
                             py_version='py3',
                             )
mnist_estimator.fit(training_data_uri)
```

Once the model has been trained, we can test how compilation works for two different hardware accelerators: a p2 instance with NVIDIA GPU devices and a c5 instance without any specialized hardware. Follow these steps:

1. For this, first, we must compile the model for the NVIDIA GPU and deploy the endpoint using the same hardware type. Note the `input_shape` parameter, which tells SageMaker what input share to use during the compilation process. You will need to convert your inference sample into the same input share at inference time:

   ```
   p2_estimator = mnist_estimator.compile_model(target_
   instance_family='ml_p2',
                                     input_shape={'data':[1,
   784]},
                                     output_path=output_path)
   ```

```
p2_predictor = p2_estimator.deploy(initial_instance
_count = 1,

instance_type = 'ml.inf1.xlarge')
```

2. To access the logs of your compilation job, you can navigate to **SageMaker | Inference | Compilation jobs** in the AWS Console. In these logs, you can find, for instance, what compilation framework SageMaker Neo is using under the hood (Apache TVM) and see the compilation status of your model operators.

3. Running compilation jobs for the c5 instance is very similar. Note that we are using the same `estimator` object that we did to compile the p2 instance. As mentioned previously, you only need to train the model once; then, you can compile it for as many target platforms as you need:

```
c5_estimator = mnist_estimator.compile_model(target_
instance_family='ml_c5',

                                input_shape={'data':[1,
784]},

                                output_path=output_path)
c5_predictor = c5_estimator.deploy(initial_instance_count
= 1,

                                                instance
_type = 'ml.c5.xlarge')
```

4. As a result of a successful compilation, the resulting model artifact will be persisted in the S3 location available upon calling the `c5_estimator.model_data` attribute.

5. Calling the endpoint with compiled models is the same as calling an uncompiled model. Here is an example of the p2 inference endpoint:

```
data = inference_data[i].reshape(1,784)
predict_response= p2_predictor.predict(data)
```

Note that we reshaped our input data so that it matches the input data that was used during the compilation process.

This brief example demonstrates how a single model can be compiled using SageMaker Neo. It's recommended to benchmark SageMaker compiled models before deploying them to production against uncompiled models to confirm latency-throughput improvements. Please note that uncompiled and compiled models may have different memory requirements.

Summary

In this chapter, we reviewed the available hardware accelerators that are suitable for running DL inference programs. We also discussed how your models can be optimized for target hardware accelerators using the TensorRT compiler for NVIDIA GPU accelerators and Neuron SDK for AWS Inferentia accelerators. Then, we reviewed the SageMaker Neo service, which allows you to compile supported models for a wide range of hardware platforms with minimal development efforts and highlighted several limitations of this service. After reading this chapter, you should be able to make decisions about which hardware accelerators to use and how to optimize them based on your specific use case requirements around latency, throughput, and cost.

Once you have selected your hardware accelerator and model optimization strategy, you will need to decide which model server to use and how to further tune your inference workload at serving time. In the next chapter, we will discuss popular model server solutions and gain practical experience in developing and deploying them on the **SageMaker Inference** service.

9
Implementing Model Servers

In *Chapter 8*, *Considering Hardware for Inference*, we discussed hardware options and optimizations for serving DL models that are available to you as part of the Amazon SageMaker platform. In this chapter, we will focus on another important aspect of engineering inference workloads – choosing and configuring model servers.

Model servers, similar to application servers for regular applications, provide a runtime context to serve your DL models. You, as a developer, deploy trained models to the model server, which exposes the deployed models as REST or gRPC endpoints. The end users of your DL models then send inference requests to established endpoints and receive a response with predictions. The model server can serve multiple end users simultaneously. It also provides configurable mechanisms to optimize inference latency and throughput to meet specific SLAs.

In *Chapter 1*, *Introducing Deep Learning with Amazon SageMaker*, we discussed that Amazon SageMaker Managed Hosting has several mechanisms to deploy models: real-time inference endpoints, batch transform jobs, and asynchronous inference. In all these cases, you will need to select a model server to manage inference runtime and model deployment. However, model server configuration for these use cases will likely be different, since they have different inference traffic profiles and latency/throughput requirements.

Amazon SageMaker provides several model server solutions as part of its DL Inference Containers. In this chapter, we will focus on three popular model servers designed to productionalize DL inference workloads: **TensorFlow Serving (TFS)**, **PyTorch TorchServe (PTS)**, and **NVIDIA Triton**.

In this chapter, we will cover the following topics:

- Using TFS
- Using PTS
- Using NVIDIA Triton

After reading this chapter, you will know how to deploy your TensorFlow and PyTorch models and configure your model servers for your inference requirements. We will also discuss the functional limitations of using model servers as part of SageMaker Managed Hosting.

Technical requirements

In this chapter, we will provide code samples so that you can develop practical skills. The full code examples are available here: https://github.com/PacktPublishing/Accelerate-Deep-Learning-Workloads-with-Amazon-SageMaker/blob/main/chapter9/.

To follow along with this code, you will need the following:

- An AWS account and IAM user with permission to manage Amazon SageMaker resources.
- Have a SageMaker Notebook, SageMaker Studio Notebook, or local SageMaker-compatible environment established.
- Access to GPU training instances in your AWS account. Each example in this chapter will provide the recommended instance types for you to use. You may need to increase your compute quota for *SageMaker Training Job* to have GPU instances enabled. In this case, please follow the instructions at https://docs.aws.amazon.com/sagemaker/latest/dg/regions-quotas.html.
- You must install the required Python libraries by running pip install -r requirements.txt. The file that contains the required libraries can be found in the chapter9 directory.
- In this chapter, we will provide examples of compiling models for inference, which requires access to specific accelerator types. Please review the instance recommendations as part of the model server examples.

Using TFS

TFS is a native model server for TensorFlow 1, TensorFlow 2, and Keras models. It is designed to provide a flexible and high-performance runtime environment with an extensive management API and operational features (such as logging and metrics). AWS provides TFS as part of TensorFlow inference containers (https://github.com/aws/deep-learning-containers/tree/master/tensorflow/inference/docker).

Reviewing TFS concepts

TFS has a concept known as **servable** that encapsulates all model and code assets required for inference. To prepare servable for TFS serving, you need to package the trained model into **SavedModel** format. A SavedModel contains a complete TensorFlow program, including trained parameters and computation. It does not require the original model building code to run, which makes it useful for sharing or deploying across the TFS ecosystem (for example, using TFLite, TensorFlow.js, or TFS). You can package more than one model as well as specific model lookups or embeddings in a single servable.

TFS loads and exposes your servable via REST or gRPC endpoints. The Server API defines a list of endpoints to perform classification and regression inference. Additionally, each servable has an associated **signature** that defines the input and output tensors for your model, as well as the model type (regression or classification). Many common models have standard signatures that depend on the type of task (for example, image classification, object detection, text classification, and so on). TFS allows you to have custom signatures as well.

Integrating TFS with SageMaker

Amazon SageMaker provides a managed hosting environment where you can manage your inference endpoints with uniform management and invocation APIs, regardless of the underlying model server. This approach sets certain limitations on native model server functionality. In this section, we will review how SageMaker integrates with TFS and the limitations you should be aware of.

When deploying TFS on SageMaker, you will not have access to TFS's native management API to manage your servable life cycle (loading and unloading models, promoting the model version, and more). Also, you will not have direct access to the TFS Serving API. Instead, you will need to call your SageMaker endpoint using the standard SageMaker invocation interface. Then, the SageMaker HTTP server (a part of the DL TFS container) translates your requests into TFS format and passes them to the TFS Serving APIs. Note that you can provide custom pre-processing, prediction, and post-processing logic in your inference script. SageMaker supports both the REST and gRPC serving APIs. The following diagram shows this TFS integration:

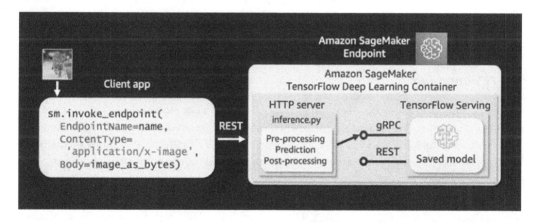

Figure 9.1 – TFS integration with SageMaker Managed Hosting

There are several things to keep in mind when working with TFS on SageMaker:

- As mentioned previously, SageMaker doesn't allow you to access the TFS Management API. However, it does allow to you provide the configuration of TFS via environmental variables.

- SageMaker supports hosting multiple models with TFS. For this, you need to prepare separate servables for each model and then create a multi-model archive.

- You can use REST headers and a request body to specify which models TFS should use to serve specific requests. For instance, the following request tells TFS to use model2 to serve this request:

```
aws sagemaker-runtime invoke-endpoint \
    --endpoint-name my-endpoint \
    --content-type 'application/json' \
    --body '{"instances": [1.0, 2.0, 5.0]}' \
    --custom-attributes 'tfs-model-name=other_model
```

SageMaker supports default TFS input and output formats for your inference requests. Additionally, SageMaker also supports application/JSON, text/CSV, and application/JSON Lines.

Note that once you deploy the endpoint with the TFS model server, you won't be able to directly change the TFS configuration or served models. For this, you will need to use the SageMaker Management API to create a new endpoint or endpoint variant with the desired configuration. We will discuss managing SageMaker inference resources in production in *Chapter 10, Operationalizing Inference Workloads*.

Optimizing TFS

TFS provides a set of mechanisms to optimize your model serving based on your requirements, the runtime environment, and available hardware resources. It implies that TFS tuning is use-case-specific and typically requires testing and benchmarking to achieve desired performance. In this section, we will review several mechanisms that you can use to tune TFS performance.

Using TFS batching

TFS supports automatic batching, where you can put several inference requests in a single batch. This can improve your server throughput, especially when using GPU instances (remember, GPUs are very good for parallel computations). How you configure batching will be different depending on the type of hardware device. TFS supports different batching schedules for different servables.

To configure TFS batching on SageMaker, you can use the following environment variables:

- SAGEMAKER_TFS_ENABLE_BATCHING to enable the TFS batching feature. This defaults to false, which means that batching is not enabled.

- SAGEMAKER_TFS_MAX_BATCH_SIZE defines the maximum size of the batch. This defaults to 8.

- SAGEMAKER_TFS_BATCH_TIMEOUT_MICROS defines how long to wait to accumulate a full batch in microseconds. This defaults to 1000.

- `SAGEMAKER_TFS_NUM_BATCH_THREADS` sets how many batches to process simultaneously. This defaults to the number of instance CPUs.

- `SAGEMAKER_TFS_MAX_ENQUEUED_BATCHES` defines how many batches can be enqueued at the same time.

You can review the detailed documentation on the TFS batching feature here: `https://github.com/tensorflow/serving/blob/master/tensorflow_serving/batching/README.md`.

Using the gRPC serving API

As discussed earlier, TFS supports two types of APIs: REST and gRPC. While both APIs have the same functionality, the gRPC API typically has better performance due to the use of HTTP/2 network protocol and more efficient payload representations via the ProtoBuf format.

While the SageMaker Invocation API only supports the REST API, you can still use gRPC for inter-container communication between SageMaker's HTTP frontend server and TFS (refer to *Figure 9.1* for an illustration of this). Note that in this case, you will need to provide some code to translate the SageMaker payload into gRPC format and send it to TFS. However, even in this case, AWS reports a decrease in the overall latency by at least 75% for image classification tasks. Refer to this article for details: `https://aws.amazon.com/blogs/machine-learning/reduce-compuer-vision-inference-latency-using-grpc-with-tensorflow-serving-on-amazon-sagemaker/`. The performance benefits will vary based on the model and payload size.

Configuring resource utilization with TFS

TFS provides the following parameters for configuring hardware resources allocation:

- `SAGEMAKER_TFS_INSTANCE_COUNT` defines how many instances of the TFS serving process will be spawned. Changing this parameter may increase your CPU and GPU utilization and ultimately improve your latency/throughput characteristics.

- `SAGEMAKER_TFS_FRACTIONAL_GPU_MEM_MARGIN` defines the fraction of GPU memory available to initialize the CUDA/cuDNN library. The remaining memory will be distributed equally between TFS processes.

- `SAGEMAKER_TFS_INTER_OP_PARALLELISM` determines how many threads are used when running independent non-blocking compute operations in your model graphs.

- `SAGEMAKER_TFS_INTRA_OP_PARALLELISM` determines how many threads are used when running operations that can be parallelized interally.

Now, let's review how we can use TFS on SageMaker using a practical example.

Implementing TFS serving

In this example, we will take one of the pre-trained models from TensorFlow Hub, convert it into **SavedModel** format, and then package it with the custom inference for deployment on SageMaker. We will review how we can use both the REST and gRPC APIs and how to define the TFS configuration when it's deployed on SageMaker Managed Hosting. For this task, we will use the popular EfficientNetV2 model architecture to classify images.

The full code is available here: `https://github.com/PacktPublishing/Accelerate-Deep-Learning-Workloads-with-Amazon-SageMaker/blob/main/chapter9/1_TensorFlow_Serving.ipynb`.

Preparing the training model

We will start by loading the model artifacts from TensorFlow Hub. You can read about the EfficientNetV2 model on its model page here: `https://tfhub.dev/google/imagenet/efficientnet_v2_imagenet1k_s/classification/2`. To download the model, we can use the TensorFlow Hub API, as shown in the following code block:

```
import tensorflow as tf
import tensorflow_hub as hub
model_handle = "https://tfhub.dev/google/imagenet/efficientnet_
v2_imagenet1k_s/classification/2"
classifier = hub.load(model_handle)
```

This model expects a dense 4D tensor of the `float32` dtype with a shape of [`batch, height, weight, color`], where `height` and `weight` have a fixed length of `384`, and `color` has a length of 3. `batch` can be variable.

To test the model locally, you need to convert the image (or a batch of images) into the expected 4D tensor, run it through the model, and apply the `softmax` function to get the label probabilities, as shown here:

```
probabilities = tf.nn.softmax(classifier(image)).numpy()
```

Now that we have performed smoke testing on the model, we need to package it in SageMaker/TFS-compatible formats.

Packaging the model artifacts

As discussed earlier, TFS expects your model to be converted into SavedModel format. Additionally, SageMaker expects the model artifact to be packaged into a `tar.gz` archive with the following structure:

```
model1
    |--[model_version_number]
```

```
            |--variables
            |--saved_model.pb
    model2
        |--[model_version_number]
            |--assets
            |--variables
            |--saved_model.pb
    code
        |--inference.py
        |--requirements.txt
```

The following code creates the appropriate directory structure and exports the trained model in SavedModel format:

```
model_name = "efficientnetv2-s"
model_dir = f"./{model_name}/1"
code_dir = f"./{model_name}/code"
os.makedirs(model_dir, exist_ok=False)
os.makedirs(code_dir, exist_ok=False)
tf.saved_model.save(classifier, model_dir)
```

Note that in our example, we will only use a single version of a single model. Next, we need to prepare an inference script for preprocessing, running predictions, and postprocessing between the SageMaker HTTP frontend and the TFS server.

Developing the inference code

SageMaker expects your processing code to be named `inference.py` and placed in the `/code` directory in the model archive. Our inference code needs to implement either the `input_handler()` and `output_handler()` functions or a single `handler()` function. In our case, we have chosen to implement a single `handler()` method to process incoming requests and send it to the appropriate TFS API:

```
def handler(data, context):
    if context.request_content_type == "application/json":
        instance = json.loads(data.read().decode("utf-8"))
    else:
        raise ValueError(
            415,
            'Unsupported content type "{}"'.format(
```

```
                    context.request_content_type or "Unknown"
            ),
        )
    if USE_GRPC:
        prediction = _predict_using_grpc(context, instance)
    else:
        inst_json = json.dumps({"instances": instance})
        response = requests.post(context.rest_uri, data=inst_
json)
        if response.status_code != 200:
            raise Exception(response.content.decode("utf-8"))
        prediction = response.content
    response_content_type = context.accept_header
    return prediction, response_content_type
```

As you can see, depending on whether we want to use the gRCP API or the REST API, the processing and prediction code will be slightly different. Note that the context namedtuple object provides necessary details about the TFS configuration, such as the endpoint path and ports, model name and version, and more.

If we choose to use the TFS REST API, we need to convert the incoming request into the expected TFS format, serialize it into JSON, and then generate a POST request.

To use the gRPC API, we will need to convert the incoming REST payload into a protobuf object. For this, we will use the following helper function:

```
from tensorflow_serving.apis import predict_pb2
from tensorflow_serving.apis import prediction_service_pb2_grpc
def _predict_using_grpc(context, instance):
    grpc_request = predict_pb2.PredictRequest()
    grpc_request.model_spec.name = "model"
    grpc_request.model_spec.signature_name = "serving_default"
    options = [
        ("grpc.max_send_message_length", MAX_GRPC_MESSAGE_
LENGTH),
        ("grpc.max_receive_message_length", MAX_GRPC_MESSAGE_
LENGTH),
    ]
    channel = grpc.insecure_channel(f"0.0.0.0:{context.grpc_
port}", options=options)
```

```
    stub = prediction_service_pb2_grpc.
PredictionServiceStub(channel)
grpc_request.inputs["input_1"].CopyFrom(tf.make_tensor_
proto(instance))
    result = stub.Predict(grpc_request, 10)
    output_shape = [dim.size for dim in result.
outputs["output_1"].tensor_shape.dim]
    np_result = np.array(result.outputs["output_1"].float_val).
reshape(output_shape)
    return json.dumps({"predictions": np_result.tolist()})
```

Here, we use the `prediction_service_pb2()` and `predict_pb2()` TFS methods to communicate with the gRPC API. Here, the `stub` object converts parameters during the RPC. The `grpc_request` object defines what TFS API to invoke and call the parameters.

To choose what TFS API to call, we implemented a simple mechanism that allows you to provide the USE_GRPC environment variable via a SageMaker Model object:

```
USE_GRPC = True if os.getenv("USE_GRPC").lower() == "true" else
False
```

Once we have our `inference.py` code ready, we can add it to the model package and create a `tar.gz` model archive. This can be done by running the following Bash code from a Jupyter notebook:

```
! cp 1_src/inference.py $code_dir
! cp 1_src/requirements.txt $code_dir
! tar -C "$PWD" -czf model.tar.gz  efficientnetv2-s/
```

Now, our model has been packaged according to TFS and SageMaker requirements and we are ready to deploy it.

Deploying the TFS model

To deploy the TFS model, follow these steps:

1. We will start by uploading our model archive to Amazon S3 so that SageMaker can download it to the serving container at deployment time. We can use a SageMaker Session() object to do this:

    ```
    import sagemaker
    from sagemaker import get_execution_role
    sagemaker_session = sagemaker.Session()
    role = get_execution_role()
    ```

```
bucket = sagemaker_session.default_bucket()
prefix = 'tf-serving'
s3_path = 's3://{}/{}'.format(bucket, prefix)
model_data = sagemaker_session.upload_data('model.tar.
gz',

                                          bucket,
                                          os.path.
join(prefix, 'model'))
```

2. Then, we can use the SageMaker SDK TensorFlowModel object to configure the TFS environment. Note that we are providing the TFS configuration via the env dictionary:

```
from sagemaker.tensorflow import TensorFlowModel
env = {
        "SAGEMAKER_TFS_ENABLE_BATCHING":"true",
        "SAGEMAKER_TFS_MAX_BATCH_SIZE":"4",
        "SAGEMAKER_TFS_BATCH_TIMEOUT_MICROS":"100000",
        "SAGEMAKER_TFS_NUM_BATCH_THREADS":"6",
        "SAGEMAKER_TFS_MAX_ENQUEUED_BATCHES":"6",
        "USE_GRPC":"true" # to switch between TFS REST and
gRCP API
        }
tensorflow_serving_model = TensorFlowModel(model_
data=model_data,

                                    name="efficientnetv2-1",
                                    role=role,
                                    framework_version='2.8',
                                    env=env,
sagemaker_session=sagemaker_session)
```

Once the model has been configured, we are ready to deploy the endpoint. Here, we will use one of the GPU instances, but you can experiment with CPU instances as well.

Before we can run predictions, we need to convert the image (or several images) into a 4D TFS tensor and then convert it into a NumPy ndarray that the .predict() method knows how to serialize into the application/JSON content type. A sample method to process images into TFS format has been provided in the sample notebook.

In the following code, we are running predictions and then mapping the resulting softmax scores to labels:

```
response_remote = predictor.predict(image.numpy())
probabilities = np.array(response_remote['predictions'])
top_5 = tf.argsort(probabilities, axis=-1,
direction="DESCENDING")[0][:5].numpy()
np_classes = np.array(classes)
# Some models include an additional 'background' class in the
predictions, so
# we must account for this when reading the class labels.
includes_background_class = probabilities.shape[1] == 1001
for i, item in enumerate(top_5):
  class_index = item if includes_background_class else item + 1
  line = f'({i+1}) {class_index:4} - {classes[class_index]}:
{probabilities[0][top_5][i]}'
  print(line)
```

After running this code, you should have an output that contains labels and their normalized probabilities.

In this section, we reviewed how to use the TFS model server on Amazon SageMaker. TFS is a highly configurable production-grade model server that should be considered a great candidate when it comes to hosting TensorFlow models. We also discussed some implementation specifics of Sagemaker/TFS integration that should be accounted for when engineering your model server. Once you have your TensorFlow model(s) running on SageMaker, it's recommended to perform benchmarking and tune the TFS configuration based on your specific use case requirements.

In the next section, we will review the native model server for PyTorch models – TorchServe.

Using PTS

PTS is a native model server for PyTorch models. PTS was developed in collaboration between Meta and AWS to provide a production-ready model server for the PyTorch ecosystem. It allows you to serve and manage multiple models and serve requests via REST or gRPC endpoints. PTS supports serving TorchScripted models for better inference performance. It also comes with utilities to collect logs and metrics and optimization tweaks. SageMaker supports PTS as part of PyTorch inference containers (https://github.com/aws/deep-learning-containers/tree/master/pytorch/inference/docker).

Integration with SageMaker

PTS is a default model server for PyTorch models on Amazon SageMaker. Similar to TFS, SageMaker doesn't expose native PTS APIs to end users for model management and inference. The following diagram shows how to integrate SageMaker and PTS:

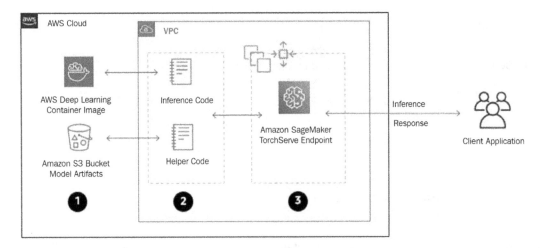

Figure 9.2 – PTS architecture on SageMaker

Let's highlight these integration details:

- SageMaker supports a limited number of PTS configs out of the box. If you need to have more flexibility with your PTS configuration, you may need to extend the SageMaker PyTorch Inference container. Alternatively, you can package the PTS configs as part of your model package and provide the path to it via the TS_CONFIG_FILE environment variable. However, with the latter approach, you won't be able to manipulate all the settings (for example, the JVM config).

- PTS requires you to package model artifacts and handler code into a MAR archive. SageMaker has slightly different requirements regarding the model archive, which we will discuss in the following code example.

- SageMaker supports hosting multiple models at the same time. For this, you need to set the ENABLE_MULTI_MODEL environment variable to true and package your models into a single archive.

SageMaker provides a mechanism to configure PTS via endpoint environmental variables. Let's review the available config parameters.

Optimizing PTS on SageMaker

PTS supports two primary mechanisms for performance optimization: server-side batching and spawning multiple model threads. These settings can be configured via the following environmental variables:

- `SAGEMAKER_TS_BATCH_SIZE` to set the maximum size of server-side batches.
- `SAGEMAKER_TS_MAX_BATCH_DELAY` to set the maximum delay that the server will wait to complete the batch in microseconds.
- `SAGEMAKER_TS_RESPONSE_TIMEOUT` sets the time delay for a timeout in seconds if an inference response is not available.
- `SAGEMAKER_TS_MIN_WORKERS` and `SAGEMAKER_TS_MAX_WORKERS` configure the minimum and the maximum number of model worker threads on CPU or GPU devices, respectively. You can read some of the considerations on setting up these in the PyTorch documentation at `https://github.com/pytorch/serve/blob/master/docs/performance_guide.md`.

Additionally, PTS supports inference profiling using the PyTorch TensorBoard plugin, which we discussed in *Chapter 7, Operationalizing Deep Learning Training*. This plugin allows you to profile your PyTorch inference code and identify potential bottlenecks.

Serving models with PTS

Let's review how to deploy PyTorch models using PTS on SageMaker. We will use the Distilbert model that has been trained on the Q&A NLP task from HuggingFace Models. The sample code is available here: `https://github.com/PacktPublishing/Accelerate-Deep-Learning-Workloads-with-Amazon-SageMaker/blob/main/chapter9/2_PyTorch_Torchserve.ipynb`.

Packaging the model for PTS on SageMaker

When using the PTS model server on SageMaker, you may choose to use one of two options:

- Deploy your model using the `PyTorchModel` class from the Python SageMaker SDK. In this case, your model archive needs to provide only the necessary model artifacts (for example, model weights, lookups, tokenizers, and so on). As part of the `PyTorchModel` object configuration, you will provide your inference code and other dependencies, and SageMaker will automatically package it for PTS.
- You can also package your model along with the inference code in a single archive. While this approach requires some additional work, it allows you to create a model package and deploy models without using the SageMaker SDK. SageMaker expects the following directory structure in this case:

```
model.tar.gz/
|- model_weights.pth
```

```
|- other_model_artifacts
|- code/
  |- inference.py
  |- requirements.txt  # optional
```

In this example, we will use the first option:

1. The following Bash script will download the required HuggingFace model artifacts and package them into a single `tar.gz archive`:

    ```
    mkdir distilbert-base-uncased-distilled-squad
    wget https://huggingface.co/distilbert-base-uncased-
    distilled-squad/resolve/main/pytorch_model.bin -P
    distilbert-base-uncased-distilled-squad
    wget https://huggingface.co/distilbert-base-uncased-
    distilled-squad/resolve/main/tokenizer.json -P
    distilbert-base-uncased-distilled-squad
    wget https://huggingface.co/distilbert-base-uncased-
    distilled-squad/resolve/main/tokenizer_config.json -P
    distilbert-base-uncased-distilled-squad
    wget https://huggingface.co/distilbert-base-uncased-
    distilled-squad/resolve/main/vocab.txt -P distilbert-
    base-uncased-distilled-squada
    wget https://huggingface.co/distilbert-base-uncased-
    distilled-squad/resolve/main/config.json -P distilbert-
    base-uncased-distilled-squad
    tar -C "$PWD" -czf distilbert-base-uncased-distilled-
    squad.tar.gz  distilbert-base-uncased-distilled-squad/
    ```

2. Then, we need to upload the model archive to Amazon S3 using the following code:

    ```python
    import sagemaker
    from sagemaker import get_execution_role
    sagemaker_session = sagemaker.Session()
    role = get_execution_role()
    bucket = sagemaker_session.default_bucket()
    prefix = 'torchserve'
    s3_path = 's3://{}/{}'.format(bucket, prefix)
    model_data = sagemaker_session.upload_data('distilbert-
    base-uncased-distilled-squad.tar.gz',bucket,os.path.
    join(prefix, 'model-artifacts'))
    ```

Next, we need to prepare some code to load models from the uploaded model artifacts and perform inference and data processing. This code is called the **inference handler** in PTS terminology.

Preparing the inference handler

SageMaker requires you to provide some code to load the model and run predictions so that you can preprocess incoming inference requests and post-process the response. To perform these operations, you need to implement the model_fn(), predict_fn(), input_fn(), and output_fn() methods. You can find implementations of the inference handler using the HuggingFace Pipeline API here: https://github.com/PacktPublishing/Accelerate-Deep-Learning-Workloads-with-Amazon-SageMaker/blob/main/chapter9/2_src/pipeline_predictor.py.

Deploying the model to a SageMaker endpoint

Deploying the model on PTS using the SageMaker SDK is straightforward. To configure PTS, we can use the "env" dictionary to set the appropriate environment variables in the serving container. Note that here, we explicitly reference the inference code via the "entry_point" parameter. Follow these steps:

1. As a prerequisite, you can add any other dependencies (for example, custom libraries or requirements.txt) to the "source_dir" location. The SageMaker SDK will automatically merge these assets with the model data into the MAR archive required by PTS:

```python
from sagemaker.pytorch import PyTorchModel
env = {
    "SAGEMAKER_TS_BATCH_SIZE": "2",
    "SAGEMAKER_TS_MAX_BATCH_DELAY": "1000",
    "SAGEMAKER_TS_RESPONSE_TIMEOUT" : "120",
    "SAGEMAKER_TS_MIN_WORKERS" : "1",
    "SAGEMAKER_TS_MAX_WORKERS" : "2"
    }
model = PyTorchModel(model_data=model_data,
                    role=role,
                    entry_point='pipeline_predictor.py',
                    source_dir='2_src',
                    framework_version='1.9.0',
                    py_version='py38',
                    env=env,
                    sagemaker_session=sagemaker_session)
```

2. Now, we can define the endpoint configuration and supported serializers and deserializers for the request/response pair:

```
from sagemaker.serializers import JSONSerializer
from sagemaker.deserializers import JSONDeserializer
remote_predictor = model.deploy(initial_
instance_count=1, instance_type="ml.
g4dn.4xlarge", serializer=JSONSerializer(),
deserializer=JSONDeserializer())
```

3. Now, we can run prediction by calling the .predict() method:

```
remote_predictor.predict(data)
```

4. We can also confirm that our PTS configurations have been applied properly. For this, you can open your SageMaker endpoint log stream and search for a log line, as shown here:

```
Model config:
{ "model": { "1.0": { "defaultVersion": true,
"marName": "model.mar", "minWorkers": 1, "maxWorkers":
2, "batchSize": 3, "maxBatchDelay": 100000,
"responseTimeout": 120 } } }
```

In this section, we discussed how PTS can be used to serve PyTorch models. In real production systems, you will probably prefer to convert your model into TorchScript format and further experiment with batching and worker scaling options to optimize your specific use case requirements.

In the next section, we will review a feature-rich framework-agnostic model server called NVIDIA Triton.

Using NVIDIA Triton

NVIDIA Triton is an open source model server developed by NVIDIA. It supports multiple DL frameworks (such as TensorFlow, PyTorch, ONNX, Python, and OpenVINO), as well various hardware platforms and runtime environments (NVIDIA GPUs, x86 and ARM CPUs, and AWS Inferentia). Triton can be used for inference in cloud and data center environments and edge or mobile devices. Triton is optimized for performance and scalability on various CPU and GPU platforms. NVIDIA provides a specialized utility for performance analysis and model analysis to improve Triton's performance.

Integration with SageMaker

You can use Triton model servers by utilizing a pre-built SageMaker DL container with it. Note that SageMaker Triton containers are not open source. You can find the latest list of Triton containers here: `https://github.com/aws/deep-learning-containers/blob/master/available_images.md#nvidia-triton-inference-containers-sm-support-only`.

SageMaker doesn't require you to provide inference custom code when deploying models on Triton. However, you will need to provide a Triton `config.pbtxt` file for each model you intend to serve. This config specifies the API contract for the inference request/response pair and other parameters on how the model needs to be served. You can review the possible configuration parameters by reading the official Triton documentation: `https://github.com/triton-inference-server/server/blob/main/docs/user_guide/model_configuration.md`.

Also, note that, unlike TFS and PTS, at the time of writing, SageMaker doesn't support hosting multiple independent models on Triton. However, you can still have multiple versions of the same model or organize several models into a pipeline.

Optimizing Triton inference

Triton provides several utilities to improve your performance:

- **Model Analyzer** allows you to understand the GPU memory utilization of your models so that you can understand how to run multiple models on a single GPU
- **Performance Analyzer** allows you to analyze your Triton inference and throughput

You won't be able to run Performance Analyzer directly against SageMaker Triton Endpoint since the SageMaker inference API doesn't match the Triton inference API. To bypass this limitation, you can run the Triton container locally on an instance of SageMaker Notebook with the target hardware accelerator and run an analysis against it.

Triton provides the following optimization features:

- **Dynamic batching**: This puts multiple inference requests into a batch to increase Triton throughput. This feature is similar to the batching we discussed for TFS and PTS model servers.
- **Model instances**: This specifies how many copies of each model will be available for inference. By default, a single instance of the model is loaded. Having more than one copy of the model typically results in better latency/throughout as it allows you to overlap memory transfer operations (for example, CPU to/from GPU) with inference compute. Having multiple instances also allows you to use all the available GPU resources more efficiently.

Both parameters can be configured via the `config.pbtxt` file. Let's gain some practical experience in using Triton on SageMaker.

Serving models with Triton on SageMaker

In this example, we will deploy the image classification PyTorch ResNet50 model using Triton. Our target hardware accelerator will be `ml.g4dn` instances. First, we need to compile the model to the TensorRT runtime; then, the compiled model will be packaged and deployed to the Triton model server. The sample code is available here: `https://github.com/PacktPublishing/Accelerate-Deep-Learning-Workloads-with-Amazon-SageMaker/blob/main/chapter9/3_NVIDIA_Triton_Server.ipynb`.

Note that the model compilation process described in the following subsection is specific to the PyTorch framework. If you choose to use the TensorFlow model, your model compilation and configuration will be different. You can refer to the Triton TensorFlow backend repository for details: `https://github.com/triton-inference-server/tensorflow_backend`.

Compiling the model for Triton

There are several ways you can compile your eager PyTorch model into TensorRT format, such as by converting your PyTorch model into ONNX format. Another way is to use the PyTorch JIT compiler to convert your eager model into TorchScript format natively. Recently, the PyTorch and NVIDIA teams have implemented an optimized way to compile your PyTorch model into a TensorRT runtime using the **Torch-TensorRT compiler**. This approach has several advantages as it allows you to use TensorRT-specific optimizations such as the GP16 and INT8 reduced precision types and NVIDIA GPU weight sparsity:

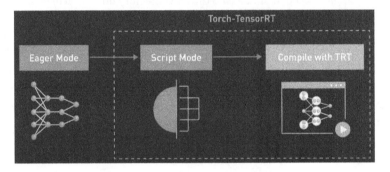

Figure 9.3 – Compiling the PyTorch model using TensorRT-Torch

To compile the PyTorch model using TensorRT-Torch, we need two components:

- A runtime environment for compilation. It's highly recommended to use NVIDIA's latest PyTorch containers for this purpose. Note that you will need to run this container on an instance with an NVIDIA GPU available. For instance, you can run this sample on a SageMaker Notebook whose type is `g4dn`.

- Compilation code. This code will be executed inside the NVIDIA PyTorch Docker container.

Now, let's review the compilation code:

1. We will start by loading the model from PyTorch Hub, setting it to evaluation mode, and placing it on the GPU device:

```
import torch
import torch_tensorrt
import os
torch.hub._validate_not_a_forked_repo = lambda a, b, c:
True
MODEL_NAME = "resnet50"
MODEL_VERSION = "1"
device = "cuda" if torch.cuda.is_available() else "cpu"
# load model
model = (torch.hub.load("pytorch/vision:v0.10.0", MODEL_
NAME, pretrained=True).eval().to(device))
```

2. Next, we will compile it using the TensorRT-Torch compiler. As part of the compiler configuration, we will specify the expected inputs and target precision. Note that since we plan to use dynamic batching for our model, we will provide several input shapes with different values for the batch dimensions:

```
# Compile with Torch TensorRT;
trt_model = torch_tensorrt.compile(
    model,
    inputs=[
        torch_tensorrt.Input(
            min_shape=(1, 3, 224, 224),
            opt_shape=(8, 3, 224, 224),
            max_shape=(16, 3, 224, 224),
            dtype=torch.float32,
        )
    ],
    enabled_precisions={ torch.float32 },
)
```

3. Finally, we will save our model to disk:

```
# Save the model
model_dir = os.path.join(os.getcwd(), "3_src", MODEL_
NAME, MODEL_VERSION)
```

```
os.makedirs(model_dir, exist_ok=True)
print(model_dir)
torch.jit.save(trt_model, os.path.join(model_dir, "model.
pt"))
```

4. To execute this script, you need to start a Docker container with the `docker run --gpus all --ipc=host --ulimit memlock=-1 --ulimit stack=67108864 -it --rm -v $PWD/chapter9/3_src:/workspace/3_src nvcr.io/nvidia/pytorch:22.05-py3` command.

5. Your console session will open inside a container, where you can execute the compilation script by running the `python 3_src/compile_tensorrt.py` command.

The resulting `model.pt` file will be available outside of the Docker container in the `3_src` directory.

Preparing the model config

Previously, we mentioned that Triton uses a configuration file with a specific convention to define model signatures and runtime configuration. The following code is for a `config.pbtxt` file that we can use to host the ResNet50 model. Here, we define batching parameters (the max batch size and dynamic batching config), input and output signatures, as well as model copies and the target hardware environment (via the `instance_group` object):

```
name: "resnet50"
platform: "pytorch_libtorch"
max_batch_size : 128
input [
  {
    name: "input__0"
    data_type: TYPE_FP32
    dims: [ 3, 224, 224 ]
  }
]
output [
  {
    name: "output__0"
    data_type: TYPE_FP32
    dims: [ 1, 1000 ,1, 1]
  }
]
dynamic_batching {
```

```
    preferred_batch_size: 128
    max_queue_delay_microseconds: 1000
  }
instance_group {
  count: 1
  kind: KIND_GPU
}
```

Refer to the Triton configuration for more details: `https://github.com/triton-inference-server/server/blob/main/docs/user_guide/model_configuration.md`.

Packaging the model artifacts

To deploy the compiled model with its configuration, we need to bundle everything into a single `tar.gz` archive and upload it to Amazon S3. The following code shows the directory structure within the model archive:

```
resnet50
|- 1
   |- model.pt
|- config.pbtxt
```

Once the model package has been uploaded to Amazon S3, we can deploy our Triton endpoint.

Deploying the Triton endpoint

The Triton inference container is not supported by the SageMaker Python SDK. Hence, we will need to use the boto3 SageMaker client to deploy the model. Follow these steps:

1. First, we need to identify the correct Triton image. Use the following code to find the Triton container URI based on your version of the Triton server (we used `22.05` for both model compilation and serving) and your AWS region:

    ```
    account_id_map = {
      # <REDACTED_FOR_BREVITY>
    }
    region = boto3.Session().region_name
    if region not in account_id_map.keys():
        raise("UNSUPPORTED REGION")
    base = "amazonaws.com.cn" if region.startswith("cn-")
    else "amazonaws.com"
    ```

```
triton_image_uri = "{account_id}.dkr.ecr.{region}.{base}/
sagemaker-tritonserver:22.05-py3".format(
    account_id=account_id_map[region], region=region,
base=base)
```

2. Next, we can create the model, which defines the model data and serving container, as well as other parameters, such as environment variables:

```
unique_id = time.strftime("%Y-%m-%d-%H-%M-%S", time.
gmtime())
sm_model_name = "triton-resnet50-" + unique_id
container = {
    "Image": triton_image_uri,
    "ModelDataUrl": model_data,
    "Environment": {"SAGEMAKER_TRITON_DEFAULT_MODEL_
NAME": "resnet50"},
}
create_model_response = sm_client.create_model(
    ModelName=sm_model_name, ExecutionRoleArn=role,
PrimaryContainer=container
)
```

3. After that, we can define the endpoint configuration:

```
endpoint_config_name = "triton-resnet50-" + unique_id
create_endpoint_config_response = sm_client.create_
endpoint_config(
    EndpointConfigName=endpoint_config_name,
    ProductionVariants=[
        {
            "InstanceType": "ml.g4dn.4xlarge",
            "InitialVariantWeight": 1,
            "InitialInstanceCount": 1,
            "ModelName": sm_model_name,
            "VariantName": "AllTraffic",
        }
    ],)
```

4. Now, we are ready to deploy our endpoint:

```
endpoint_name = "triton-resnet50-" + unique_id
create_endpoint_response = sm_client.create_endpoint(
    EndpointName=endpoint_name,
EndpointConfigName=endpoint_config_name)
```

Once the endpoint has been deployed, you can check SageMaker's endpoint logs to confirm that the Triton server has started and that the model was successfully loaded.

Running inference

To run inference, we must construct a payload according to the model signature defined in config. pbtxt. Take a look at the following inference call. The response will follow a defined output signature as well:

```
payload = {
    "inputs": [
        {
            "name": "input__0",
            "shape": [1, 3, 224, 224],
            "datatype": "FP32",
            "data": get_sample_image(),
        }
    ]
}
response = runtime_sm_client.invoke_
endpoint(    EndpointName=endpoint_name,
ContentType="application/octet-stream", Body=json.
dumps(payload))
predictions = json.loads(response["Body"].read().
decode("utf8"))
```

This section described the basic functionality of the Triton model server and how to use it on Amazon SageMaker. It's recommended that you refer to the Triton documentation to learn advanced features and optimization techniques. Keep in mind that depending on your chosen model format and DL framework, your model configuration will be different. You can review the AWS detailed benchmarking for the Triton server for the BERT model at https://aws.amazon.com/blogs/machine-learning/achieve-hyperscale-performance-for-model-serving-using-nvidia-triton-inference-server-on-amazon-sagemaker/. These benchmarks provide a good starting point for experimenting with and tuning Triton-hosted models.

Summary

In this chapter, we discussed how to use popular model servers – TensorFlow Serving, PyTorch TorchServe, and NVIDIA Triton – on Amazon SageMaker. Each model server provides rich functionality to deploy and tune your model inference. The choice of a specific model server may be driven by the DL framework, target hardware and runtime environments, and other preferences. NVIDIA Triton supports multiple model formats, target hardware platforms, and runtimes. At the same time, TensorFlow Serving and TorchServe provide native integration with their respective DL frameworks. Regardless of which model server you choose, to ensure optimal utilization of compute resources and inference performance, it's recommended to plan how you load test and benchmark your model with various server configurations.

In the next chapter, *Chapter 10, Operationalizing Inference Workloads*, we will discuss how to move and manage inference workloads in production environments. We will review SageMaker's capabilities for optimizing your inference workload costs, perform A/B testing, scale in and out endpoint resources based on inference traffic patterns, and advanced deployment patterns such as multi-model and multi-container endpoints.

10

Operationalizing Inference Workloads

In *Chapter 8, Considering Hardware for Inference*, and *Chapter 9, Implementing Model Servers*, we discussed how to engineer your **deep learning** (**DL**) inference workloads on Amazon SageMaker. We also reviewed how to select appropriate hardware for inference workloads, optimize model performance, and tune model servers based on specific use case requirements. In this chapter, we will focus on how to operationalize your DL inference workloads once they have been deployed to test and production environments.

In this chapter, we will start by reviewing advanced model hosting options such as **multi-model**, **multi-container**, and **Serverless Inference** endpoints to optimize your resource utilization and workload costs. Then, we will cover the **Application Auto Scaling** service for SageMaker, which provides another mechanism to improve resource utilization. Auto Scaling allows you to dynamically match your inference traffic requirements with provisioned inference resources.

After that, we will discuss how to continuously promote models and model versions without this impacting your end users. We will also cover some advanced deployment patterns required for A/B testing and quality assurance of model candidates. For this, we will review SageMaker's **Model Variant** and **Deployment Guardrails** capabilities.

Then, we review how to monitor model and inference data quality using SageMaker **Model Monitor**. We will close this chapter by discussing how to select an optimal inference workload configuration based on your use case type, its business, and technical requirements.

In this chapter, we will cover the following topics:

- Managing inference deployments
- Monitoring inference workloads
- Selecting your workload configuration

By the end of this chapter, you will have an understanding and practical skills on how to operationalize SageMaker inference workloads.

Technical requirements

In this chapter, we will provide code samples so that you can develop practical skills. The full code examples are available here: `https://github.com/PacktPublishing/Accelerate-Deep-Learning-Workloads-with-Amazon-SageMaker/blob/main/chapter10/`.

To follow along with this code, you will need the following:

- An AWS account and IAM user with permission to manage Amazon SageMaker resources.

- A SageMaker Notebook, SageMaker Studio Notebook, or local SageMaker-compatible environment established.

- Access to GPU training instances in your AWS account. Each example in this chapter will provide the recommended instance types to use. You may need to increase your compute quota for *SageMaker Training Job* to have GPU instances enabled. In this case, please follow the instructions at `https://docs.aws.amazon.com/sagemaker/latest/dg/regions-quotas.html`.

- You will need to install the required Python libraries by running `pip install -r requirements.txt`. The file that contains the required libraries can be found in the `chapter10` directory.

- In this chapter, we will provide examples of compiling models for inference, which requires access to specific accelerator types. Please review the instance recommendations as part of the model server examples.

Managing inference deployments

In *Chapter 1*, *Introducing Deep Learning with Amazon SageMaker*, we discussed that SageMaker provides several options when it comes to running your inference workloads, depending on your use case's requirements, as follows:

- **Real-time endpoints** are designed for inference use cases with low latency requirements. It comes with certain limitations on payload size (up to 5 MB) and response latency (up to 60 seconds).

- **Batch transform jobs** are an option for processing large-scale batched inference requests in an offline fashion.

- **Asynchronous endpoints** allow you to queue and process inference requests in near-real time. It also has a much higher limit on inference payload size (up to 1 GB) compared to real-time endpoints.

So far in this book, we have covered how to deploy a **single model** for your inference workload. This is supported by all three inference options listed previously.

However, for real-time endpoints, it's possible to package and deploy several models and model versions (known as **production variants**) behind a single endpoint. In this section, we will dive deeper into these model deployment strategies and highlight implementation details, their advantages, and certain limitations.

Additionally, we will review the recently introduced **Serverless Inference** endpoints. Like real-time endpoints, serverless endpoints are designed to serve users in real time. However, in the case of serverless endpoints, you will have access to compute resources without the need to choose provision and scale inference instances.

Considering model deployment options

In many situations, hosting a single model behind a dedicated SageMaker real-time endpoint can lead to sub-optimal resource utilization and additional costs that can be avoided. For example, when you need to simultaneously host a fleet of models, each with low resource requirements, hosting each model behind an individual endpoint would be a major avoidable cost.

SageMaker provides a range of model deployment options that can address more complex use cases. In the following subsections, we will discuss their target use cases, advantages, and limitations.

Multi-model endpoints

A **multi-model endpoint** (MME) is a special type of SageMaker model endpoint that allows you to host thousands of models behind a single endpoint simultaneously. This type of endpoint is suitable for scenarios for similarly sized models with relatively low resource requirements that can be served from the same inference container.

MMEs and their underlying model servers manage resource allocation, such as unloading infrequently used models and loading requested ones when an instance runs out of memory. This leads to additional inference latency when the user requests a model that is currently not loaded into memory. Hence, MMEs may not be a good fit for scenarios where consistently low latency is required. This additional latency can increase when hosting large models with evenly distributed traffic patterns as this will lead to frequent unloading and loading of models.

To provision an MME, you need to package each model (model artifacts and inference code) into a separate archive and upload it to Amazon S3. Once the MME instance has been provisioned, it is downloaded from the S3 location to the instance disk, which loads the models into instance memory. By default, if the MME runs out of instance disk space and/or instance memory, SageMaker deletes the least recently used models from the local disk and/or unloads models from memory to accommodate the requested models.

The following diagram shows the MME architecture:

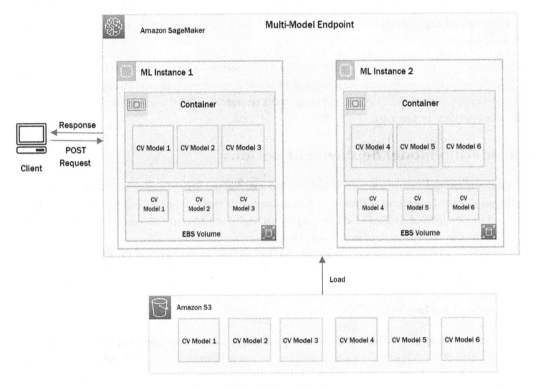

Figure 10.1 – MME architecture

MMEs are supported by PyTorch and TensorFlow inference containers. You can also automatically scale MMEs in and out to match your inference traffic. MMEs allow you to directly invoke models as well as inference pipelines comprising several models.

When selecting an instance type and family, consider the following aspects:

- Instance memory defines how many models can be loaded simultaneously
- Instance disk size defines how many models can be cached locally to avoid expensive download procedures from S3
- The number of vCPUs defines how many inference requests can be handled simultaneously

Note that GPU-based instances are not supported for MMEs, which limits what model architectures can be served using MMEs within reasonable SLAs.

Now, let's learn how to implement an MME.

Implementing an MME

In this code sample, we will learn how to deploy two NLP models simultaneously using an MME. One model analyzes the sentiment of German text, while the other analyzes the sentiment of English text. We will use the HuggingFace PyTorch container for this. The full code is available here: `https://github.com/PacktPublishing/Accelerate-Deep-Learning-Workloads-with-Amazon-SageMaker/blob/main/chapter10/1_Multi_Model_Endpoint.ipynb`.

For this task, we will use two models, trained to predict the sentiment of English and German texts: `distilbert-base-uncased-finetuned-sst-2-english` and `oliverguhr/german-sentiment-bert`, respectively. Follow these steps:

1. We will start by fetching the models from the HuggingFace Model hub and saving them locally. The following code shows the English model:

    ```
    import torch
    from transformers import DistilBertTokenizer,
    DistilBertForSequenceClassification
    en_tokenizer = DistilBertTokenizer.from_pretrained(EN_
    MODEL)
    en_model = DistilBertForSequenceClassification.from_
    pretrained(EN_MODEL)
    en_model_path = "models/english_sentiment"
    os.makedirs(en_model_path, exist_ok=True)
    en_model.save_pretrained(save_directory=en_model_path)
    en_tokenizer.save_pretrained(save_directory=en_model_
    path)
    ```

    As a result, the following artifacts are downloaded:

    ```
    ('models/english_sentiment/tokenizer_config.json',
     'models/english_sentiment/special_tokens_map.json',
     'models/english_sentiment/vocab.txt',
     'models/english_sentiment/added_tokens.json')
    ```

    These model artifacts will be added to the model data package later. But first, we need to develop the inference script.

2. An MME has the same requirements as those for the inference scripts of single-model endpoints. The following code shows the inference script for the English model, which implements the required methods for model loading, inference, and data pre-/post-processing:

    ```
    def model_fn(model_dir):
        tokenizer = DistilBertTokenizer.from_
    pretrained(model_dir)
    ```

```
      model = DistilBertForSequenceClassification.from_
pretrained(model_dir)
      return model, tokenizer
def input_fn(serialized_input_data, content_type=JSON_
CONTENT_TYPE):
      if content_type == JSON_CONTENT_TYPE:
          input_data = json.loads(serialized_input_data)
          return input_data
      else:
          Exception("Requested unsupported ContentType in
Accept: " + content_type)
def predict_fn(input_data, model_tokenizer_tuple):
      model, tokenizer = model_tokenizer_tuple
      inputs = tokenizer(input_data, return_tensors="pt")
      with torch.no_grad():
          logits = model(**inputs).logits
      predicted_class_id = logits.argmax().item()
      predictions = model.config.id2label[predicted_class_
id]
      return predictions
def output_fn(prediction_output, accept=JSON_CONTENT_
TYPE):
      if accept == JSON_CONTENT_TYPE:
          return json.dumps(prediction_output), accept
      raise Exception("Requested unsupported ContentType in
Accept: " + accept)
```

3. Next, we need to package the model and inference code for the MME. SageMaker requests a specific directory structure that varies for PyTorch and TensorFlow containers. For PyTorch containers, the model and code should be packaged into a single `tar.gz` archive and have the following structure:

```
model.tar.gz/
              |- model.pth # and any other model artifacts
              |- code/
                      |- inference.py
                      |- requirements.txt # optional
```

Each model should have a model package. Once the packages have been prepared locally, we need to upload them to Amazon S3 and save the respective URI:

```
en_model_data = sagemaker_session.upload_data('models/
english_sentiment.tar.gz', bucket=bucket,key_
prefix=prefix)
ger_model_data = sagemaker_session.upload_data('models/
german_sentiment.tar.gz', bucket=bucket,key_
prefix=prefix)
```

4. Once the data has been uploaded, we need to define the respective serving container and configure it to be used for the MME. The following code locates the PyTorch container based on the desired runtime configuration and task (inference):

```
from sagemaker import image_uris
HF_VERSION = '4.17.0'
PT_VERSION = 'pytorch1.10.2'
pt_container_uri = image_uris.
retrieve(framework='huggingface',
                                    region=region,
                                    version=HF_VERSION,
                                    image_scope='inference',
                                    base_framework_
version=PT_VERSION,
                                    instance_type='ml.
c5.xlarge')
```

5. Then, we need to configure the MME parameters. Specifically, we must define the MultiModel mode. Note that we provide two specific environment variables – SAGEMAKER_PROGRAM and SAGEMAKER_SUBMIT_DIRECTORY – so that the SageMaker inference framework knows how to register the model handler:

```
container  = {
    'Image': pt_container_uri,
    'ContainerHostname': 'MultiModel',
    'Mode': 'MultiModel',
    'ModelDataUrl': mm_data_path,
    'Environment': {
    'SAGEMAKER_PROGRAM':'inference.py',
    'SAGEMAKER_SUBMIT_DIRECTORY':mm_data_path
    }
}
```

6. The last step of configuring the MME is to create a SageMaker model instance, endpoint configuration, and the endpoint itself. When creating the model, we must provide the `MultiModel`-enabled container from the preceding step. We have omitted the creation of the endpoint configuration and endpoint for brevity:

```
unique_id = datetime.datetime.now().strftime("%Y-%m-%d%H-
%M-%S")
model_name = f"mme-sentiment-model-{unique_id}"
create_model_response = sm_client.create_model(
    ModelName=model_name,
    PrimaryContainer=container,
    ExecutionRoleArn=role,
)
```

7. Once the endpoint has been created, we can run and invoke our models. For this, in the invocation request, we need to supply a special parameter called `TargetModel`, as follows:

```
ger_response = runtime_sm_client.invoke_endpoint(
    EndpointName=endpoint_name,
    ContentType="application/json",
    Accept="application/json",
    TargetModel="german_sentiment.tar.gz",
    Body=json.dumps(ger_input),
)
```

While the MME capability provides a convenient way to optimize your inference costs when running multiple similar models, it requires models to have the same runtime environment (in other words, they must use the same inference container). To address scenarios where you need to host multiple models within different inference containers, SageMaker supports **multi-container endpoints** (**MCEs**), as shown in the next section.

Multi-Container Endpoints

An MCE allows you to host up to 15 inference containers simultaneously. In this case, each container would serve its own model. MCEs are a good fit for use cases where models require different runtime environments/containers but not every single model can fully utilize the available instance resources. Another scenario is when models are called at different times.

Unlike an MME, an MCE doesn't cache or unload containers based on their invocation patterns. Hence, you need to ensure that the inference containers will collectively have enough resources to run on the endpoint instance. If the instance resources (for example, instance memory) are not enough to run all containers, you may see an error during MCE creation time. Hence, you need to consider the total resource requirements of all the inference containers when choosing an instance configuration. Each inference container will have a proportional amount of resources available for it. The following diagram shows the MCE architecture:

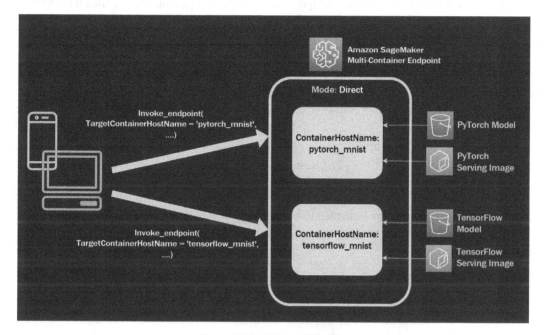

Figure 10.2 – MCE architecture

You can automatically scale an MCE. It supports **Direct** mode (invoking inference containers directly) or **Serial** mode (invoking several containers sequentially).

At the time of writing this book, MCEs don't support GPU-based instances.

Now, let's learn how to create an MCE by using a simple example of running TensorFlow and PyTorch models simultaneously. This will give you some practical skills in terms of how to create and use an MCE.

Implementing an MCE

In this example, we will run an inference workload with two NLP models using different runtime environments: TensorFlow and PyTorch. We will host the Q&A model in a TensorFlow container and the text summarization model in a PyTorch container.

Creating an MCE is very similar to creating an MME with a few notable exceptions, which we will highlight in the following steps:

1. Fetching the model data, inference scripts, and model packaging is identical to what we did for the MME. Note that since one of our endpoints will run the TensorFlow container, the Q&A model should comply with the following directory structure:

```
model.tar.gz/
             |--[model_version_number]/
                                      |--variables
                                      |--saved_model.pb
         code/
             |--inference.py
             |--requirements.txt # optional
```

2. Next, we will configure the container and create the model package. Note that we provide two containers and endpoint mode, Direct, while creating the model package:

```
model_name = f"mce-nlp-model-{unique_id}"
create_model_response = sm_client.create_model(
    ModelName=model_name,
    Containers=[tensorflow_container, pytorch_container],
    InferenceExecutionConfig={"Mode": "Direct"},
    ExecutionRoleArn=role,
)
```

3. Then, we will create the endpoint configuration and endpoint. This step is similar to that for the MME, so we have omitted the code snippet for brevity.

4. Once the endpoint has been deployed, we are ready to send inference traffic. Note that we supply the TargetContainerHostname header so that SageMaker knows where to route our inference request:

```
tf_response = runtime_sm_client.invoke_endpoint(
    EndpointName=endpoint_name,
    ContentType="application/json",
    Accept="application/json",
    TargetContainerHostname="tensorflow-distilbert-qa",
    Body=json.dumps(qa_inputs),
)
```

So far, we have discussed how to host multiple models on SageMaker. Next, we will discuss how to safely promote a new version of the model (or a different model altogether) while keeping the endpoint operational for end users. For this, we will review SageMaker multi-variant endpoints.

Multi-variant endpoints

A production variant is a SageMaker-specific concept that defines a combination of the model, its container, and the resources required to run this model. As such, this is an extremely flexible concept that can be used for different use cases, such as the following:

- Different model versions with the same runtime and resource requirements
- Different models with different runtimes and/or resource requirements
- The same model with different runtimes and/or resource requirements

Additionally, as part of the variant configuration, you also define its traffic weights, which can be then updated without them having any impact on endpoint availability. Once deployed, the production variant can be invoked directly (so you can bypass SageMaker traffic shaping) or as part of the SageMaker endpoint call (then, SageMaker traffic shaping is not bypassed). The following diagram provides more details:

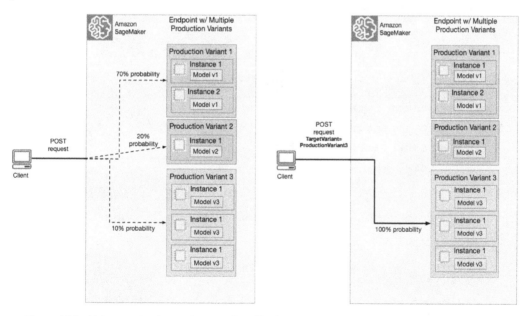

Figure 10.3 – Using production variants with traffic shaping (left) and with a direct invocation (right)

When updating production variants, the real-time endpoint stays available and no interruption occurs for the end users. This also means that you will incur additional costs, as each production variant will have an associated cost.

Now, let's see how we can use production variants to test a new production variant.

Using production variants for A/B testing

In this example, we will register two different models for the same Q&A NLP task. Then, we will shape the inference traffic using the production variant weights and invoke the models directly. The full code is available here: `https://github.com/PacktPublishing/Accelerate-Deep-Learning-Workloads-with-Amazon-SageMaker/blob/main/chapter10/4_AB_Testing.ipynb`. Follow these steps:

1. We will start by creating two HuggingFace models using the `HuggingFaceModel` class. We have omitted this for brevity.

2. Then, we will create two different endpoint variants. We start with the equal weights parameter, which tells SageMaker that inference traffic should split evenly between model variants:

```python
from sagemaker.session import production_variant
variant1 = production_variant(
    model_name=model1_name,
    instance_type="ml.c5.4xlarge",
    initial_instance_count=1,
    variant_name="Variant1",
    initial_weight=1,
)
variant2 = production_variant(
    model_name=model2_name,
    instance_type="ml.c5.4xlarge",
    initial_instance_count=1,
    variant_name="Variant2",
    initial_weight=1,
)
```

3. After that, we create the endpoint based on our configured production variants:

```python
from datetime import datetime
endpoint_name = f"ab-testing-{datetime.now():%Y-%m-%d-%H-%M-%S}"
sagemaker_session.endpoint_from_production_variants(
    name=endpoint_name, production_variants=[variant1,
variant2]))
```

4. Once the endpoint has been deployed, we can run inference against the newly created endpoint. Once you run the following code, the resulting statistics should show that each production variant served ~50% of inference traffic:

```
results = {"Variant1": 0, "Variant2": 0, "total_count":
0}
for i in range(20):
    response = sm_runtime_client.invoke_
endpoint(EndpointName=endpoint_name,
ContentType="application/json", Body=json.dumps(data))
    results[response['InvokedProductionVariant']] += 1
    results["total_count"] += 1
```

5. Next, we can update the weights of our endpoint variants. Re-running the previous inference test loop should now show that only ~10% of traffic is served by `"Variant1"`, which is expected based on the provided variant traffic weights:

```
sm_client.update_endpoint_weights_and_capacities(
    EndpointName=endpoint_name,
    DesiredWeightsAndCapacities=[
        {"DesiredWeight": 10, "VariantName": "Variant1"},
        {"DesiredWeight": 90, "VariantName":
"Variant2"},])
```

6. We can also bypass SageMaker traffic shaping and directly invoke a specific variant by using the `TargetVariant` parameter, as follows:

```
sm_runtime_client.invoke_endpoint(EndpointName=endpoint_
name, TargetVariant="Variant2", ContentType="application/
json", Body=json.dumps(data))
```

SageMaker's production variants provide you with a flexible mechanism to operate your inference workloads in production or production-like environments.

Serverless inference endpoints

Using **serverless inference endpoints (SIEs)** is another deployment option available on SageMaker. It allows you to provision real-time inference endpoints without the need to provision and configure the underlying endpoint instances. SageMaker automatically provisions and scales the underlying available compute resources based on your inference traffic. Your SIE can scale them down to 0 in cases where there is no inference traffic.

SIEs are a good fit for scenarios where there's an uneven traffic pattern and you can tolerate short periods of elevated latency during a **cold start**. A cold start period specifies the time needed to provision new serverless resources and deploy your model runtime environment. Since larger models generally have longer deployment times than smaller ones, they will have longer cold start periods too. One potential use case for Serverless Inference is using it in test and sandbox environments. With an SIE, you pay only for the time that the SIE takes to process the inference request.

Serverless Inference is functionally similar to SageMaker real-time inference. It supports many types of inference containers, including PyTorch and TensorFlow inference containers. However, Serverless Inference also has several limitations, including the following:

- No GPU resources are available

- The instance disk size is 5 GB

- The maximum concurrency for the endpoint is 200; requests beyond this limit will be throttled by SageMaker

- The cold start period depends on your model size and inference container start time

When creating SIE resources, you can choose from the list of available memory options, and SageMaker will automatically assign the proportional number of vCPUs. During the memory configuration, you will need the size of the memory to be at least slightly higher than your model size, and the minimum memory size must be 1,024 MB; the maximum is 6,144 MB. If your model performance is CPU-bound, you may choose a bigger memory configuration to have more vCPU resources.

Now, let's see how we can deploy a serverless endpoint using the SageMaker Python SDK.

Deploying a serverless endpoint

In this example, we will deploy the Q&A NLP model from the HuggingFace Model hub. The full code is available here: `https://github.com/PacktPublishing/Accelerate-Deep-Learning-Workloads-with-Amazon-SageMaker/blob/main/chapter10/3_Serverless_Inference.ipynb`. Follow these steps:

1. We will start by defining the SageMaker model to deploy. For this, we will fetch a CPU version of the HuggingFace inference container using the built-in `image_uris` method, as follows:

```
From sagemaker import image_uris
HF_VERSION = '4.17.0'
PT_VERSION = 'pytorch1.10.2'
hf_container_uri = image_uris.
retrieve(framework='huggingface',
                         region=region,
                              version=HF_VERSION,
```

```
                                          image_scope='inference',
                                          base_framework_
version=PT_VERSION,
                                          instance_type='ml.
c5.xlarge')
```

2. Then, we will use the `HuggingFaceModel` instance to configure the model architecture and target NLP task:

```
Hub = {
    'HF_MODEL_ID':'distilbert-base-uncased-distilled-
squad',
    'HF_TASK':'question-answering'
}
huggingface_model = HuggingFaceModel(
    env=hub,
    role= role,
    transformers_version=HF_VERSION,
    pytorch_version=PT_VERSION,
    image_uri=hf_container_uri,
)
```

3. Next, we will define the serverless configuration and deploy our first endpoint. Here, the `memory_size_in_mb` parameter defines the initial memory behind your endpoint and the `max_concurrency` parameter defines the maximum number of concurrent invocations your endpoint can handle before inference traffic gets throttled by SageMaker:

```
Serverless_config = ServerlessInferenceConfig(
    memory_size_in_mb=4096, max_concurrency=10,
)
predictor = huggingface_model.deploy(
    serverless_inference_config=serverless_config
)
```

That's it! In several minutes, your endpoint will be deployed. After that, you can use it as any other real-time endpoint.

With Serverless Inference, SageMaker automatically scales in and out of your endpoints without much input from your side other than the memory sizing and concurrency. In the next section, we will review the endpoint autoscaling capability, which provides you more with fine-grained control over scaling behavior.

Advanced model deployment techniques

In this section, we will discuss some advanced techniques for managing your SageMaker inference resources, namely autoscaling and blue/green deployments.

Autoscaling endpoints

SageMaker allows you to automatically scale out (increase the number of instances) and scale in (decrease the number of instances) for real-time endpoints and asynchronous endpoints. When inference traffic increases, scaling out maintains steady endpoint performance while keeping costs to a minimum. When inference traffic decreases, scaling in allows you to minimize the inference costs. For real-time endpoints, the minimum instance size is 1; asynchronous endpoints can scale to 0 instances. The following diagram shows this:

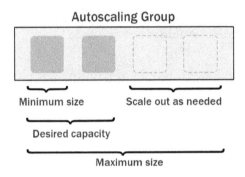

Figure 10.4 – Autoscaling concepts

During scaling events, SageMaker endpoints remain fully available for end users. In the case of downsizing an endpoint, SageMaker automatically drains traffic from instances so that they can be removed. To ensure additional resiliency, SageMaker places instances in different **availability zones**.

To autoscale your endpoint, you need to create a production variant for your model. After that, you must define the desired scaling behavior in the **autoscaling policy**. SageMaker supports four types of scaling policies, as follows:

- **Simple scaling** (or `TargetTrackingScaling`) allows you to scale endpoints based on the value of specific Amazon CloudWatch metrics. SageMaker supports several endpoint metrics out of the box, but you can also use your own custom metrics. The **CPUUtilization**, **GPUUtilization**, and **SageMakerVariantInvocationsPerInstance** metrics are usually good starting choices.

- **Step scaling** is a more advanced scaling policy that allows you to have finer control over how many instances are provisioned based on the size of the metric value change. This policy requires careful configuration and testing with various load profile values.

- **Scheduled scaling** allows you to scale endpoints based on a predefined schedule. For instance, you can scale in after hours, and scale out during peak work hours.

- **On-Demand scaling** changes the endpoint instance count based on explicit user requests.

When selecting and configuring autoscaling policies, you may start by analyzing your traffic patterns and how they correlate with your endpoint metrics. Load profiles define which type of scaling policy to choose, while correlating to endpoint metrics allows you to select good tracking metrics. It's recommended that you start with a simple baseline (for example, simple scaling with the CPUUtilization tracking metric). Then, you can fine-tune it over time as you observe other traffic patterns and how autoscaling reacts to them.

In the following example, we will learn how to apply autoscaling policies to a SageMaker real-time endpoint.

Implementing autoscaling for inference endpoints

In this example, we will learn how to apply the target tracking autoscaling policy to a real-time endpoint. The full code is available here: `https://github.com/PacktPublishing/Accelerate-Deep-Learning-Workloads-with-Amazon-SageMaker/blob/main/chapter10/5_AutoScaling.ipynb`. Follow these steps:

1. We will start by creating a regular SageMaker real-time endpoint. We have omitted this code for brevity.

2. Next, we will create two autoscaling resources: a **scalable target** and a **scaling policy**. The scalable target defines a specific AWS resource that we want to scale using the Application Auto Scaling service.

   In the following code snippet, we are instantiating the client for the Application Auto Scaling service and registering our SageMaker endpoint as a scalable target. Note that the `ResourceId` parameter defines a reference to a specific endpoint and production variant. The `ScalableDimension` parameter for SageMaker resources always references the number of instances behind the production variant. `MinCapacity` and `MaxCapacity` define the instance scaling range:

   ```
   import boto3
   as_client = boto3.client('application-autoscaling')
   resource_id=f"endpoint/{predictor.endpoint_name}/variant/
   AllTraffic"
   policy_name = f'Request-ScalingPolicy-{predictor.
   endpoint_name}'
   scalable_dimension =
   'sagemaker:variant:DesiredInstanceCount'
   # scaling configuration
   response = as_client.register_scalable_target(
   ```

```
    ServiceNamespace='sagemaker', #
    ResourceId=resource_id,
    ScalableDimension='sagemaker:variant:DesiredInstance
Count',
    MinCapacity=1,
    MaxCapacity=4
)
```

3. Next, we will create a policy for our scalable target. Here, we chose to use the target tracking policy type with the following parameters:

```
response = as_client.put_scaling_policy(
    PolicyName=policy_name,
    ServiceNamespace='sagemaker',
    ResourceId=resource_id,
    ScalableDimension=scalable_dimension,
    PolicyType='TargetTrackingScaling',
    TargetTrackingScalingPolicyConfiguration={
        'TargetValue': 10.0, # Threshold
        'PredefinedMetricSpecification': {
            'PredefinedMetricType':
'SageMakerVariantInvocationsPerInstance',
        },
        'ScaleInCooldown': 300, # duration until scale in
        'ScaleOutCooldown': 60 # duration between scale
out
    }
)
```

4. Once the policy is in place, we can test it. For this, we need to generate sufficient inference traffic to breach the target metric value for a duration longer than the scale-out cooldown period. For this purpose, we can use the Locust.io load testing framework (https://locust.io/), which provides a simple mechanism to mimic various load patterns. Follow the instructions in the notebook to create a Locust configuration for your endpoint and provide your AWS credentials for authorization purposes.

5. Once the configuration is complete, you can start your Locust client to generate load using the following terminal command. It generates an inference load of up to 20 concurrent users for 5 minutes. This load profile should trigger a scaling-out event for our endpoint:

```
locust -f ../utils/load_testing/locustfile.py --headless
-u 20 -r 1 --run-time 5m
```

6. During the load test, you can observe your endpoint status as well as the associated scaling alerts in the Amazon CloudWatch console. First, you can see that scale-out and scale-in alerts have been configured based on the provided cooldown periods and target metric value:

	Name	State	Last state update	Conditions
☐	TargetTracking-endpoint/qa-tensorflow-2022-08-28-17-17-39-297/variant/AllTraffic-AlarmLow-1397a1f4-2a7f-474f-8425-341bc8a0359a	⊘ OK	2022-08-28 13:27:07	InvocationsPerInstance < 9 for 15 datapoints within 15 minutes
☐	TargetTracking-endpoint/qa-tensorflow-2022-08-28-17-17-39-297/variant/AllTraffic-AlarmHigh-21e525f5-6c42-4a6b-9d1a-137814037b48	⊘ OK	2022-08-28 13:22:42	InvocationsPerInstance > 10 for 3 datapoints within 3 minutes

Figure 10.5 – Autoscaling alerts for SageMaker endpoints

7. After the initial scale-out cooldown period has passed, the scale-out alert switches to the **In alarm** state, which causes the endpoint to scale out. Note that in the following screenshot, the red line is the desired value of the tracking metric, while the blue line is the number of invocations per endpoint instance:

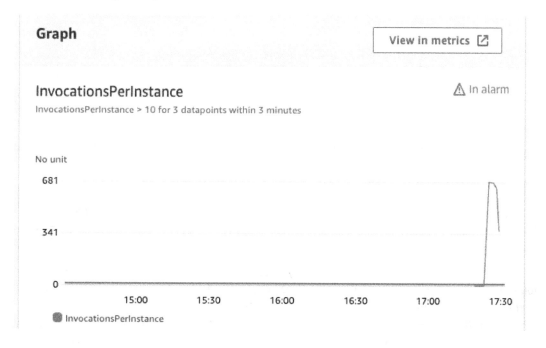

Figure 10.6 – Triggered a scaling-out alert

8. After triggering scaling out, your endpoint status will change from `in Service` to `Updating`. Now, we can run the `describe_endpoint()` method to confirm that the number of instances has been increased. Since we are generating a sufficiently large concurrent load in a short period, SageMaker immediately scaled our endpoint to the maximum number of instances. The following code is for the `describe_endpoint()` method:

```
. . .
"ProductionVariants": [
  {
    "VariantName": "AllTraffic",
    . . .
  ],
    "CurrentWeight": 1,
    "DesiredWeight": 1,
    "CurrentInstanceCount": 1,
    "DesiredInstanceCount": 4
  }
]
'EndpointStatus': 'Updating'
. . .
```

Since we are no longer running an inference traffic generator, we should expect our endpoint to scale in once the scale-in cooldown period has passed.

In the next section, we will review how to securely and reliably deploy model candidates using SageMaker Deployment Guardrails.

Using blue/green deployment patterns

So far, we have discussed how to deploy and update SageMaker endpoints via APIs or SDK calls. However, this approach may not fit when you're updating mission-critical workloads in production, where you need to have additional checks to ensure smooth production rollout.

SageMaker **Deployment Guardrails** is a fully managed endpoint promotion mechanism. Guardrails follows the blue/green deployment concept, which is common for DevOps practices. Here, the blue fleet is the old deployment (the production variant in the case of SageMaker endpoints), while the green fleet is the new version to be deployed. SageMaker provisions a green fleet next to the blue fleet. Once the green fleet is ready and healthy, SageMaker starts shifting traffic according to the predefined rules from the blue fleet to the green fleet.

Deployment Guardrails supports several modes of traffic shifting:

- **All at once** mode shifts all traffic from blue to green in one step once the green fleet is up and healthy. At this point, SageMaker decommissions the blue fleet.

- **Canary** mode shifts a small portion of traffic to the green fleet. Then, if the canaries are healthy, SageMaker shifts the remainder of the traffic to the green fleet. After that, SageMaker decommissions the blue fleet.

- **Linear** mode gradually shifts the traffic from the blue fleet to the green fleet.

Note that during a blue-green deployment, you will incur costs for both the blue and green fleets while they are running. If, during the rollout, the green fleet becomes unhealthy, SageMaker will execute an automatic rollback to the initial deployment to avoid any impact on the end user experience.

Deployment Guardrails doesn't support the following features:

- Marketplace containers

- Multi-container endpoints

- Multi-model endpoints

- Multi-variant endpoints

- Endpoints that use Inferentia-based instances

- Endpoints that use Amazon SageMaker Model Monitor (with data capture enabled)

Practicing setting up deployment guardrails is outside the scope of this book, as these types of tasks are typically performed by dedicated DevOps/MLOps teams. However, it's important to understand that SageMaker supports such capabilities out of the box.

Monitoring inference workloads

In this section, we will cover the available mechanisms for monitoring inference workloads.

Using Amazon CloudWatch

Throughout this book, we have frequently referenced Amazon CloudWatch. SageMaker relies on it for all monitoring needs, specifically the following:

- Uses CloudWatch Logs to collect, organize, and manage SageMaker logs (for example, your model server logs)

- Uses CloudWatch Metrics to measure endpoint characteristics such as latency, resource utilization, and others

- Uses CloudWatch alarms to trigger autoscaling events

SageMaker inference workloads support several metrics out of the box. Depending on the chosen inference workload option and deployment pattern, your default SageMaker metrics may vary. For instance, for an MME, you will have additional default metrics to measure some specific characteristics, such as the model's performance and loading time. We recommend that you refer to the SageMaker documentation for the most up-to-date information on default SageMaker metrics: `https://docs.aws.amazon.com/sagemaker/latest/dg/monitoring-cloudwatch.html`.

If, for some reason, the out-of-the-box metrics are not sufficient for your use case, you can always create custom metrics. Some scenarios where custom metrics can be useful are as follows:

- Your model and model server require custom metrics for appropriate scaling.
- You need a higher resolution of metrics. Note that SageMaker default metrics to a 1-second resolution.
- You need to do custom metrics pre-processing. For instance, you may need to apply a sliding window average that's not supported by CloudWatch.

You can also create custom CloudWatch alarms. Note that you can create alarms for both metrics and logs. CloudWatch alarms can be used to notify you about specific events via email or text notifications (this will require integrating your alarms with the Amazon SNS service).

Another popular use case for CloudWatch alarms is to perform actions once an alarm is triggered. We have already seen how CloudWatch alarms are used to scale your SageMaker endpoint in and out. However, you can use alarms for any other custom logic. For example, you may integrate your custom alarm with an Amazon Lambda serverless function. Your function and its custom logic (for example, an endpoint update action) will be executed once the alarms is triggered.

Monitoring inference workload quality

SageMaker Model Monitor is a purpose-built capability for measuring and continuously monitoring the quality of your inference. It allows you to calculate baseline statistics for your inference inputs and model outputs and then monitor how your models perform against baseline statistics in near-real time. In the case of significant deviations from the predefined statistical constraints, SageMaker Model Monitor will generate an alert to notify you that your model may be not performing according to the desired quality metrics.

Model Monitor comprises several components for monitoring different aspects of your inference quality:

- **Data quality monitoring** allows you to detect **data drift** between data used to train your model and real inference traffic against the deployed model. Data drift usually results in a lower-than-expected quality of your model predictions. To detect data drift, Model Monitor calculates statistics for the training data (baseline), captures the inference traffic, and continuously compares these statistics to the baseline.

- **Model quality monitoring** allows you to compare your model predictions to the predefined ground truth labels. If your model predictions violate the ground truth predictions by predefined constraints, Model Monitor will generate an alert.

- **Bias drift monitoring** allows you to detect bias in your model predictions and how it changes over time. Model bias can be introduced when inference traffic is different from the data used for model training. To detect bias, Model Monitor calculates a specific bias metric called **Difference in Positive Proportions in Predicted Label** (DPPL). When the DPPL metric violates a predefined range of values, an alert is generated.

- **Model feature attribution monitoring** is another way to ensure that new bias is not introduced during model deployment. Feature attribution drift means that the influence that a specific feature has over an inference result changes over time.

> **Note**
> Model Monitor only supports tabular data as inference inputs. This limits its applicability to DL inference since in most cases, DL models are used to perform inference on unstructured data, such as images or text.

There are several scenarios where Model Monitor can apply to DL inference:

- If you are using DL models to run classification or regression inference tasks. In practice, this rarely happens since classical **machine learning** (ML) algorithms (for example, XGBoost) often outperform DL models on such tasks and require a fraction of the resources for training and inference compared to more expensive DL models.

- If your inference input can be converted from an unstructured format into a structured format before it's sent to the SageMaker inference resource – for example, if you convert your unstructured text into a tokenized input and send it for inference. In this case, the tokenized input can be represented as a tabular dataset so that it can be used with Model Monitor.

Note that you can still use Model Monitor to ensure your model accuracy with DL workloads for scenarios where your model has either classification or regression outputs.

Selecting your workload configuration

In the previous three chapters, we reviewed the different capabilities Amazon SageMaker provides to engineer and operate inference workloads: from selecting optimal compute instances and runtime environments to configuring model servers and managing and monitoring deployed models.

In this section, we will summarize various selection criteria that you can use when selecting inference workload configurations. Then, we will suggest a simple algorithm that will guide the decision-making process when you're choosing your inference configuration.

When engineering your inference workload, you may consider the following selection criteria:

- **Business use case**: This allows you to understand your business opportunity and end user experience by using your inference service. Analyzing your use case drives important decisions such as selecting the right SageMaker inference option and end user SLAs.

- **Inference SLAs**: We have discussed two key inference SLAs in this book: latency and throughput. Understanding the desired SLAs drives decisions such as which instance type to use, model server configuration, and others.

- **Budget and cost**: It's important to forecast both the inference budget and the setup mechanisms to monitor for budget usage (the running cost of inference). In the case of a budget overrun, you may want to have a mechanism to react to such an event (for example, sending a notification, scaling down an endpoint, and so on).

- **Compute instances**: When you choose compute instances, you need to consider multiple factors, such as which model architecture you intend to use, your SLAs, and others. The process of selecting an instance type is called rightsizing and requires load tests and benchmarking to be performed.

- **Input data and inference traffic**: You need to understand your data size (for offline inference) and inference traffic patterns (for online inference). For instance, if your traffic is seasonality patterns, you may be able to use endpoint autoscaling to minimize your inference costs.

- **Model runtime and deployment**: Depending on your model characteristics, inference traffic patterns, and chosen compute instances, you need to choose specific SageMaker containers and model packaging configurations (single model versus several models behind an endpoint). Another aspect to explore is the model promotion strategy and quality assurance in productions. For instance, earlier in this chapter, we discussed how to organize A/B testing on live SageMaker endpoints using production variants.

The following table highlights the key characteristics of the available SageMaker inference options:

	Real-Time Inference	**Batch Transform**	**Asynchronous Inference**	**Serverless Inference**
Inference Type	Online (real-time response).	Offline.	Online (near-real-time inference, cold start during scale out from 0).	Online (cold start during scale out from 0).

	Real-Time Inference	Batch Transform	Asynchronous Inference	Serverless Inference
Resource Scaling	1 to hundreds of instances behind a single endpoint.	1 to hundreds of instances in one inference job.	0 to hundreds of instances.	0 to 200 concurrent inference requests.
Payload Size	Up to 6 MB.	Up to 100 MB.	Up to 1 GB.	Up to 4 MB.
Inference Timeout	60 seconds.	No.	Up to 15 minutes.	60 seconds.
Multi-Model/ Multi-Container Support	Yes.	No.	No.	No.
Target Use Case	When you need to have consistent real-time inference latency. Supports a wide range of compute instances and model servers.	Offline inference or processing when the input dataset is available upfront.	When you need to handle larger payload sizes and/or processing times and additional inference latency is acceptable. There is a cost-saving opportunity to scale to 0 when there is no inference traffic.	When you need to have real-time inference with the lowest management overhead and associated costs. Pay only for served inference requests. You can scale to 0.

Figure 10.7 – Comparing SageMaker inference options

In the following diagram, we have organized several decision points you need to be aware of when selecting your inference workload implementation:

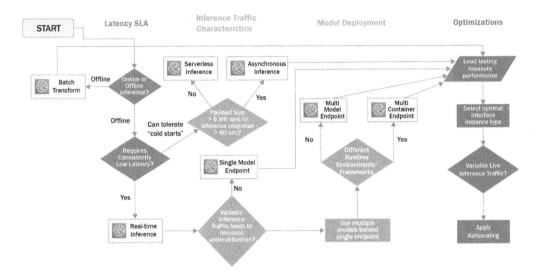

Figure 10.8 – Selection algorithm for inference options

Note that your workload configuration is not static. Some non-extensive examples that may require you to reconsider your workload configuration choices include the following:

- Traffic pattern changes may result in changes in your scaling policies

- Changes in user SLAs may result in changes in the selected compute instances and/or updates in scaling policies

- New versions of the model architecture and/or available compute instances may require benchmarking against the baseline to measure potential accuracy or performance gains

Hence, you should plan and budget for continuous monitoring and workload optimizations as part of your initial workload design.

Using SageMaker Inference Recommender

Choosing an optimal inference configuration requires considerable engineering and testing efforts. To simplify this process, AWS recently introduced **SageMaker Inference Recommender**, which provides you with a simple way to assess your inference performance and costs for real-time endpoints in different configurations.

Inference Recommender deploys your model to real-time endpoints with different configurations, runs load testing against those endpoints, and then provides latency and throughput measures, as well as associated costs. Based on the generated measures, you can select the most appropriate configuration based on your SLAs and cost budget. SageMaker Inference Recommender provides the following benchmarks:

- End-to-end **model latency** in milliseconds
- **Maximum invocations** per minute
- **Cost per hour** and **cost per inference**

SageMaker Inference Recommender is well suited for the following use cases:

- Finding the optimal instance type. Note that you can either provide your own list of instance types you are interested in benchmarking or let SageMaker benchmark this list across all supported instances.
- Benchmarking compiled by SageMaker Neo models. Here, you can compare the performance of your original model to the performance of the compiled model variant.
- Running a custom load test. Inference Recommender supports modeling different traffic patterns to benchmark your endpoint performance under different conditions. Hence, you can use SageMaker Inference Recommender to benchmark and fine-tune your model server configurations, different model versions, and more.

Note that at the time of writing, Inference Recommender only supports real-time endpoints. So, if you need to benchmark different inference options (for instance, Serverless Inference), you may need to use the custom benchmarking and load testing facilities. Also, benchmark statistics by Inference Recommender as well as the supported traffic patterns are limited.

Summary

In this chapter, we discussed how to operationalize and optimize your inference workloads. We covered various inference options offered by Amazon SageMaker and model hosting options, such as multi-model, multi-container, and Serverless Inference. Then, we reviewed how to promote and test model candidates using the Production Variant capability.

After that, we provided a high-level overview of advanced model deployment strategies using SageMaker Deployment Guardrails, as well as workload monitoring using the Amazon CloudWatch service and SageMaker's Model Monitor capability. Finally, we summarized the key selection criteria and algorithms you should use when defining your inference workload configuration.

Index

N

`Packt.com`

Subscribe to our online digital library for full access to over 7,000 books and videos, as well as industry leading tools to help you plan your personal development and advance your career. For more information, please visit our website.

Why subscribe?

- Spend less time learning and more time coding with practical eBooks and Videos from over 4,000 industry professionals

- Improve your learning with Skill Plans built especially for you

- Get a free eBook or video every month

- Fully searchable for easy access to vital information

- Copy and paste, print, and bookmark content

Did you know that Packt offers eBook versions of every book published, with PDF and ePub files available? You can upgrade to the eBook version at `packt.com` and as a print book customer, you are entitled to a discount on the eBook copy. Get in touch with us at `customercare@packtpub.com` for more details.

At `www.packt.com`, you can also read a collection of free technical articles, sign up for a range of free newsletters, and receive exclusive discounts and offers on Packt books and eBooks.

Other Books You May Enjoy

If you enjoyed this book, you may be interested in these other books by Packt:

Learn Amazon SageMaker - Second Edition

Julien Simon

ISBN: 978-1-80181-795-0

- Become well-versed with data annotation and preparation techniques
- Use AutoML features to build and train machine learning models with AutoPilot
- Create models using built-in algorithms and frameworks and your own code
- Train computer vision and natural language processing (NLP) models using real-world examples
- Cover training techniques for scaling, model optimization, model debugging, and cost optimization
- Automate deployment tasks in a variety of configurations using SDK and several automation tools

Amazon SageMaker Best Practices

Sireesha Muppala, Randy DeFauw, Shelbee Eigenbrode

ISBN: 978-1-80107-052-2

- Perform data bias detection with AWS Data Wrangler and SageMaker Clarify
- Speed up data processing with SageMaker Feature Store
- Overcome labeling bias with SageMaker Ground Truth
- Improve training time with the monitoring and profiling capabilities of SageMaker Debugger
- Address the challenge of model deployment automation with CI/CD using the SageMaker model registry
- Explore SageMaker Neo for model optimization
- Implement data and model quality monitoring with Amazon Model Monitor
- Improve training time and reduce costs with SageMaker data and model parallelism

Packt is searching for authors like you

If you're interested in becoming an author for Packt, please visit `authors.packtpub.com` and apply today. We have worked with thousands of developers and tech professionals, just like you, to help them share their insight with the global tech community. You can make a general application, apply for a specific hot topic that we are recruiting an author for, or submit your own idea.

Share Your Thoughts

Now you've finished *Accelerate Deep Learning Workloads with Amazon SageMaker*, we'd love to hear your thoughts! Scan the QR code below to go straight to the Amazon review page for this book and share your feedback or leave a review on the site that you purchased it from.

`https://packt.link/r/1-801-81644-1`

Your review is important to us and the tech community and will help us make sure we're delivering excellent quality content.

Download a free PDF copy of this book

Thanks for purchasing this book!

Do you like to read on the go but are unable to carry your print books everywhere? Is your eBook purchase not compatible with the device of your choice?

Don't worry, now with every Packt book you get a DRM-free PDF version of that book at no cost.

Read anywhere, any place, on any device. Search, copy, and paste code from your favorite technical books directly into your application.

The perks don't stop there, you can get exclusive access to discounts, newsletters, and great free content in your inbox daily

Follow these simple steps to get the benefits:

1. Scan the QR code or visit the link below

https://packt.link/free-ebook/9781801816441

2. Submit your proof of purchase
3. That's it! We'll send your free PDF and other benefits to your email directly